# PLANNING

### AND

# DESIGNING

# SCHOOLS

# PLANNING
## AND
# DESIGNING
# SCHOOLS

## C. WILLIAM BRUBAKER

**Raymond Bordwell, AIA**
**(Perkins & Will, Chicago)**

**Gaylaird Christopher, AIA**
**(Perkins & Will, Pasadena)**

**McGraw-Hill**

New York   San Francisco   Washington, D.C.   Auckland   Bogotá
Caracas   Lisbon   London   Madrid   Mexico City   Milan
Montreal   New Delhi   San Juan   Singapore
Sydney   Tokyo   Toronto

**Library of Congress Cataloging-in-Publication Data**

Brubaker, C. William.
   Planning and designing schools/C. William Brubaker.
      p.    cm.
   Includes index.
   ISBN 0-07-049405-3
   1. School buildings—United States—Design and construction.
2. School buildings—United States—Planning.   3. School
environment—United States.   I. Title.
LB3218.A1B78   1998
371.6′2′0973—dc21                                        97-35484
                                                                    CIP

*McGraw-Hill*

A Division of The **McGraw·Hill** Companies

   2 3 4 5 6 7 8 9 0   KGP/KGP   9 0 2 1 0 9 8

ISBN 0-07-049405-3

The sponsoring editor for this book was Wendy Lochner, the editing
supervisor was Penny Linskey, and the production supervisor was Sherri
Souffrance. Interior design and composition by North Market Street
Graphics

Printed and bound by Quebecor/Kingsport Press.

McGraw-Hill books are available at special quantity discounts to use as pre-
miums and sales promotions, or for use in corporate training programs. For
more information, please write to the Director of Special Sales, McGraw-Hill,
11 West 19th Street, New York, NY 10011. Or contact your local bookstore.

To the educators, board members,

citizens, students, fellow architects,

engineers, consultants and builders

who strive to achieve high quality

imaginative architecture for education

# CONTENTS

# PREFACE

When I was a young architecture student at the University of Texas in Austin, Professor Martin Kermacy suggested that I take a summer job in an architect's office to get some on-the-job experience and learn how projects were developed through the design and construction documents phases. It was good advice, but good intentions do not always spark action. Martin, however, took action: He called Larry Perkins and Phil Will and recommended me for a job in Chicago. They responded with an invitation to work at Perkins & Will for the summer.

Occurring between the third and fourth years of the five-year program, the Chicago experience was wonderful. I worked on drawings for two schools and then went out to the construction site to get some muddy-boots experience.

Something else happened: I was suddenly even more interested in my architecture courses at the University of Texas and was eager to graduate and become an architect for schools, colleges, and universities and for urban mixed-use developments (which, of course, would include schools, colleges, and universities—this was the education age).

That was a new professional goal. Earlier I had graduated from Leesburg High School in northern Indiana, near Warsaw, in a class with only a dozen students. I wanted to study engineering, and so I enrolled at Purdue University. One year, followed by a year in the U.S. Navy (with time to read books on architecture, planning, and design), convinced me that I should switch from engineering to studies that focused on people and planning and buildings, and so

I transferred from engineering at Purdue to architecture at Texas.

During my summer job at Perkins & Will, something else emerged: I was hooked on Chicago!

Chicago, I discovered, was a great place to live and work. Especially for architecture students, the city was an exciting place to visit, explore, photograph, and sketch. (I hope there are lots of students who feel the same way in the year 2000 and the year 2100.)

I had known Chicago as a small child when my parents had taken me to the 1933 "Century of Progress" World's Fair. I thought the buildings and spaces and the "sky-ride" were wonderful, but it did not occur to me that one could choose to be an architect and design such urban places. My parents also introduced me to the Art Institute of Chicago later on.

As an architecture student, my horizons were broader. I discovered Oak Park and Unity Temple and the Frank Lloyd Wright houses. To be near those wonderful houses of the 1890s and 1900s I found a small apartment near Unity Temple. It was a great neighborhood of revolutionary houses identified as "the Prairie School of Architecture," with beautiful houses designed by Frank Lloyd Wright and his contemporaries.

The lakefront proved to be as interesting as I could have imagined, and Daniel Burnham in his Chicago Plan of 1908 had created a bold plan for it which others, such as Montgomery Ward, fought to protect and follow.

The Museum of Science and Industry was known to most visitors to Chicago, but the University of Chicago quadrangles were not, and so it was fun to explore that Oxbridge environment.

The most exciting part of the city to explore was "the Loop" with its splendid collection of landmark-quality office buildings and other structures. The "Second School of Chicago Architecture" was and is famous as the inventor of the skyscraper. World-class high-rise buildings survive; the Monadnock, the Reliance, the Marquette, and famous buildings by Adler & Sullivan, including the Carson Pirie Scott store and the auditorium, are in this walkable central business district.

Mies van der Rohe's 860 and 880 North Lake Shore Drive apartment towers were under construction. Crow Island School in Winnetka had been completed in 1940. More on that landmark later.

It was a great summer to work in Chicago.

Martin Kermacy, a University of Texas professor, and other teachers at the School of Architecture—especially Hugo Leipziger and Raleigh Roesner—had pushed me in two important directions: an interest in architecture for education (my fifth-year thesis project was an art school for a university) and a love affair with Chicago.

Martin and his wife, Eve, introduced me to another love: my future wife. Martin is the kind of teacher we need more of. He would walk through the design studio and invite the late toilers to stop at his house for a beer. Meanwhile, Eve would invite students from other disciplines. I met my wife there: Elizabeth Rogers from Dayton, Ohio, who was working on a master's degree in economics.

Somewhere along the way I said, "If you're ever in Chicago, look me up." She did, and we have been happily married for forty-two years. Our children, Rogers (a social scientist at UCLA), Elizabeth (an environmentalist in Toronto), and Robert (an ophthalmic technician in Chicago), are interested in architecture, even though none decided to make it a career.

For thirty-eight years we've lived in Winnetka across the street from New Trier High School where 3,500 students learn under one big roof. New Trier, an academic model for big schools, was good for our three children. In the 1960s Perkins & Will, in association with the Architects Collaborative, designed a new campus, New Trier West, which has become a community center for adult education, the arts, and physical fitness in response to the fact that New Trier's enrollment declined in the 1970s and 1980s. Recently,

demographers have predicted enrollment increases again, and so New Trier Township probably will become a two-campus district after the year 2000.

I would like to thank dozens of my associates at Perkins & Will, who have made school projects an award-winning pleasure. Initially, Larry Perkins and Phil Will encouraged me to pursue my interest in architecture for education and Lee Cochran gave me experience in school design as both a designer and a project manager (relatively easy for smaller elementary schools but too difficult for large high schools, and so a planning and design team must evolve). Other design team members have been important mentors, as have the other architects with whom we have associated for specific projects, along with the many consultants who have brought valuable special experience and knowledge to the work.

Some of these architects and consultants have been associates for decades. Burgess & Niple, Ohio engineers and architects, have been team members on six projects; in Fort Myers, Florida, Parker-Mudgett-Smith have been associates and friends since 1962. The educational consultant Stanton Leggett and I have worked on projects together for decades, and Hedrich-Blessing, renowned architectural photographers, have photographed Perkins & Will schools since 1940, when their assignment was Crow Island School in Winnetka, Illinois. The most important people are the clients, who have a program of space needs and the resources to finance each enterprise, along with their ideas, understanding, and dreams. This is particularly important for schools, which are planned with many clients in mind: students, teachers, administrators, board members, and, increasingly, the community. The goal of an effective design team should be to create a functional, safe, flexible, and beautiful building.

I have had the satisfaction of working in many different positions on a great variety of design teams: draftsman, field representative, project architect, designer, partner in charge, officer in charge (different states require different organizations), vice president, president, chairman of the board, and most recently vice chairman.

Perkins & Will's early years (1940s–1950s) were school design years, but in the 1960s and 1970s colleges and universities and hospitals and office buildings were also important fields for Perkins & Will, giving me broader experience in architecture for education. For example, New Trier West High School and the First National Bank of Chicago were planned in the 1960s; both were done in association with other architects. I worked on the design for both projects and served as partner in charge of design for Perkins & Will for the bank, in association with C.F. Murphy Associates. I believe that both projects benefited from this teamwork.

In the 1970s and 1980s health care and education work was important, and Perkins & Will designed school and university projects from coast to coast in the United States as well as in the Middle East and elsewhere in the world. We designed new campuses in Egypt, Greece, Iran, Iraq, Saudi Arabia, and Mexico. I especially enjoyed working on our first overseas project—Cairo American College in Maadi, Egypt—and on the campus for the college of agriculture near Mexico City. This international experience proved to be a valuable source for work as school enrollment in the United States unexpectedly declined.

During those years school-building projects in many parts of the United States disappeared as the demographics changed and some communities found that they had surplus school space. Then the numbers and trends changed, and new elementary schools were needed again in the 1980s. Those students grew up, creating a growing demand for secondary schools in the 1990s.

Perkins & Will was fortunate to be selected for a new high school in Santa Fe, New Mexico, in 1984. My partner, Ralph Johnson, and I teamed up with the Santa Fe firm Mimbres and worked with Kass Germanas of that firm. Very few new high schools were being planned in 1984. We developed some fresh new ideas for the school, designing it in response to the local culture and in the Santa Fe style and spirit, emphasizing patios, portals, New Mexico materials such as stucco on concrete block, and desert colors.

Meanwhile, for the Gadsden district west of El Paso, near the Mexican border, the same team designed the Desert View elementary school, a prototype that was built three times on similar sites. This very low-cost school was awarded a national AIA Honor Award in 1985; in the following year the high school in Santa Fe also won that award.

We were off to a fresh start in school design. Schools for Warsaw, Indiana, and Troy, Michigan, followed, and we formed new teams with associated architects for schools at Perry and Solon, Ohio; Fort Collins, Colorado; North Fort Myers, Florida; New

Albany, Ohio; Raleigh, North Carolina; Williamsburg, Virginia; Fort Worth, Texas; Woodlands, Texas; Sauk Rapids, Minnesota; Saint Paul, Minnesota; Chelsea, Massachusetts; and Mashpee, Massachusetts (on Cape Cod) and Crystal Lake, Illinois (a northwestern suburb of Chicago)—all designed in the 12-year period from 1983 to 1995. Concurrently, we planned additions and renovations at existing schools (a high priority for the new century) and planned multischool systems such as that for the Irvine Unified School District in Orange County, California, working closely with the school administrator, the city of Irvine, and the Irvine Company's planning department. What emerged for the 2-square-mile village of Woodbridge is a system of two high schools, four middle schools, and eight elementary schools.

Hundreds of people, especially educators and architects, should be acknowledged for helping me along the way. An effective design team includes the superintendent of schools and/or the assistant superintendents. An architect cannot design and complete a good school without a good client, and the administrators determine the flavor and fate of the school design process more than anyone else with the possible exception of an outstanding board member, a brilliant teacher who recognizes the importance of good design, or a local citizen who works with the school district to achieve better schools for the community.

I have worked with dozens of outstanding clients throughout the years and have learned a lot from them; in fact, this has been my continuing education program for almost fifty years.

To cite one recent example, the Saint Paul public schools experience designing the new Arlington High School included on the design team three brilliant administrators who have worked effectively with the superintendent of schools and the board of education while planning the school with the community and working with the architects, engineers, and consultants. The administrative team included Bill Dunn, who had been appointed principal of the new high school when planning for it began; Carole Snyder, who was in charge of curriculum from the beginning; and Leon Hakilla, who was in charge of Saint Paul's school facilities and therefore was to be responsible for maintaining the campus.

My thanks go to the dozens of architects, engineers, and administrators at Perkins & Will who have helped me look good to our clients. In the early decades of my career Phil Will and Larry Perkins encouraged me to pursue school design as a career, but many other associates, from young designers to experienced officers, have been helpful in recent years. Since ours is a large firm with offices in many cities, mentioning all my associates would extend these acknowledgments too far, but I do want to thank my Chicago partners, Ralph Johnson, Raymond Bordwell, and August Battaglia, and the designers Jerry Johnson, Vojo Narancic, and Brian Junge, who produced many of the drawings in this book. In our education studio, Jan Fletcher, the administrative assistant, recognized my word-processing limitations and helped keep me organized and put all my texts on disk. Also, in the New York City office, thanks go to Mark Chen, and in our Pasadena, California, office, to Gaylaird Christopher. Ray Bordwell and Gaylaird Christopher contributed three chapters which bring their broad experience in school design to the readers of this book.

Perkins & Will has a global partner, Dar Al-Handasah Consultants, and I thank Dr. Kamal Shair for his support. I also recognize and thank James ("Sandy") Stevenson, president of Perkins & Will, for his encouragement.

Many Perkins & Will projects are planned in association with other firms of architects and engineers. Some of these associations are ongoing working agreements that continue for decades. I have been working with Parker Mudgett Smith of Fort Myers, Florida, for thirty-five years. The most recent joint project is North Fort Myers High School, which is illustrated in Chapter 3.

Professional associations also have been influential in my career I am especially grateful to the American Institute of Architects' Committee on Architecture for Education and the Council of Educational Facilities Planners International for managing effective programs for continuing education.

Professional magazines are valuable sources of information for school design. Many of my completed projects have found their way into the leading architectural magazines—*Architectural Record* and *Architecture*—and into education publications.

Educational consultants have been of great assistance. Special thanks go to Stanton Leggett for participating in significant projects with me for forty years. Other projects have enjoyed the services of Dwayne Gardner, Paul Abramson, William DeJong, and C. William Day.

In addition to a good client, architect, and consultants, a successful school project needs a good contractor or construction manager and/or a program manager. We have been fortunate to attract and work with excellent builders and suppliers.

When the construction work is finished, the talents of a superb photographer are necessary if the project is to be published, shown at conventions, and explained in seminars. We have been fortunate to be able to tap the photography skills of Hedrich-Blessing for many of our schools.

Finally, McGraw-Hill continues to be a great publisher. I am most grateful to Wendy Lochner, Robin Gardner, and Penny Linskey for their guidance and assistance in publishing this book on school design.

Architecture for education is important to students and to communities. Twenty-first-century schools will be planned, designed, and built on a firm foundation and will enjoy a rich heritage as they strive to create a wonderful learning environment for our children and grandchildren. I am pleased to be part of that endeavor.

*C. William Brubaker*

# PLANNING
## AND
# DESIGNING
# SCHOOLS

# CHAPTER

# OUR HERITAGE

## A BRIEF HISTORY OF SCHOOL DESIGN IN THE NINETEENTH AND TWENTIETH CENTURIES

When we think about nineteenth-century school buildings, we tend to visualize a nineteenth-century one-room schoolhouse in a rural setting and ignore the urban schools of that era, which were planned for growing cities. Some buildings from the nineteenth century are still in use and many have been sympathetically restored, while other hundred-year-old schools have been demolished. The best surviving examples are worthy of landmark status.

### Baltimore Schools: 1850s–1920s

Baltimore school buildings serve as a good example of the urban schools built during the last half of the nineteenth century. Brick walls, axial plans, pitched roofs, historical styles, two to four stories, and very small sites (a response to rising land costs) characterize these structures. Elementary schools were erected on sites barely big enough for the buildings, with "playgrounds" and any kind of landscaping almost ignored. A ten-classroom school from the 1850s through the 1880s typically was built on a site of only a quarter of

an acre with a playground one-tenth of an acre. The building would be two stories in height with a pitched-roof attic. By 1890, sixteen-classroom three-story schools were more common and the sites were larger. Also noteworthy is the fact that early American schools were "classical" in design, with pediments and a temple front for the principal facade. By 1890 this had changed; instead of being characterized by classical simplicity, school buildings were exuberant in design, with Victorian and other details borrowed from earlier cultures. Then, beginning in the 1920s, Baltimore-area schools were more often placed in the suburbs on relatively spacious sites of 5 to 10 acres. These "suburban" schools were less formal, with one or two stories, and were situated on access roads with romantic names like Wildwood Parkway.

The depression and World War II interrupted this evolution of school design.

In the late 1940s and 1950s school building increased dramatically. School boards approved new construction because the existing buildings had become too crowded.

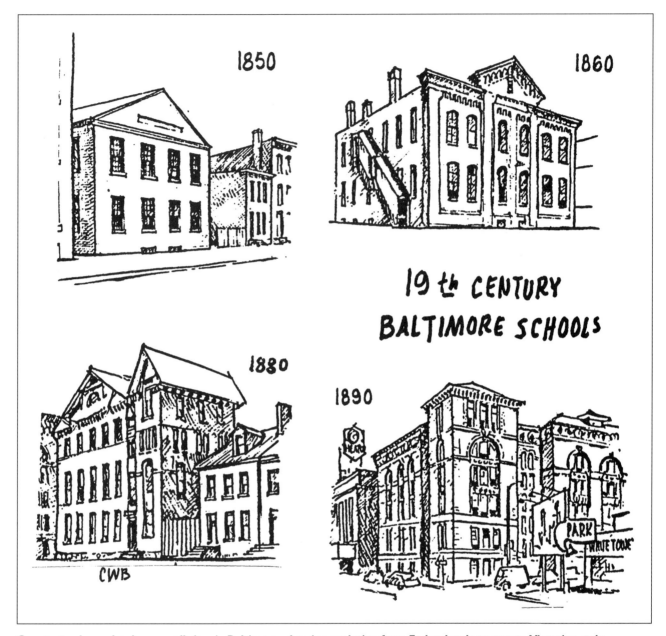

**Compact urban schools on small sites in Baltimore, showing evolution from Federal style to ornate Victorian style.**

Meanwhile, a new style in architecture was dominating design theories. "Modern architecture" was quickly adopted for schools because it generated simple boxy buildings that were easy to plan and inexpensive to build. Some masterpieces were created, but unfortunately, not all boards, administrators, and architects were sensitive to the existing community environment and its need for well-designed buildings and green open space.

Modern architecture too often produced industrial-looking, unadorned, flat-roofed shoe-box school build-

ings. City schools did not escape this national trend toward the bare-bones construction of big boxes. The repetition of metal and glass curtain walls, with no sense of orientation and a lack of thoughtful landscaping, made some citizens critical of school and community design in the 1960s.

## Cleveland Schools: 1850s–1920s

People continued to move westward, and the focus of school design shifted to cities such as Cleveland and

Chicago, where a large number of school buildings were built a generation or two later than they were in Baltimore.

In 1916 an interesting little book, *School Buildings and Equipment,* was published as part of a "Cleveland Education Survey." The book provided a one-page review of a typical school building in each decade from 1850 to 1910.

Cleveland's Alabama School of the 1850s was a three-story cube with three classrooms on each floor and nothing else—no corridors (only stairs), no wardrobes, no office, no toilets. Each classroom accommodated (if that is the right word) 100 children. As the city continued to expand, school enrollment grew, and 200 children were sometimes shoehorned into each room. The authors of this fascinating book observed that "there was hardly a square foot of waste space in these buildings." We have come a long way from Alabama.

Sterling School of the 1860s was a better plan. Architectural design enjoyed new prominence; note the roof lines, arched entrances, and "Gothic" windows. The six classrooms per floor are consistent with today's image of "the state of the art." Maybe we have not come a long way, after all. Sterling has a curiously complicated corridor exit stair plan.

Giddings School of the 1880s generates within us the feeling that we've been there. At the center of the compact plan is an "expanded hall" or auditorium. Eight classrooms on the first floor are clustered around this space, and eight more classrooms on the second floor surround it. "The expanded hall proved most unsatisfactory as an auditorium," the 1971 book, *School Buildings and Equipment,* reported; the acoustics were chaotic.

In the next example, the auditorium was moved up to the third floor attic under a big roof, which represented an improvement. However, almost everyone

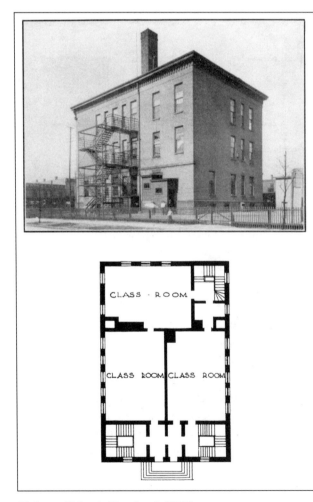

**Alabama School, Cleveland, 1850's**

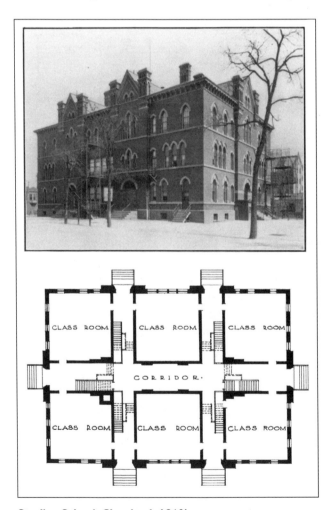

**Sterling School, Cleveland, 1860's**

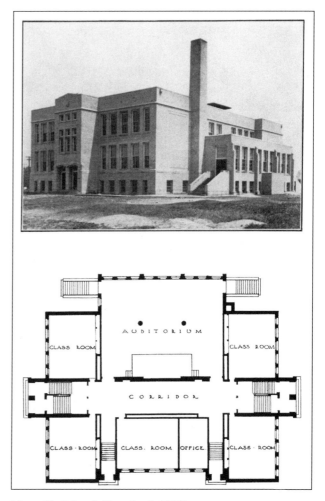

**Giddings School, Cleveland, 1880's**

**Memphis School, Cleveland, 1900's**

was more satisfied with the Memphis School of the 1900s, in which the auditorium was brought back down to the first floor as a separate sound-isolated space.

The next step in this evolutionary process was to locate two large spaces on the central cross-axis flanked by symmetrical classroom wings, a plan which the authors of *School Buildings and Equipment* thought was "the most modern type of school architecture."

## Chicago Schools: 1880s–1930s

A dozen sketches of typical Chicago schools remind us of the character of the schools built in our cities. Most of these schools are still in use. Some have been renovated and/or added to. Some have been demolished as enrollment in inner-city neighborhoods has declined.

Compare the nineteenth-century Thomas Jefferson School, which has four stories on a small site, with the twentieth-century Elizabeth Sutherland School, which has only two stories and is on a larger site. The Sutherland School is not urban in character; it is suburban, with a pitched roof and a cupola.

Note the locations of the schools on the accompanying maps. Jefferson School was in an old inner-city neighborhood near what is now the University of Illinois Medical Center. As health facilities expanded into a square-mile campus (a mile west of the University of Illinois at Chicago campus), neighborhoods lost residential units and students, and so only a few old school buildings survive. Compare the location of the Sutherland School—it is at the outer edge of Chicago and therefore is newer, lower, more spacious, and more suburban in character—in a residential neighborhood. Also, note the Kate Kellogg School with its

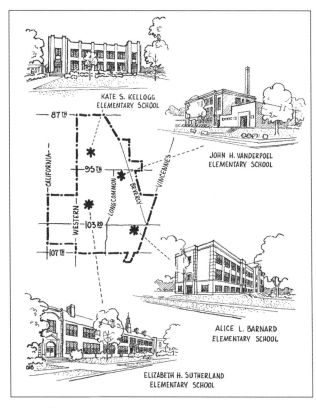

**Typical South side Chicago schools**

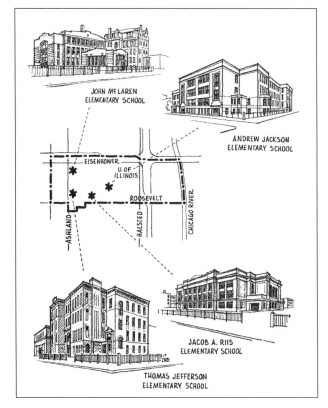

**Typical West side Chicago schools**

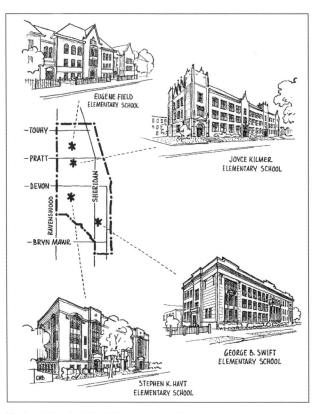

**Typical North side Chicago schools**

appealing design, appropriate scale, and well-detailed brick walls and windows; it should be useful as an educational facility for another 100 years if it is well maintained. If they are not maintained with tender loving care, these schools will deteriorate and be demolished.

Some of these old buildings, however, not only are in poor physical condition but are educationally obsolete. Restoration would be too costly. Each property must be examined and evaluated on an individual basis to establish a likely useful life span, estimate the cost of bringing it up to date, and compare that estimate with the cost of new construction.

## Chicago and Suburban Schools Designed by Perkins, Fellows and Hamilton: 1900s–1930s

Dwight Perkins was the father of Lawrence B. Perkins, a cofounder of Perkins & Will. In the 1920s, Dwight Perkins was famous for school design for several interrelated reasons. First, he was the manager of Daniel Burnham's office in Chicago when Burnham was busy planning the 1983 World's Columbia Exposition and working closely with Wright and was influenced by the "Prairie School" style, which included long horizontal lines of brick, wood, and stucco; continuous bands of windows sheltered by large roof overhangs; and new nontraditional forms and details.

With encouragement from Burnham, Dwight Perkins rented space in a new building, Steinway Hall, and invited his young and able architect friends to share space in the building and to form associations as new design opportunities appeared. The architects worked for each other, especially during the production of working drawings in a "federation of small offices." The participating young architects included Frank Lloyd Wright, Walter Burley Griffin, Marian Mahoney Griffin, Solon S. Beman, and Myron Hunt. Dwight Perkins was then only twenty-seven years old. These architects were later called the "Prairie School Architects." They worked closely with Frank Lloyd Wright, who was associated with Louis Sullivan.

Dwight Perkins also was a cofounder of the firm Perkins, Fellows and Hamilton, which designed superb schools in the Collegiate Gothic manner and the Prairie School style. Their high schools in the

**Offices of Perkins, Fellows and Hamilton, at the Chicago Water Tower, 1917**

Chicago suburbs included Evanston Township High School and New Trier Township High School in Winnetka. Perkins, Fellows and Hamilton developed a national and international practice which included high schools in Mishawaka, Indiana; Manitowoc, Wisconsin; St. Clair, Michigan; Bay City, Michigan; Whiting, Indiana; Pontiac, Michigan; Danville, Kentucky; and Hinsdale, Illinois. They also designed the University of Nanking.

Dwight Perkins was also the in-house architect for the Chicago public schools from 1905 to 1910. In that position he designed some wonderful schools for Chicago. The masterpiece is Carl Schurz High School of 1910 on Milwaukee Avenue between Cicero Avenue and Pulaski Road, which continues to serve its neighborhood well. It was and is a beautiful school set back from the street lines with a lawn and old trees in the

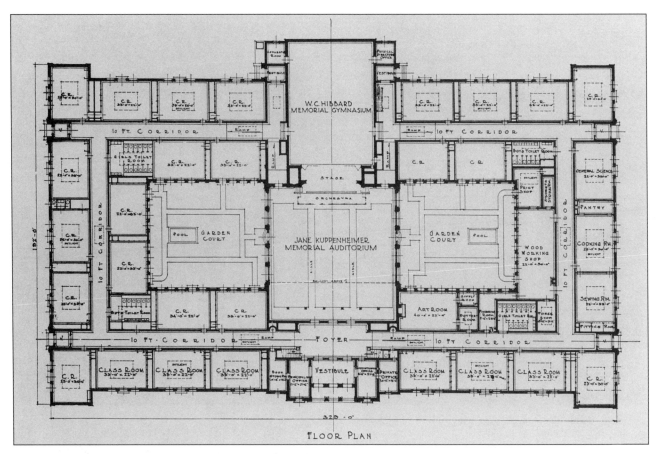

Skokie School, Winnetka, IL. Perkins, Fellows and Hamilton, architects. Classrooms with outside doors to gardens. Classrooms with skylights.

Hubbard Woods School, Winnetka, IL. Big sheltering roof; Prairie School of Architecture. Perkins, Fellows and Hamilton, architects.

**Evanston Township High School, Evanston, IL. Collegiate Gothic. Perkins, Fellows and Hamilton, architect.**

front yard. The design is in the Prairie School style, rather oriental in character, and is dominated by a huge tile roof which overhangs and shelters the three- and four-story brick walls. Before Perkins, Fellows and Hamilton's work of the first three decades of the twentieth century, school buildings were often poorly lighted and ventilated, had crude plumbing, were on nearly treeless sites, and were often big standard boxes with an unimaginative institutional character. Dwight Perkins designed over forty new schools in Chicago which changed school design in Chicago and many midwestern cities and paved the way for the innovative modern schools of the 1940s through the 1990s that gave Perkins & Will a rich heritage.

## Perkins & Will: Since 1935— Nationwide and Worldwide

Perkins & Will was founded in 1935 and celebrated its fiftieth anniversary in 1985. The cofounders were Lawrence B. Perkins and Philip Will, Jr., who had been friends and fraternity brothers at Cornell University.

**Gymnasium entrance at New Trier Township High School, Winnetka, IL. Elegant brick work detailing by Perkins, Fellows and Hamilton, architect.**

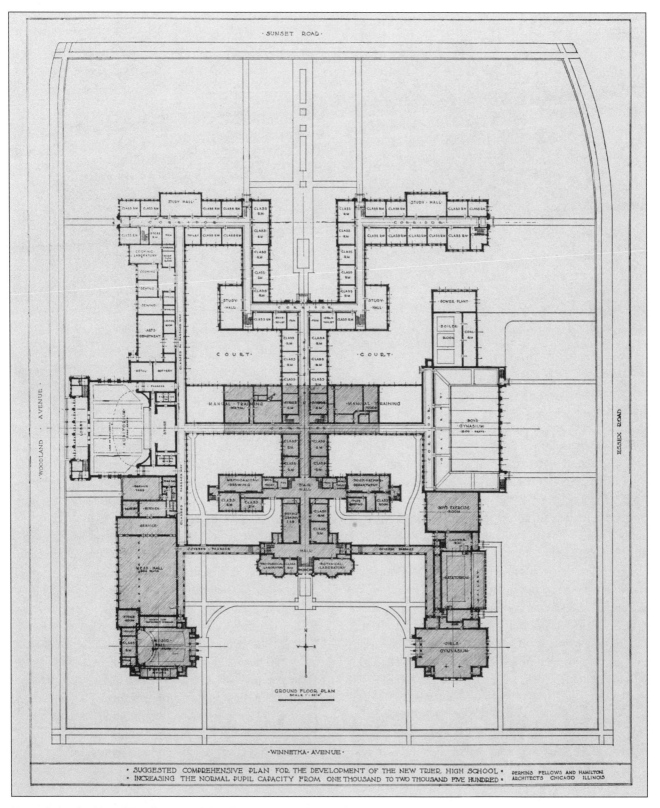

**Master plan for New Trier Township High School, Winnetka, IL. Perkins, Fellows and Hamilton, architect.**

**Bowen High School, Chicago, IL under construction 1910. Great sheltering roofs protect three and four story walls of brick and windows in the Prairie School style. Dwight Perkins, architect.**

In 1935 the prospects were not bright for young architects, but the crucial step (opening a new office) was taken, and during the last years of the depression the new firm found work and grew slowly but steadily. (A new partner joined the firm—E. Todd Wheeler—but during the war years, when work was slow, he left to become the state architect and plan a huge medical center on the west side of Chicago.) Perkins Wheeler & Will designed good-quality houses, both traditional and modern. Many of those houses were in Winnetka, and so it wasn't surprising that Perkins Wheeler & Will was interviewed when Winnetka found that it needed to build a new elementary school. Winnetka already had completed two schools designed by Perkins, Fellows & Hamilton: Hubbard Woods School in 1915 and Skokie School in 1922.

Skokie School was built with funds raised by popular subscription (i.e., cash gifts), not with tax money. This innovative school has classrooms around two courtyards, and every classroom has an outdoor entrance and a skylight. Hubbard Woods School has an elegant design with a big sheltering roof and bold ventilation towers. The school was designed to be built in sections; the first section opened in 1915. The school board members liked Perkins Wheeler & Will's

residential work but asked the firm if it would invite a noteworthy and more experienced architect to join the team. The superintendent of schools, Carleton Washburne, asked whether Eliel Saarinen might be the right person. A phone call to Saarinen revealed that he was interested. His reply, Larry Perkins remembers, was, "It's a job, isn't it?"

Crow Island School on Willow Road in Winnetka was a great success when it opened in 1940. It usually is identified as the first modern school. It certainly demonstrated a new kind of architecture for education. In contrast to the formal, axial, traditional, multistory, heavy masonry institutional buildings of the 1900s through the 1920s, Crow Island was an informal one-story modern school built of modest materials, especially common brick, with a "clock tower" (actually the chimney) marking the main entrance. The clock was asymmetrically located on the chimney, a detail that generated much controversy even as the local citizens welcomed modern architecture to Winnetka.

The more significant fact was Winnetka's progressive and innovative educational program; its outstanding superintendent of schools, Carleton Washburne, supported by an enthusiastic faculty and board of education, aimed high. Superintendent Washburne made

**Crow Island School, Winnetka, IL 1940. Perkins, Wheeler and Will, in association with Eliel and Eero Saarinen. (Color Photo)**

it all happen. He wanted to achieve three things with the Crow Island design process:

1. Create a significant example of modern architecture

2. Perform a restudy of Winnetka's educational system

3. Redirect the learning process and the architecture it generated, recognizing the importance of how to teach and where to teach

Larry Perkins and Superintendent Washburne headed a great team from the beginning. Larry "went to school," sitting in on classes and learning all about the spaces, the equipment needed, and the kinds of activities an architect should design for.

This has become a tradition that has served Perkins & Will well over the years. Crow Island School was completed and opened in 1940—before World

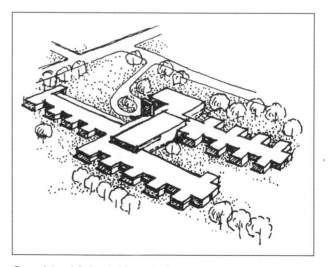

**Crow Island School. Mass study.**

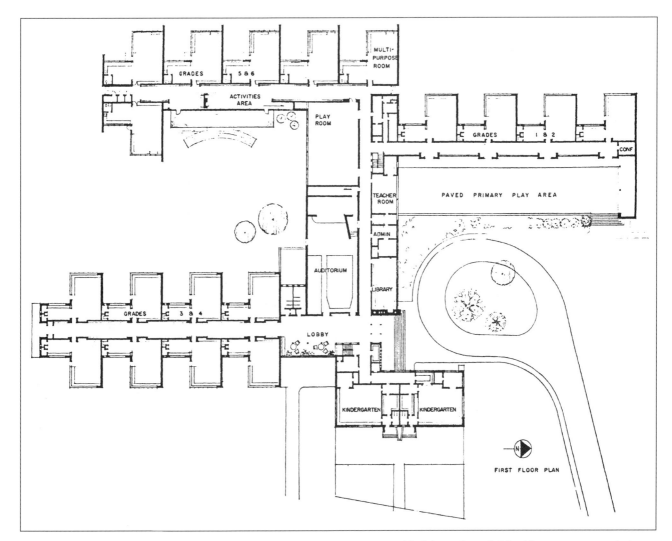

**Crow Island School. Floor plan. A large library and resource center was added, later, in unfinished basement space below the play room.**

**Crow Island School before the trees grew up.**

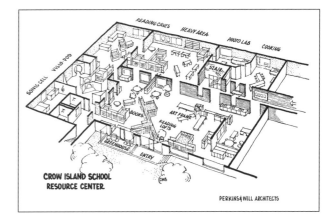

**Crow Island School resource center.**

**Students enjoy Crow Island School's Pioneer Room**

War II—and received extensive publicity as a new kind of school. It received the prestigious "25-Year Award" from the American Institute of Architects in the 1970s.

After World War II ended, the baby boom began and thousands of new schools were needed. Crow

**Crow Island School resource center.**

Island served as a model for many schools, and its influence was nationwide.

Creative school design work evolved in southern and western states in the 1950s. For example, for a school in Oklahoma, Perkins & Will worked in association with a Bryan, Texas, firm, Caudill Rowlett & Scott (CRS). John Lyon Reid and Partners designed the flexible Hillsdale High School in San Mateo, California, using industrial materials and systems. Ernest Kump planned fine "finger-plan" schools with good natural lighting and ventilation. In Florida, the Sarasota schools were innovative, and in New England, TAC and other architects designed significant schools.

Meanwhile, with the arrival of jet airplane service, some architects expanded geographically to become nationwide, including Perkins & Will (P&W). It is interesting to note the ways in which P&W grew:

1. Geographically from the Chicago office to a New York City office and a Washington, D.C. office, then in the locations needed for specific projects, such as California, Florida, North Carolina, Georgia, and Minnesota

2. By expanding from elementary schools to secondary schools as children grew up and then moving on to colleges and universities

3. By offering wider services, beginning with architecture and then adding interior design; structural engineering; mechanical, electrical, and civil engineering; construction; management; and other services not often imagined in the 1950s

4. By expanding into different building markets, such as health care, civic buildings, hotels, airports, office buildings, and housing and shopping centers

All that is indeed a rich heritage for architects who were primarily interested in elementary and secondary school design and college and university design. When this book was planned, the idea of including higher education was considered, but a decision was made to focus on elementary schools, middle schools, and high schools; college and university planning and design would more appropriately be the subject of another book.

Before the media explosion, the library was a place for books, periodicals, and study. Princeton Day School, Princeton, NJ.

Dundee Elementary School, Greenwich, CT, serving one of the booming suburbs in the New York metropolitan area. Perkins & Will.

The last half of the twentieth century saw many changes in education and therefore many changes in architecture for education. At the risk of oversimplifying these changes, we now summarize the five decades that followed World War II.

## THE 1950S

The record-breaking baby boom produced a huge increase in enrollments and a sudden and growing demand for new elementary schools. The new schools in most parts of the nation were no longer classic, traditional, colonial, Georgian, Gothic, or eclectic but were "modern," often meaning that they were one-story and flat-roofed with glass and metal window walls and brick or concrete walls. Some 1950s schools were air-conditioned, a trend that would continue in the following decades. Widely influenced by the Crow Island School, which was completed in 1940, the 1950s began an age of innovation in school design, but some school boards missed the opportunity to create better school facilities while they struggled to keep up with increasing enrollment. Too often, 1950s schools were built too cheaply for true economy, since yearly maintenance and operation costs were not properly calculated. Lightweight structures, poorly insulated roofs and walls, cheap hardware, poor-quality lighting, minimal ventilation systems, and endlessly repeated standardized plans and elevations characterized many school buildings of that era.

Keokuk, IA built a dramatic modern high school in the 1950's. Perkins & Will.

Not all the new schools were excessively cheap or unimaginative. Some were innovative, well built, and beautiful. One of the most interesting reviews of architecture for education in the 1950s was the book *Schoolhouse,* edited by Walter McQuade. The team of writers and editors included color photographs (unusual in that decade) of the new American schools they most admired, including the following:

1. Wilbur Snow Elementary School in Middletown, Connecticut, by the architect Warren Ashley: four classroom buildings scattered on a wooded site in a collegelike master plan

2. Hillsdale High School in San Mateo, California, by the architects John Lyon Reid & Partners: an innovative and flexible loft, high-tech in spirit and prophetic of things to come

3. Phyllis Wheatley Elementary School in New Orleans, Louisiana, by the architect Charles Colbert: an urban school on stilts above a playground, representing a sensible response to a hot and rainy climate

4. Acalanes Union High School in Lafayette, California, by Franklin & Kump: a finger-plan school mixing classrooms and greenery in an appealing design for a benign climate

5. Crow Island School in Winnetka, Illinois, by Perkins, Wheeler and Will with Eliel and Eero Saarinen

It is also appropriate to note the fact that in the 1950s Caudill Rowlett and Scott emerged as a significant school design firm.

## THE 1960S

The children who were in the first grade in 1954 grew up and became high school seniors in 1965. Not surprisingly, the principal demand for new schools changed to high schools.

The decade was dominated by the "research and extension" activities of foundations, especially the work of Educational Facilities Laboratories (EFL), funded by the Ford Foundation.

EFL encouraged innovation in school architecture by giving planning grants to schools and consultants, issuing its findings in attractive publications, and holding conferences on elementary and secondary educational facilities—buildings, equipment, and sites—as they relate to communities.

Among its many research activities, EFL, working with educators, architects, and suppliers, (1) studied and promoted the use of folding and movable walls to

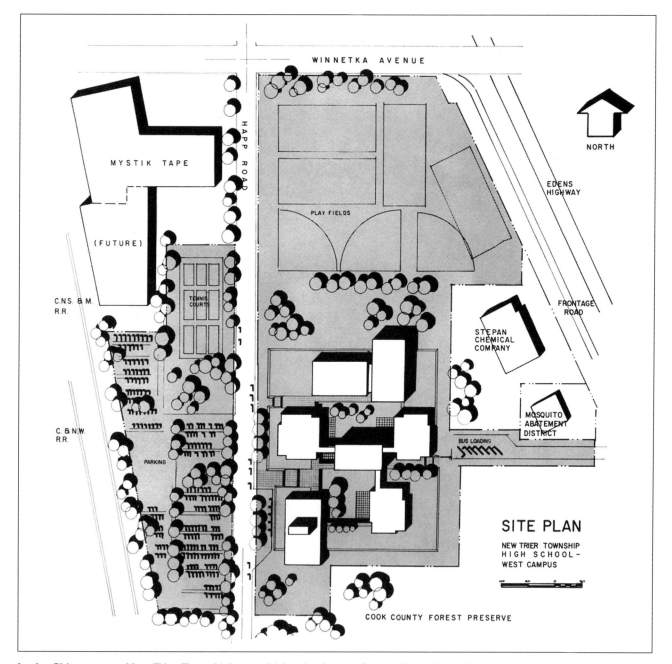

**In the Chicago area, New Trier Township's west high school was influenced by college design—a cluster of seven buildings, around two courtyards—designed by Perkins & Will in association with The Architects Collaborative 1965.**

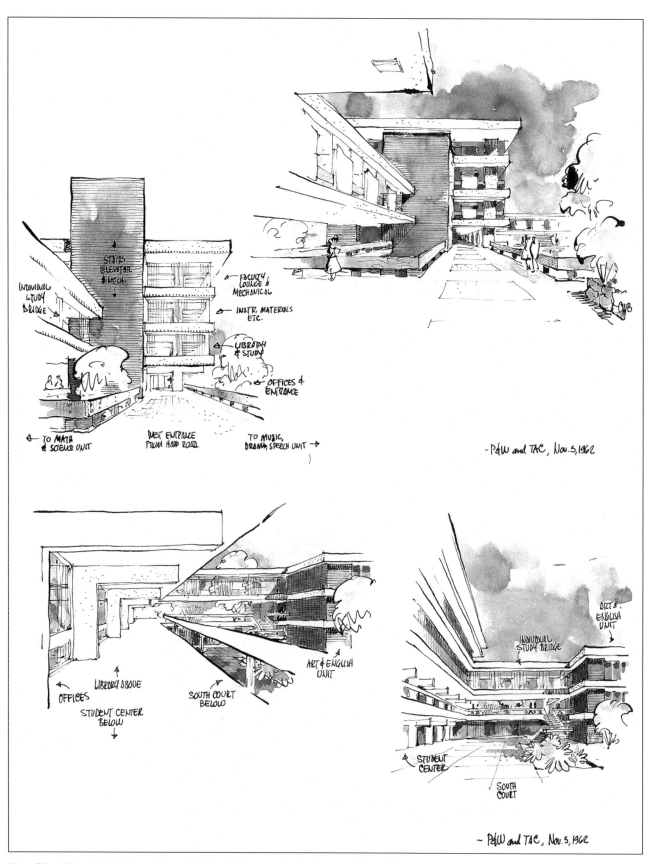

**New Trier West High School, Northfield, IL. Uses study bridges to link buildings.**

New Trier's concrete structured frame is expressed in the design, and infill walls of brick and windows help make this a classic modern campus.

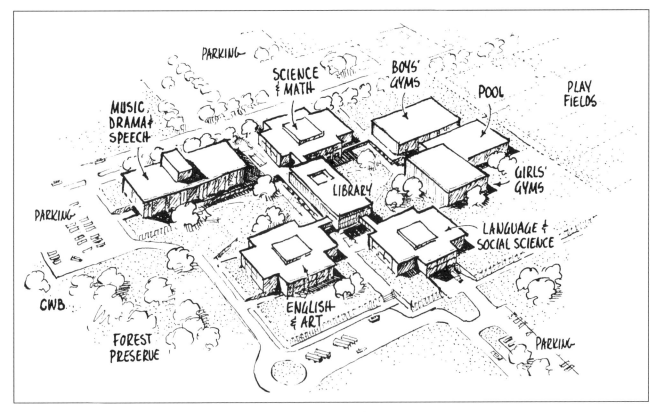

Around the New Trier West High School's library are three academic units.

City schools were also designed and built in the 1960 decade. Anthony Overton Public School in Chicago was a prototype for the city.

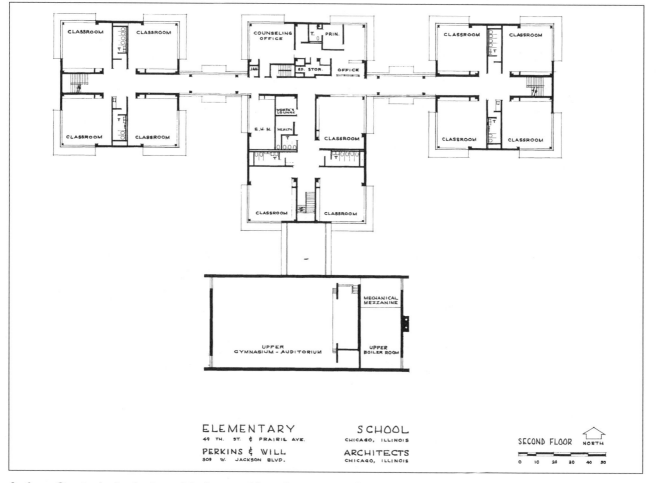

ELEMENTARY SCHOOL
49 TH. ST. & PRAIRIE AVE. CHICAGO, ILLINOIS
PERKINS & WILL ARCHITECTS
809 W. JACKSON BLVD. CHICAGO, ILLINOIS

SECOND FLOOR NORTH
0 10 20 20 40 50

Anthony Overton's classic plan, with clusters of four classrooms each.

**Jones Commercial High School, downtown Chicago, over a subway station, was designed for vertical expansion by adding as many as ten floors.**

gain the advantages of flexible space, (2) investigated and funded examples of "system" building components to build schools faster, cheaper, and better (a goal that was not completely achieved), (3) explored the use of new media, especially television, and studied how they might influence school design, and (4) encouraged school systems to try new organizational methods such as team teaching, new curricula, and new relationships with their communities. Dr. Harold Gores was the leader of this exciting partnership between the foundation and schools, which influenced school design nationwide and in Canada. Thousands of educators, planners, engineers, and architects were influenced by EFL, and that influence continues today. Jonathan King and Ben Graves were also at the center

of EFL innovation. Ben Graves was also the author of *Schoolways,* which was published in 1993 by McGraw-Hill.

One of EFL's most important innovations was the development of the "open plan," a concept that influenced the basic design of thousands of schools in the 1960s. This idea was easily understood: Instead of being designed with dozens of identical, boxy, and rigid classrooms ("the egg-crate plan" serving a program that was based on "cells and bells," Harold Gores and his associates delighted in reminding us), the school of the future should be planned with large, open, and therefore flexible spaces. Without many inflexible walls, the open space would constantly adapt to the changing needs of the educational teams. Instead of having almost all academic activities in 30-foot by 30-foot permanent classrooms with one-hour segments of time regardless of the nature of the curriculum, the open spaces would be adaptable to changing educational needs.

The open plan idea and its concept of flexibility were an important innovation in the 1960s, but unfortunately, the idea was unacceptable to some teachers, administrators, and architects who didn't want to change. In the following years most open plan schools returned to the old and comfortable programs. Open space was chopped up into classrooms with doors that could be shut.

This happened to most of the open plan schools—most but not all.

Some open space schools have survived. We'd guess that only a small percentage of these schools are still "open," and a few more have been built in recent years. Others are being planned.

An example of an open space school that has continued to be "open" is the Disney Magnet School on Lake Shore Drive near Montrose Harbor in Chicago. The school as it was constructed is shown on a typical floor plan for a three-story school. Other alternative plans show how the 90-foot by 90-foot open spaces (served by generous faculty team offices—workrooms) may be partitioned for traditional 30-foot by 30-foot classrooms. That hasn't happened yet, and the school is twenty-seven years old!

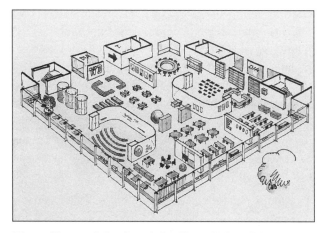

Disney Magnet School, on Lake Shore Drive, Chicago, IL. Designed as a series of 90 feet by 90 feet open spaces. One option, group of thirty students.

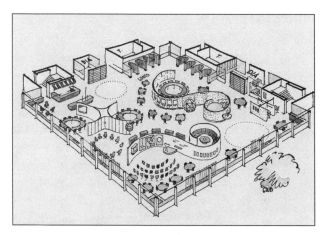

A more imaginative concept for one of the 8,100 sq. ft. open spaces at Disney Magnet School. The open plan has survived!

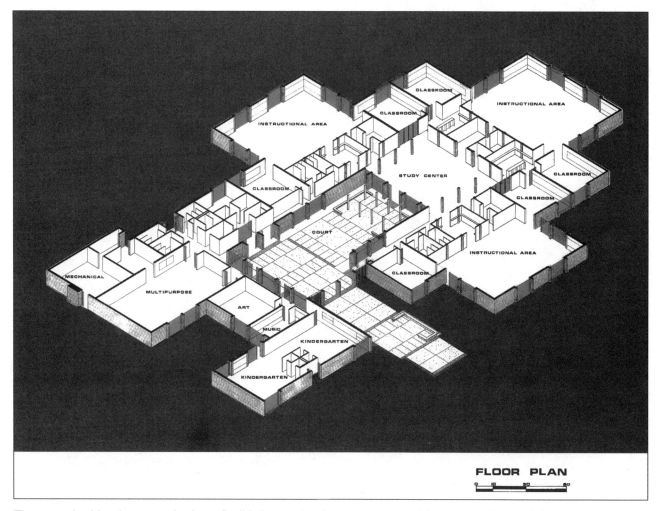

The open plan idea, incorporating large flexible instructional areas, was an exciting concept in the 1960's. Butternut Elementary School in North Olmsted, OH, was planned by Lesko Associates in association with Perkins & Will.

## THE 1970S

A lot of important design activity occurred in California in the 1960s and 1970s. Many significant schools were planned and constructed by growing school districts. The Irvine Unified School District in Orange County built prize-winning and parent-pleasing elementary, middle, and high schools designed by the Blurock office and by others. We prepared a master plan for the educational facilities for the village of Woodbridge, working with three clients: (1) the Irvine Company, which was the developer, (2) the city of Irvine, and (3) the Irvine Unified School District. Different architects were selected to design specific buildings. We designed Woodbridge High School, a villagelike cluster of one- and two-story shed-roofed structures, using wood construction, which also was used for houses and commercial buildings because it was agreeable in character and because wood structures have good earthquake-resisting qualities.

The enrollment boom began to cool down, the number of students dropped nationwide, and school districts found that they had too much space. They had surplus schools. A new challenge faced school planners: what to do with school buildings that were no longer needed for traditional education.

Some very imaginative solutions were developed.

Some surplus buildings were torn down, a perfectly reasonable action if the school buildings were junkers. However, some existing buildings are gems, or at least not bad. In that case four possible solutions can be considered:

1. Sell the building to another public or private owner.

2. Lease the building to another public or private user.

3. Keep the building but use it for new programs (such as adult education).

4. Keep the building but mothball it.

Well-known examples include the following:

1. A beautiful high school in Claremont, California, became a shopping center.

UNIT A (BELOW INTERSTATE)
ADULT EDUCATION, DAY CARE,
HEALTH SUITE, ELDERLY CENTER
UNIT B
CLASSROOMS, STUDIOS,
MEDIA CENTER, PUBLIC LIBRARY
AUDITORIUM, CAFETERIA
UNIT C (BELOW RAILROAD)
COMMUNITY SERVICES, CRAFTS,
COUNSELING, ADMINISTRATION
UNIT D
GYMNASIUM, POOL, LOCKERS

**NEW NORTH COMMUNITY SCHOOL**
SPRINGFIELD, MASSACHUSETTS

PERKINS & WILL ARCHITECTS

**Problem: The site for the New North Community School in Springfield, MA, was divided by Interstate 91 and a railroad. Solution: A lower level walkway lined with community offices links three buildings and two neighborhoods.**

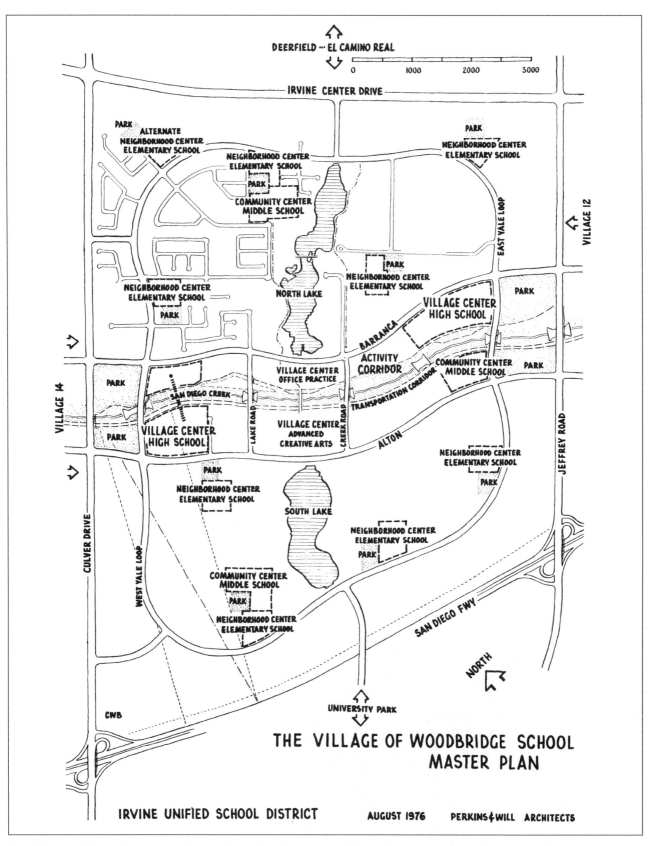

**THE VILLAGE OF WOODBRIDGE SCHOOL MASTER PLAN**

IRVINE UNIFIED SCHOOL DISTRICT    AUGUST 1976    PERKINS & WILL ARCHITECTS

**The Village of Woodbridge School Master Plan:** Two high schools (Village Centers), four middle schools (Community Centers), and eight elementary schools (Neighborhood Centers). Irvine, CA.

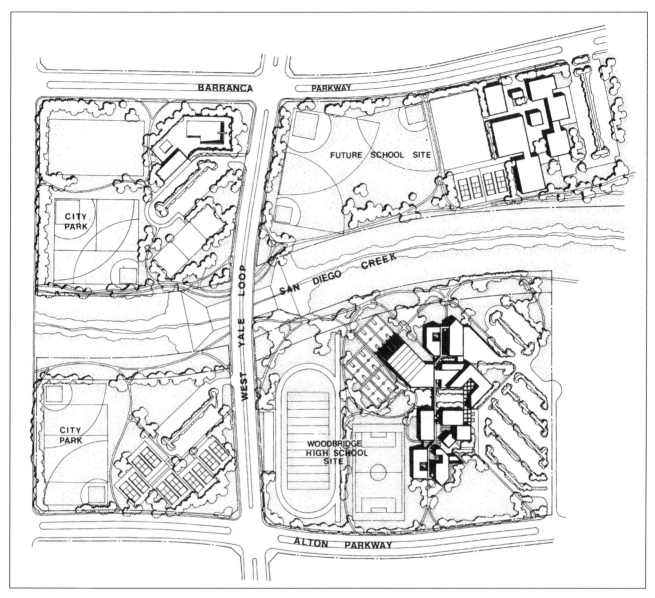

Village of Woodbridge School Master Plan detail. The high school is "village-like." Site facilities are shared with parks.

The plaza at Woodbridge High School.

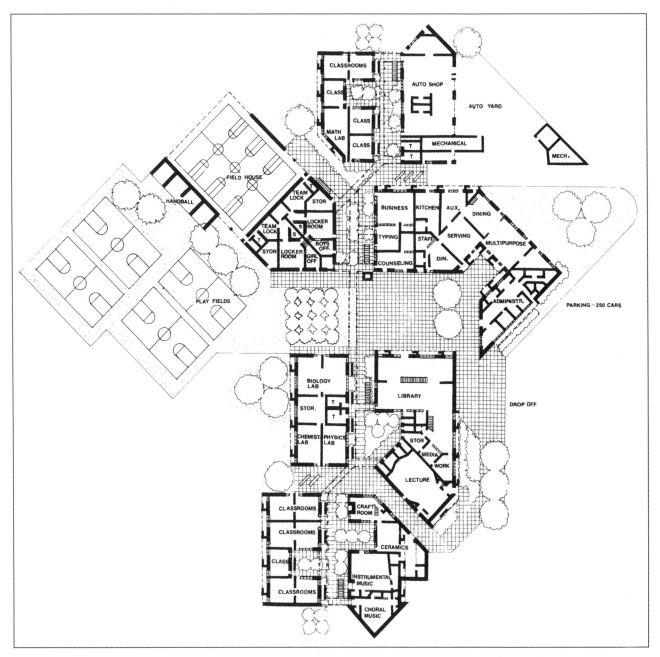

**Woodbridge High School. First floor plan.**

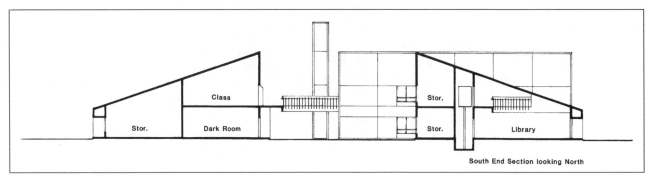

**Typical cross section.**

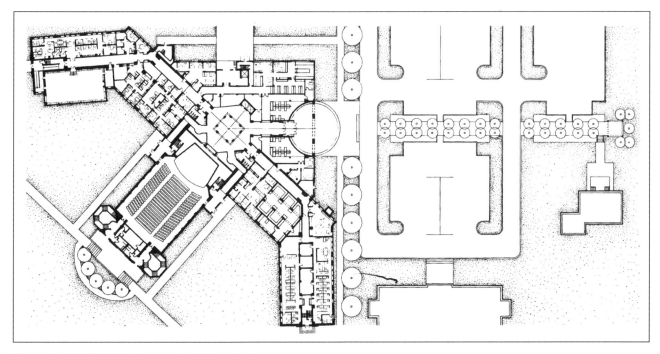

**Norwalk, CT, City Hall. A re-cycled high school.**

2. A late 1880s school in downtown Dallas, Texas, is now corporate offices.

3. Perkins School in Boston has been converted to apartments.

4. A school in Norwalk, Connecticut, became a city hall.

5. New Trier West High School west of Winnetka, Illinois, in recent years has been a community center for fitness, arts, and offices but may become a high school again as enrollment increases.

One of the problems caused by declining enrollment and surplus school space is the fact that tax-paying citizens are not inclined to vote for school facility improvements when they read that their school systems have unused classrooms. Therefore, existing school buildings deteriorate since funds for maintenance, repairs, and replacement are not available. Deferred maintenance was a serious problem in many communities in the 1970s and 1980s, and in the 1990s this situation joined the list of "crises" American society was facing. The scope of the problem was beginning to be recognized as we entered the 1980s.

## THE 1980S

Generally, things changed from declining numbers of students to gains in enrollment as the demographic pendulum swung back and forth. School administrators and boards of education found that they didn't have enough space at the elementary school level.

**The mall for the Dade County facility that serves students and adults from a large region south of Miami.**

**Robert Morgan Vocational—Technical Institute, Dade Co., FL.**

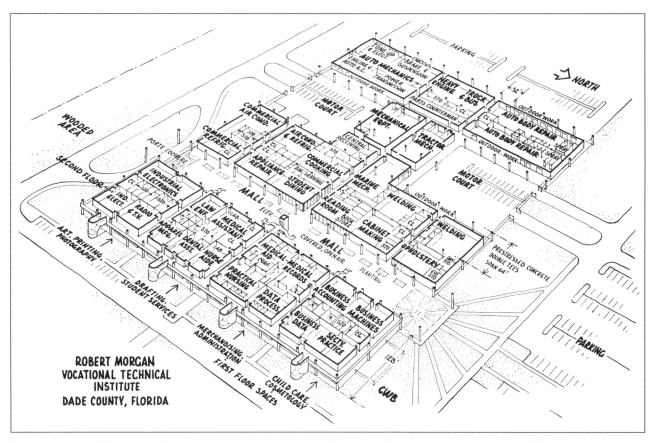

**The mall (covered, but open air) or student street, is the focal point, serving one story shops on one side and two story labs on the other side.**

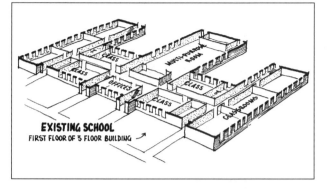

**Existing School: Surplus space. How might it serve the community?**

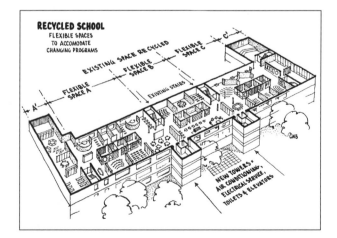

**Recycled School and Community Center—a new focal point and cultural, recreational and educational center for the community.**

Some communities experienced overcrowded classrooms and double sessions, just as they had thirty years earlier. Classrooms were added to existing elementary schools, and new schools were planned; this surprised not only citizens but also architects, engineers, and builders who thought that architecture for education was a topic that could interest only a few educational facilities planners.

However, a closer inspection of demographic trends showed that many new schools were needed

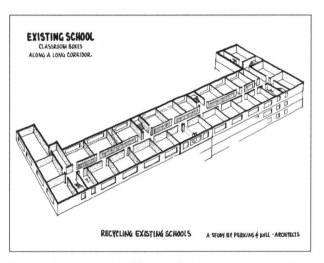

**Typical classroom wing. How might the existing space be re-deployed?**

and that the demand for new buildings would continue into the twenty-first century. The trends included a rise in the birthrate, the movement of people to the south and west, the growth of some cities and states, greater use of school facilities by more people, reawakened interest in better education, and satisfaction of the pent-up demand for high-quality buildings.

During the latter years of the 1980s the emphasis in new construction began to change from elementary schools to secondary

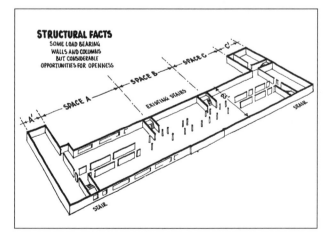

**First, examine the structure to determine how flexible the space is.**

**Then, re-plan the space following a new educational program.**

schools. The "miniboom" enrollments affected high schools, and demographic analysts projected new records in the number of high school students anticipated in the 1990s and beyond.

Planning and architecture for secondary education gained new importance as educators projected the need for thousands of new high schools nationwide to accommodate the increased numbers of students. In addition, the entire stock of existing buildings was in need of evaluation and, usually, improvement. The "old" schools, constructed from late in the nineteenth century to late in the twentieth century, ranged from the heavyweight, ornate, multistory brick and stone wall "classical" schools of the 1890s and 1900s, to the lightweight, plain, one-story steel and glass wall "modern" schools of the 1950s, to the postmodern, two- and three-story, more appealing schools of the 1990s. Most of these schools had obvious shortcomings when evaluated in terms of teaching and learning technology, energy conservation, safety, flexibility, handicapped accessibility, acoustics, indoor air qual-ity, and site concerns (size, location, accessibility, community use).

In the 1980s we found that there were many exciting new challenges in both designing and building new schools and updating existing buildings. One way to look at this new interest in architecture for education is to compare the topics featured at the conventions of the AASA (American Association of School Administrators), ASBO (Association of School Business Officials), and NSBA (National School Boards Association). During the last half of the 1970s, when we were all considering what to do with surplus space, these conventions had practically no sessions on school design. In the 1980s some programs on elementary school planning and design appeared, and during the last half of the decade sessions on secondary school planning and design began to be scheduled.

Concurrently, the AIA (American Institute of Architects) conventions acknowledged the new importance of education by including programs on school design.

# 2

# ARCHITECTURE

## FOR

# EDUCATION

This chapter will discuss some of the issues, trends, and ideas we all will confront in the twenty-first century.

Architecture for education does not occur in a vacuum. Education, and therefore school architecture, is responsive to changes in demographics, changes in culture and the economy, new social and environmental demands, and competition—local, statewide, national, and now global. American students are linked to students worldwide, especially as transportation, telephone, television, and computer networks and the Internet expand.

**Issues, Trends and Ideas**

## Flexibility

Architects who design schools are always confronted by the following questions: How can we best plan for the future? How can we build spaces that are appropriate for the first year of occupancy while anticipating the future need for space of the school? If we don't know the program for tomorrow, how can we design schools to accommodate the educational specifications of future users?

The modern American office building has solved the problem of not knowing who future tenants will be. The key words are *flexibility* and *adaptability*. The owner-developer of an office building often builds space for the unknown tenants of tomorrow. The general nature of the space requirements is known from

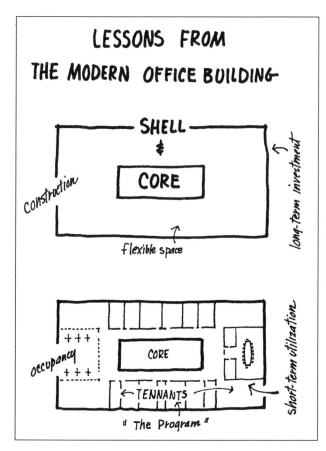

**Flexible space between outer shell and inner core.**

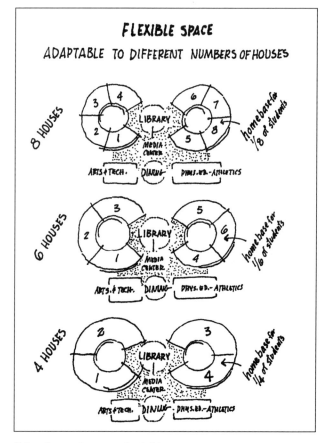

**Schools need some adaptable space.**

current experience with similar projects. The owner-developer knows that one floor of office space may be used by an insurance company that needs open and flexible working space with room for lots of electronic communications equipment. Another floor might consist of suites of doctors' and dentists' offices with many small spaces and lots of plumbing potential. The design of the building's services must be adaptable to these different space needs. The HVAC (heating, ventilating, and air-conditioning) system must be designed to make future changes in occupancy relatively easy and inexpensive. The electrical system and the communication systems ("technology") and computers also must meet those requirements.

Design experience in office building helps generate the form of a building. For example, most people want windows with a view, and work spaces are best situated when they are within 30 or 40 feet of windows. In the northern hemisphere, south-facing and north-facing windows are best. Windows facing the south can be protected from the sun by roof overhangs that shade walls from high summer sun, while windows facing the north do not have a sun control problem. East-facing windows provide early morning warmth, but west-facing windows are sometimes difficult to control. A glassy office tower in a southern city too often has the same glass curtain wall on the west eleva-

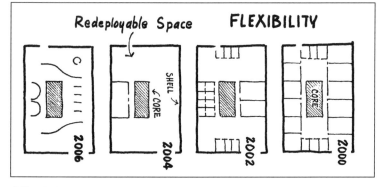

**Office buildings provide re-deployable space.**

tion that it has on the other three elevations. Both comfort and energy efficiency are sacrificed if the architects fail to recognize the problem and opportunity of orientation.

Shifting that experience to school design is relatively easy once the advantages are understood. Education can use flexible space just as business and government use it.

An interesting test of flexible space occurs when a company takes over a surplus school and adapts it to its own space needs. Good examples are seen in many parts of the United States. In Wilmette, Illinois, a northern suburb of Chicago, "Office in the Park" is an adaptive reuse of a modern 1960s two-story elementary school. The developer removed all the interior walls and replanned the space; a new floor was built in the gym, creating two stories of offices around a small skylighted atrium. The original space proved to be flexible.

In Dallas the SEDCO Oil Drilling Company restored the 1890s downtown Cumberland School for its corporate headquarters. Norwalk, Connecticut, redeveloped its obsolete high school to create a "new" city hall.

In Saint Paul, Minnesota, an impending classroom shortage generated an innovative solution to the need for 200 elementary school classrooms. To provide some of those classrooms, the school district purchased an existing building which was relatively new, vacant, and for sale. It had been a 265,000-square-

foot Control Data Corporation distribution center. The district purchased the building and the 14-acre site for $8.3 million and spent $16 million on renovation and technological improvements to create the Rondo Educational Center. The compact two-story building had a large footprint of 520 feet by 350 feet, and so the architects, Pope Associates, working with the school's facility planning managers created four courtyards to bring daylight and views into the space. The building was able to accommodate eleven programs, including early childhood, kindergarten through sixth grade (K–6) and kindergarten through eighth grade (K–8) schools, and family education, for a total of 2,265 students. Shared spaces that are accessible from each of the eleven programs include gyms, health facilities, and the instructional materials center. This is a beautiful example of recycling existing space for new uses, in this case, elementary education.

It works both ways. Some schools successfully use buildings that originally were built to be offices, labs, factories, or warehouses. In Boston, the architects Pierce, Pierce and Kramer converted a fifty-year old "four-story factory" into a fine school and community center. In Tacoma, a 1910 department store was recycled for a law school, and in Dallas, El Centro, the downtown community college is situated in a former department store.

There are a number of lessons from such experiences in terms of achieving flexibility for a broad range of needs, from simple changes in partitioning in one wing of an existing building to the total redesign of an entire building:

> Twentieth-century buildings, both traditional and modern, often provide space which is reasonably adaptable to new needs. Some nineteenth-century buildings also provide such space but sometimes do not satisfy modern fire and exit codes and may be costly to restore.
>
> Space is flexible when it is by nature open and not irrevocably committed to only one plan of rooms and when mechanical and electrical systems are easily modified to satisfy new needs.
>
> Schools can reuse both existing school buildings and other kinds of structures, such as low-rise office buildings. The reasons for doing this not only are financial (in fact, colleges and universities often find that restoring "Old Main" costs more than new

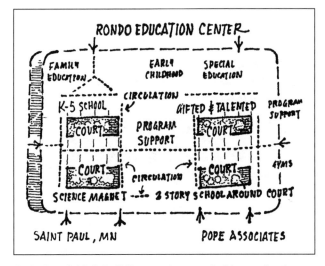

**An industrial loft building can be recycled into school space.**

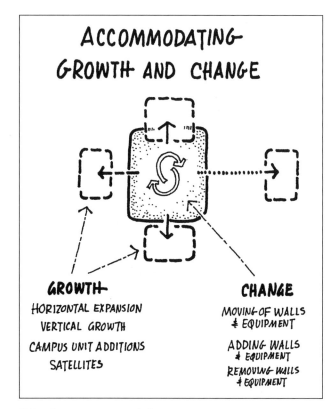

**Schools must grow and change.**

The school of the future will be planned with future reuse in mind. So far, almost no examples exist, but planners should consider how a school might be reused when enrollment plunges as it did in the 1970s. The nature of the neighborhood will determine who the next users will be. If the school is located in a commercial area, the reuse is obvious. If it is in a residential area, conversion to apartments will be a logical solution to the problem of decreasing enrollment and surplus space.

For an area that is already built up, a surplus school should be leased for ten years and not sold, because no other sites will be available when enrollment begins to rise again.

## The Two Big Form Generators

The plan and shape of a school building—its form—are determined by the program of space requirements (the educational specifications) and by the site (the size, shape, and characteristics of the land and the neighboring properties).

This simple and straightforward fact is recognized by architects, engineers, and planners but is not widely appreciated by laypeople, who may believe that

construction) but can save an institution time when schedules are tight. Historical preservation may be the motive for reuse.

Twenty-first-century schools are going to utilize both new buildings which satisfy contemporary and future space needs and recycled buildings from the twentieth century but also from the nineteenth century as entirely new interiors within the preserved and restored shells of landmark structures. This rich mix of architecture for education will give educational facilities more personality and more individuality and will encourage innovation. Students and parents will choose the most promising school from a broad range of options, including great old buildings and great new buildings.

Some schools *should* be demolished or sold to other users. A good school in a poor location suggests two options: (1) close the school and open a new or recycled school at a good location or (2) solve the poor location problem, whether it is an environmental, social, or other condition.

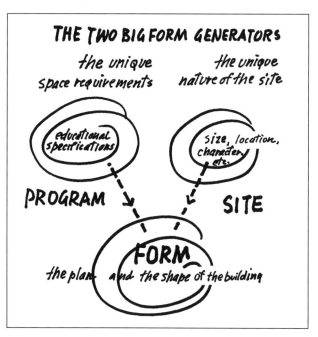

**The form of a building is generated by its program and its site.**

the designer or design team more or less arbitrarily selects a form for a school building. Of course, the form of some schools is unrelated to the program and site, but such structures are seldom deemed appropriate.

When the architect and the other members of the design team understand and support the unique nature of the program and the unique nature of the site, the prospects are good for the achievement of excellence in school design.

In the past, the forms of some schools were determined by arbitrary selection (such as choosing between "Collegiate Gothic" and "Collegiate Georgian") or by fashion (such as choosing between "boxy modern" and "postmodern"). In the future, the program and site will have a greater impact on design, and this will generate architecture for education that is more regional and more responsive to local needs.

## The Issue of Size

A school or a system of related schools cannot be envisioned, planned, designed, and built without facing the issue of size. Are large schools or small schools more appropriate for a specific situation? Can a network of small general schools be served by a number of specialized facilities, somewhat like a cluster of small colleges, set around special facilities which may include the library and media center, the arts center, and the fitness center?

Meanwhile, high schools in some cities have grown to accommodate 3,000 or more students or are planned for future growth to that size. One issue that is not always recognized as a problem is the popularity of high school football in many states and cities. A large student enrollment gives the football coaches a large number of potential players. Some educators, however, have challenged the advisability of large size or at least have questioned the issues that affect the decision-making process. In 1995 Valerie Lee at the University of Michigan and Julia Smith at the University of Rochester published research which showed that the ideal high school is in the range of 600 to 900 students. One of their most important conclusions is, "In large high schools, especially those enrolling over 2100 students, they learn consistently less."

The building design implications of this issue are so important that we will return to this topic later in this chapter.

## Basic Assumptions Reconsidered

Schools will have a new flavor as some of the basic assumptions change in response to societal changes. Old ideas about the time for education, the place for education, the grade system, the schedule egg crate, and the effectiveness of teachers will be questioned. New answers will help create new kinds of schools.

Teachers will again play a key role, but this time they will have better workplaces and equipment. Remember that currently only a few teachers have a telephone, let alone more exotic equipment such as a fax machine, a computer, printer, voice mail, and E-mail. There are many calls for new forms of teaching and learning, but we don't use the telephone imaginatively. The equipment is too often down the hall in a faculty work and preparation room. A better place would be the heart of a small cluster of classrooms or the equivalent space in an open plan configuration. Wait! Did someone say "open plan"? The concept was discredited in the 1970s, when some teachers resisted change in the school format. We will return to this topic later in this chapter.

## Space for Individual Learning

An individualized schedule for every student would have significant implications for school planning and design. Identical classrooms lined up along identical corridors or clusters of identical spaces with identical prefabricated portable classrooms would no longer be appreciated. Instead, adaptable space would be needed to accommodate a great variety of learning styles: individually, in small groups (including office-size spaces for teams of 5 students), in medium-size groups of 10 to 25 students, and large group spaces for 50 to 200 students, plus a theater, a dining room, a multipurpose room, and a gymnasium which can seat the entire student body, whether it consists of 600, 1,200, or 2,400 students.

We have been especially interested in the future prospects for "space for individual learning" since 1959, when we published in *School Executive and*

**SPACE FOR INDIVIDUAL LEARNING**

**Turf: five students' place for individual learning.**

the only place for teaching and learning. Schools will be seen as places where individuals and whole families learn basic skills, do research, prepare presentations, and learn about occupations, business and history, and art and languages. These are things which could be done at home, on the school bus, or on the job, but the school concentrates on teaching and learning and organizes the vast array of things to be learned by grouping relative topics, using both print and electronic media, and assembling diverse curricula to meet the unique needs of each individual. The school also provides a meeting place for cooperative learning and a social environment that can encourage and facilitate learning.

The English developed their own kind of neighborhood social center, the pub. That's where friends meet and where local news is heard. The United States isn't ready to include beer in most neighborhood centers, but the prospect of viewing the school as the community education center serving people of all ages, including preschoolers and senior citizens, should appeal to most people. More individuals will have a stake in the center.

*Educational Business* magazine a sixteen-page sketchbook which explored "Q-Space" (one student's place for an individual quest) mixed with teachers' studies and group spaces of various kinds.

Later, in 1968, we published an expanded version of this idea. A thirty-two-page sketchbook set some kind of record for visualizing a new kind of learning environment, by developing sketches for presenting a concept for the future. We visualized the "turf concept," which would give five students an office-size home base for individual study, projects, computer work, small group sessions, and meetings with faculty members. This is an idea that is still evolving. It has been adopted by a number of school planners and architects throughout the country as a model for the school of the future.

### Places Where People Want to Be

When thoughtfully planned, constructed, and managed, schools will be places where people worldwide, young and old, want to be. The school will continue to be the prime place for education, though it will not be

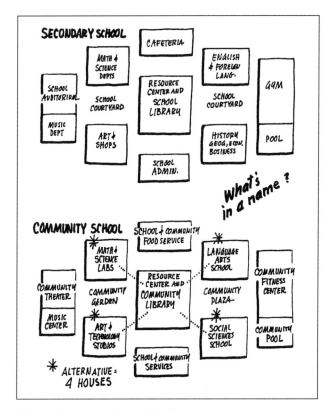

**Places where people want to be.**

## The Need for Innovation

Merriam-Webster's Collegiate Dictionary defines *innovation* as "the introduction of something new," "a new idea, method, or device," and "novelty." Americans are comfortable with the word *new* (and often believe that new is better than old) but are not so comfortable with *novelty,* which in addition to signifying *new* implies that something new may not be valuable or useful but instead may be capricious or even damaging. This is an issue that school and college planners and architects face every day: how to be innovative in designing educational facilities, to get the most effectiveness for the dollar in terms of social goals, while avoiding school building innovations that do not enhance the learning environment.

We can agree that being innovative in school planning and design is risky, but it is important to take risks in school design. It is not advisable to let well enough alone. Experiments are necessary. If they are truly innovative, they may not be successful; in fact, one could argue that most innovations in design are not successful, since more often than not they fail to make learning more effective (which is the measure of success). However, experiments may be successful. An innovative idea may be so successful that it may change the way we do things. It may be downright revolutionary!

Some examples of successful innovation in school design in the nineteenth and twentieth centuries were classrooms for thirty students more or less, specialized shops and laboratories, computer technology, flexible and adaptable space of the kind one finds in modern office buildings, the community school concept, and team teaching.

When an architecture for education innovation catches on, it can spread and change the way we plan, design, and use school buildings and the equipment schoolhouses contain. To discourage innovation would be to signal that experimentation and changes in school design are not welcome; stagnation (motionless, dull, inactive, stale conditions) then would dominate the educational institutions and the buildings and equipment they use.

To foster a healthy and stimulating society, the need for innovation is apparent; to create effective schools, innovation in the design of educational facilities is essential.

## Schools Will Be Larger/Schools Will Be Smaller

The size of tomorrow's schools will be influenced by two trends:

1. Schools will be larger in the twenty-first century. This is supported by the belief that economies of scale favor larger and larger institutions. Costs will be lower, it is argued, because teachers and specialized laboratories and machines are expensive.

2. Schools will be smaller in the twenty-first century. This is supported by the belief that schools are too large, too impersonal, and overpowering in scale and do not always effectively serve the needs of individual students.

You can have the advantages of both larger and smaller schools. Large schools, their supporters insist, utilize facilities more efficiently. A swimming pool for a 1,200-student high school stands idle for many hours of the day and evening. In a school 50 percent larger (1,800 students) the pool is used for more hours. A well-equipped Russian language lab and classroom, along with a Russian teacher, may have a better chance for survival in a larger school. Bigger and better studios for the arts are another argument for big schools. However, the learning environment in a large school may be overwhelming to some students. Those who prefer small schools point out that such schools give more students more opportunities to participate in student government, the paper, the yearbook, drama, the orchestra, athletics, and student government.

## Schools within a School

A concept that deserves our attention is that of schools within a school, or the "house plan," in which a larger school is subdivided into three to six smaller schools, each with its own space and identity.

Sketched here is a concept for a middle school. This school has not been constructed; it is a concept, an idea for a new school that consists of a two-story unit with a ramp connecting four, five, or six small schools clustered around a midlevel media center. Each school within a school consists of four generalized learning spaces around a faculty office and workroom. The four schools also share some specialized

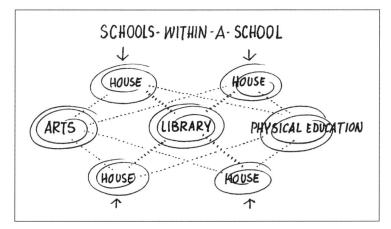

**The house plan is composed of small schools.**

The site can be relatively small if it is adjacent to another school and to a community park which includes a neighborhood swimming pool, tennis courts, and a system of paths and bicycle trails which connect the various facilities. The shared facilities make good sense.

## Larger and Smaller: We Need Both

Schools are often larger than they were in the past and often deliver appropriate educational opportunities. The matter of size, however, suggests that large schools make even more specialized facilities available for some of the disciplines (physical education and athletics, theater and music, science and technology) but do not necessarily provide better spaces for the humanities, social sciences, English, and foreign languages.

learning areas—science, home arts, arts and crafts, technical education, and music—and, in adjacent but separate units, a community multipurpose room and physical education spaces.

The four schools are in a two-story residential-scaled unit, with the media center midway between the houses. A ramp connects the three levels.

The reasons for large schools are complex and may be economic, social, cultural, or competitive. In many

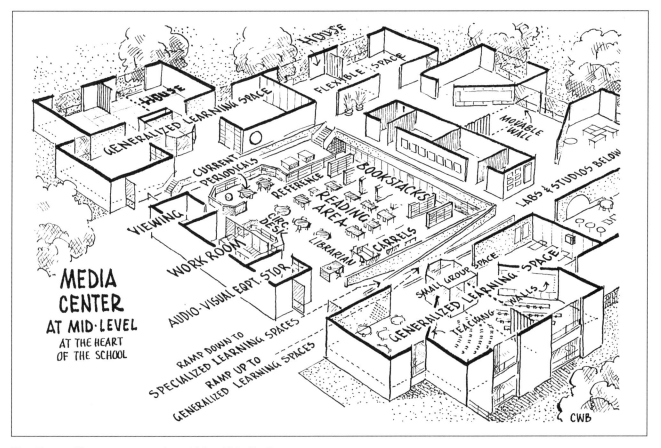

**Two floors of houses surround a mid-level Media Center.**

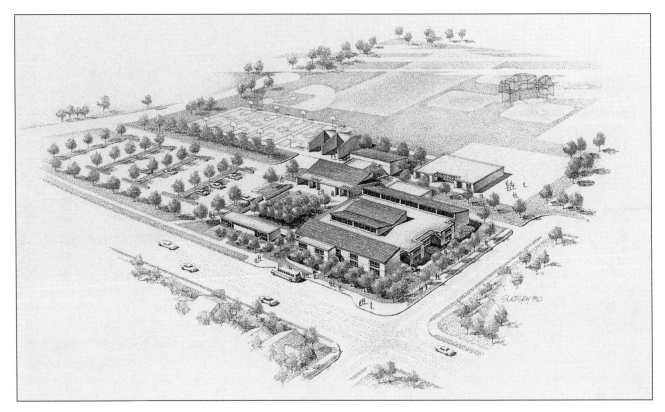

**Village scale.**

states high school football is a very popular sport for both students and citizens. A large enrollment means a larger pool of potential athletes. In Indiana, it's basketball. Meanwhile, some citizens wonder why the emphasis is on football and basketball, instead of on "lifetime sports," especially tennis, handball, swimming, golf, jogging, and walking—sports which adults enjoy. The response is clear: Americans do indeed favor football, basketball, and baseball at the school, at the arena, and on television.

Bigger schools mean larger attendance areas, more school buses, greater consumption of energy, and less walking because in big districts fewer students and staff members can walk to school. Fewer opportunities to plan a school with broader community needs in mind also may be a problem with big schools. The scale and impact of a 3,000- or 4,000-student high school can be overpowering to the street, the neighborhood, and the individual students and staff members.

It is interesting to note that a 3,000-student college is considered "large" and almost always consists of a number of small buildings arranged among green and forested open outdoor spaces. Students go outdoors to walk from one part of the campus to another. The college system of small buildings mixed with various open spaces creates a very agreeable learning environment.

Contrast that with some 3,000-student secondary schools, which often are nearly windowless, usually consisting of many additions without the benefit of a thoughtful master plan, creating a single-building "megastructure." The students move through the corridors of the various floor levels, going up and down exit stairs designed by firefighters. This scenario, however, should branch into two or more optional scenarios:

1. The big school is entirely too "institutional," with boxes of space jammed together as a multistory blockbuster.

2. The big school is planned around varied open spaces with interior daylight, views, and drama—flexible spaces which allow changes in programs on a daily basis—and the school is subdivided into a half dozen schools within a school (houses).

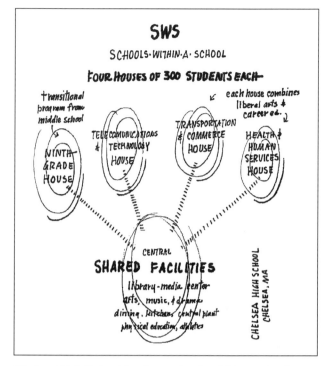

**SWS**

SCHOOLS·WITHIN·A·SCHOOL

**FOUR HOUSES OF 300 STUDENTS EACH**

transitional program from middle school

each house combines liberal arts & career ed.

NINTH GRADE HOUSE

TELECOMMUNICATIONS & TECHNOLOGY HOUSE

TRANSPORTATION & COMMERCE HOUSE

HEALTH & HUMAN SERVICES HOUSE

CENTRAL **SHARED FACILITIES**

library - media center
arts, music, & drama
dining, kitchen, central plant
physical education, athletics

CHELSEA HIGH SCHOOL CHELSEA, MA

**Chelsea High School has four schools-within-a-school.**

In other words, a big school presents a special design challenge to an architect, whether it is a high-density megastructure on an urban site or a low-density cluster of smaller buildings on a spacious suburban site.

One should remember that a large school of 3,000 or 4,000 students is a different kind of school and represents a different kind of planning and design problem and opportunity. The Conroe Independent School District north of Houston has completed its 3,000-student Woodlands High School. A high school of that size is not unusual in Texas. It is an interesting solution to the problem of size, creating an environment that benefits from the advantages of a large high school and those of a small school. A half dozen major building units (including a circular three-story academic unit) are related closely to each other for convenience but are separated by a fine circular courtyard and other open spaces. Students at Woodlands enjoy classrooms with windows and views of the big trees which surround the site and can take advantage of the broad range of education options a large school offers.

When "consolidation" was a nationwide process which created larger school districts, small schools were considered a thing of the past. Most people associated bigger with better. High schools with only a few

dozen students were consolidated into schools with hundreds or even thousands of students. This occurred in a context of the replacement of one-room and other very small schools nationwide.

We must ask whether there is a desirable limit to consolidation. We must ask whether the further combination of existing smaller schools into larger schools would be beneficial. We must explore the possibility of revitalizing the idea of a small school.

One of the most obvious problems with small schools is the presence of a very small faculty in each school. There is a possible answer, however, to the question of how to bring other resources into a small school to supplement the small staff and limited facilities: learning technology. Computers, television, distance learning, fax, laptops, telephones, and weekly visits to other education centers can make a small school as good as a larger school.

Dr. Stanton Leggett, an educational consultant, has been a consistent advocate for small schools where "each student is really needed, an important counter balance to our impersonal culture." His ideas are based on the premise that small schools can compete successfully with larger ones.

Dr. Leggett was the educational consultant for the Evanston Township High School in the 1960s, when increasing enrollments made it necessary to add to the classic Collegiate Gothic building of the 1920s, where the site was large and centrally located, or to build a second high school at a new location. The insurmountable problem consisted of finding a site for a second high school of 2,500 to 3,000 students, a need which the demographers had forecasted. Since Evanston is a completely built up suburb just north of Chicago, the board decided to expand the existing high school to 5,000 or 6,000 students. Concurrently, it was decided to adopt the schools within a school organization plan by including four houses of 1,250 to 1,500 students each, with each house having its own quadrant of classrooms and labs and sharing certain large and central facilities, especially physical education and athletics; fine arts, including a large auditorium; and a central resource center around which were four house libraries where most teachers offices would be located. The completed complex is a wonderful campus.

One prediction, however, turned out to be wrong. The demographics changed, the high school never reached 6,000 students, and when enrollment declined, the house plan was modified. The lessons were clear, but almost everyone agreed that the schools within a school concept was still a worthy option for the future. Now that the enrollment is increasing again, the idea of returning to the house plan can be entertained because the facilities are flexible and adaptable enough to accommodate any number of ideas for the future. Evanston will continue to promote high-quality education. Superb space will help make that possible.

## The Multilocation School

Students in most secondary schools spend nearly all their time at one school location. This routine is relieved occasionally by a bus ride to another high school for an athletic event or an infrequent visit to an office, lab, or museum. Contrast that all-at-one-location high school system to a college freshman's schedule, which every day involves many different sites—the dormitory, the dining room, the library, classrooms, labs, studios, the gym and pool, and off-campus restaurant or movie—one or more bus rides, and considerable walking.

This suggests more freedom, more variety in scheduling, more locations, and more self-responsibility for twelfth-graders. Students could get more of their education at off-campus sites: the government office building, private offices, banks, labs, factories, newspaper offices, hospitals, local libraries, museums, concert halls, and local community college and university campuses. This was an important innovation in Philadelphia in the late 1960s which was widely publicized as the "Parkway School."

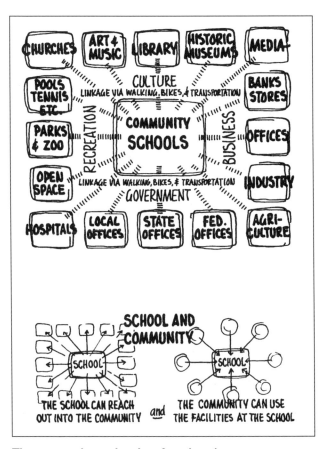

The community as the place for education.

impose standards on architecture for education. The fact is that similar building solutions make no sense in widely different localities. New England has to plan for vigorous winters; the benign climate of Southern California makes outdoor circulation feasible, but that layout is inappropriate for Chicago. New Mexico's Indian and Hispanic culture includes an important architectural heritage. Alaska and northern Canada have to

## Regionalism

The United States and Canada are large nations that encompass a broad range of cultures, climates, geographic features, historical backgrounds, resources, industries, occupations, and degrees of urbanization. There is no reasonable way to assume that one kind of school design would be appropriate for even a small percentage of the schools in North America. However, there is a danger that school facilities planners will attempt to

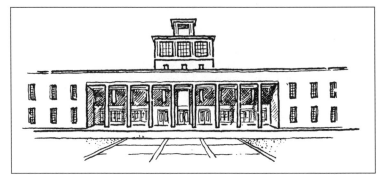

**Capital High School in Santa Fe. Regional character.**

design foundations for permafrost. Florida is hot and humid, and so a campus in Miami can be a tropical paradise. Each location needs its own special architecture.

The next chapter is illustrated with photographs and drawings of schools in different parts of the United States.

## Every School Should Have Its Own Special Character

Schools are like snowflakes. No two are exactly alike, but each has certain characteristics which are common to all snowflakes, especially the hexagonal structure. Schools are also like the people they serve. No two people are identical. (No two identical twins are identical after a year of kindergarten because of the thousands of new encounters each child has.)

Every school is affected daily by hundreds of students, dozens of faculty members, visitors to the school building, and the neighborhood. The educational program is influenced by the experiences of these hundreds of people.

If one focuses on an individual student, it is reasonable to believe that that student's learning experience will be most effective if he or she has a program that has been custom designed for his or her needs.

That idea might have been appealing to many people in earlier decades, but there were too many obstacles. We had inherited the gridiron scheduling system that mandated one hour, or fifty minutes, or any other rigid time box for almost all the activities at a school. We also inherited the idea that most teaching should occur in classes of thirty students or, if the children were lucky, twenty-four students in a square classroom situated along the wall of a long corridor.

But now, looking ahead to the twenty-first century, we may have found a way to plan and manage individual programs for every student. Technology has come to our rescue. With the help of the computer, the school administration people and the school's counseling center, each student can have an individualized schedule. Don't expect to see an egg-crate schedule and its partner, the egg-crate building with rows of identical classrooms.

## Enrollment Projections Up and Down: The 1950s and 1960s

In the 1950s and 1960s many new schools were built in response to the baby boom. In every one of those years more than 4 million children were born in the United States.

Other concurrent forces created a strong demand for new schools. People moved from old city neighborhoods to new suburbs and from old northeastern states to southeastern, southwestern, and western states. These geographic changes would have caused many new schools to be built even without the demand caused by increases in the birthrate.

A third force for new schools was pent-up demand. Only a few new schools were created in the 1930s and 1940s. This situation was caused by the depression and World War II. Most school districts saved money by cutting back on maintenance. Existing buildings were from 20 years old to over 100 years old. New schools were needed, but few could be financed. In summary, the aging school problem, combined with enrollment increases and geographic shifts in population, created a demand for thousands of new schools. An innovative era of school building ensued.

The 1950s and 1960s were exciting and challenging decades for school planners and designers. New ideas about curricula, teaching methods, and community involvement and evolving concepts of architecture, engineering, and construction made school design

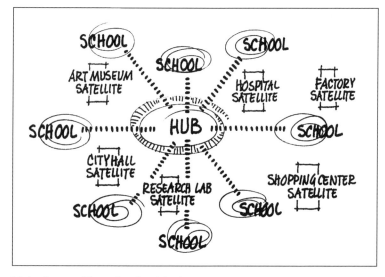

**Hub plus satellite schools with character.**

an important topic. A center for innovation was EFL, the Educational Facilities Laboratories, financed by the Ford Foundation, which became a major force for change by promoting research and financing studies on how to plan better schools. The president of EFL, Dr. Harold Gores, inspired educators and architects to explore new concepts for school buildings, sites, equipment, and curricula.

Sadly, almost no one is continuing the EFL vision. For the twenty-first century a new EFL is needed to reinforce and encourage innovative design. Since school facilities will continue to be a hot topic in the twenty-first century, there is an opportunity for this type of foundation. EFL supported the need for flexible space, folding and sliding walls, building systems, large and small groups of students, all-year schools, community schools, community use of facilities, and team teaching using the new media, and almost everyone benefited from its fresh ideas.

## Enrollment Projections Up and Down: The 1970s and 1980s

The 1970s featured a change in demography, especially a change in enrollment projections.

The demographers decided that they had been wrong on the subject of how much and how fast schools would grow.

Instead of projecting future upward trends, many experts on enrollment said that enrollment projections had to be revised downward because the birthrate had gone down. Announcements of this type caused a profound change in the prospects for new schools. First, the demographers' latest projections proved to be correct—enrollments fell. Many classrooms stood empty, and some schools were closed (but were imaginatively recycled for other community uses). Second, citizens, seeing empty classrooms and hearing reports about school designs, were not in the mood to pay for any improvement in the education infrastructure. Therefore, school boards and administrators were forced to spend as little as possible on maintaining existing schools and making new additions to buildings as communities turned down bond issues.

In the 1980s, the prospects for new schools improved as the economy improved, and the enrollment figures moved upward again. Elementary schools were the first to be influenced. A minor baby boom continues and is now affecting secondary schools.

## Enrollment Projections Up and Down: The 1990s and 2000s

Schools are being built again. The American Institute of Architects points out that school construction has increased every year since 1983, and rising enrollment will keep the market strong for the next decade. Elementary schools took off first, then middle schools, and then high schools. Assuming ten months for the program and the design and construction documents and twenty months for construction, a school that would be completed on January 1, 2000, had to start program and design work in mid-1997. A high school senior in 2000 had been in kindergarten thirteen years earlier—in 1987—when each student could be counted by the demographers and projections about the future could be made.

Our projection is that new schools will be needed in the year 2000 and that extensive renovation will be needed for hundreds of thousands of existing schools.

The renovation (renewal, remodeling, recycling) of existing schools requires new ideas, up-to-date analyses, and future-oriented syntheses. The title for this section could be changed to "New Schools Are Being Built Again, and Thousands of Existing Schools Are in Need of Extensive Renovation."

## The Enduring Classroom

This discussion leads to a broader investigation of how classrooms are designed, how they relate to other classrooms, how large they should be, what shape they should have, what size they should be, the nature of equipment to be used, probable seating and work space patterns, and the prospects for change.

Educators have predicted the demise of the classroom for generations. The boldest predictions came from EFL in the 1960s and 1970s and from studies by Dr. Lloyd Trump, who brought to our attention his belief that individuals learn most effectively as independent students proceeding at their own rates in both small groups (5 to 20 students) and large groups (60 to 100 students or more). In this concept, the classroom of thirty students does not exist. Its functions have been taken over by small and large groups, as happens in law schools, where the big lecture assembly is the best place for law students to hear lectures by the in-house faculty and by visitors, with independent study occurring in the adjacent law library, in other campus buildings, and at each student's residence.

The Trump plan was interesting and innovative, but it has not revolutionized school planning or school design. At least not yet.

The standard classroom survived. Efforts to change it, cluster it, add technology, subdivide and reconfigure it, and reshape it have met with some success, but the classroom for thirty students (or for twenty-eight or twenty-four or twenty) still exists in almost all public and private schools. It usually is rectangular or square, may or may not have windows, and usually has a door designed to keep the class in and both the neighborhood and the world out.

The following dozen sketches are meant to illustrate the design spirit of a dozen different options for planning classrooms or their successors. In each option learning spaces are clustered in alternative ways.

Consider some of the options for classrooms:

1. *Compact gridiron plan.* Since air-conditioning appeared, many one- and two-story schools have big footprints; formal, mechanistic, wide, and long floor plans; windowless classrooms; and a modular design (ingredients leading to a repetitive and institutional character). The gridiron prevails—no surprises. With the help of the computer, copying such plans is relatively easy and common. Without care, such overly compact buildings can be oppressive, and the learning environment will suffer.

2. *Organic plan.* The opposite is informal, organic architecture—rambling plans with great variety in terms of rooms, materials, and details. Each room has its own special character. The school continuously adapts to the changing space needs of new people. Classrooms are never finished.

3. *Double-loaded corridor with assigned classrooms.* Classrooms "belong" to teachers (especially in elementary schools) and classes of, say, twenty-five students. The classroom is also the teacher's office and workroom. The classroom is personal and expresses one teacher's personality.

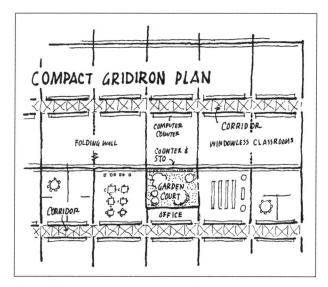

**The gridiron plan dominates school planning.**

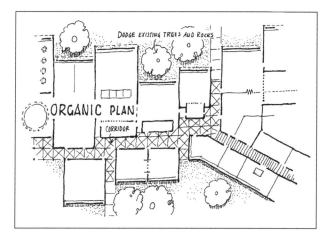

**In contrast, the organic plan adapts, changes.**

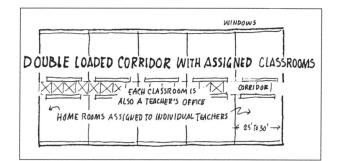

**Classrooms "belong" to teachers, as in elementary schools.**

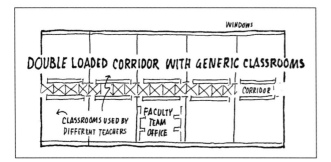

**Classrooms are used by various teachers, as in college.**

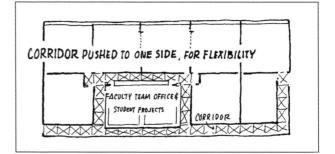

**Wider space, for clustering.**

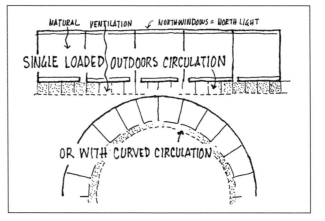

**Outdoor circulation. The most efficient plan.**

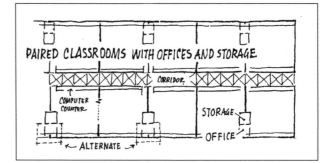

**Shared office and conference room.**

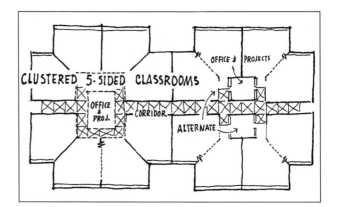

**Challenging the gridiron.**

4. *Double-loaded corridor with generic classrooms.* Classrooms are generic; they do not belong to one teacher (especially in colleges and universities). A number of different teachers and classes use the classroom. It is not one teacher's office. "Down the hall" one finds a faculty office where teachers from different disciplines meet and work together. Classrooms are impersonal.

5. *Corridor pushed to one side for wider flexible space.* This is the "Fort Collins plan": Instead of a central corridor, circulation is pushed to one side to achieve more adaptability. The corridor can be enclosed or open to learning spaces and/or to the outdoors.

6. *Single-loaded outdoor circulation.* This is a very efficient plan in which climate encourages a campus plan with very few, if any, interior corridors. All classrooms, labs, and other large spaces have windows, views, natural light, and natural cross-ventilation. This is still a good idea in areas where a benign climate makes outdoor circulation a pleasure. It has been a popular plan before and after the introduction of air-conditioning in the southern and western states.

7. *Paired classrooms sharing an office–conference room and storage.* Each pair of classrooms shares an office–conference room and storage room. This design is popular with teachers who need an acoustically separate place for private conversations and phone calls and a place for small group activities.

8. *Clustered five-sided classrooms.* Four pentagonal classrooms set around an office–conference room decrease the length of the corridor and provide cluster identity. Classrooms can be partially

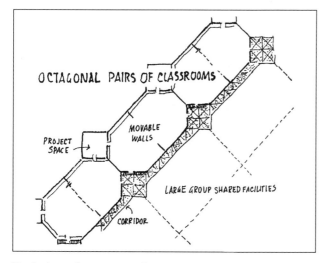

**Exploring other geometrics.**

"open" with different kinds of teaching walls and with or without doors.

9. *Hexagonal or octagonal classrooms.* This was tried in the 1960s. Expect new examples to appear in the twenty-first century. One problem is that furnishings and equipment are not widely available for hexagonal plans. Some of these plans were inspired by Frank Lloyd Wright.

10. *Small house plans (the schools within a school concept).* An example would be a multidisciplinary house for 125 students, as at the Solon Middle School in Solon, Ohio. A house has one classroom each for English, languages, social studies, science, and math, plus a multidisciplinary faculty team office.

11. *Medium-size house for 200 students.* This concept involves larger schools within a school, equivalent to eight classrooms, plus offices and a house resource center. A flexible, shared central space in the spirit of the modern office building is 30 feet wide and 100 feet long, or 3,000 square feet, a gross area of only 15 square feet per student. Imagine the possibilities for using this house resource center.

12. *Space for individual learning and the open plan reconsidered.* "The enduring classroom" evolves in small increments in response to curriculum changes, the influence of teaching and learning technology, and changes in the organization of high schools, slowly transforming the school program and school design.

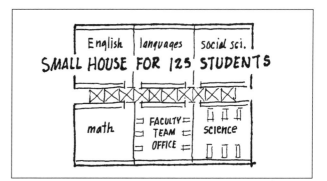

**Schools-within-a-school.**

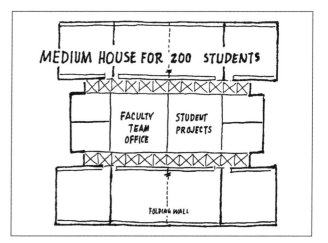

**Medium size houses.**

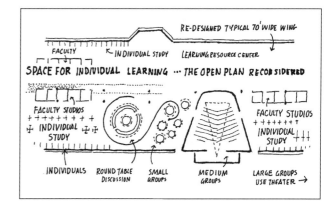

**The open plan re-considered.**

## The Community School

In the section on the multilocation school above, we explored the possibility of having the school reach out into the community; the other side of that coin is the fact that citizens in the community use school facilities more often now. Adults in some places see schools as

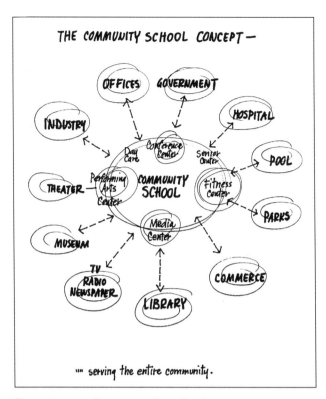

**Success story: the community school.**

places for adult education, consider the physical education facilities a community fitness center, and think of the school auditorium as a community cultural center. This new attitude affects elementary, middle, and high schools.

Instead of a school serving only middle school–age pupils, it can become a community center. Many facilities will be shared, and new relationships will emerge. Sometimes the "school library" and the "community library" will merge, and the new library–resource center will send its services electronically to homes as well as classrooms.

## The New Libraries

The school campus library will be the school's resource center and also will be one of the community's resource centers. Students and their parents will know where the resources are and will know that assistance is always available; if something is not immediately accessible, the library staff will scan the resources of the community, the state, the nation, and, the world. A partnership between community schools and local library systems is a possibility.

Recognizing the possibilities of learning throughout the community, on the job, via television, and at home, students and adults will think of school and community libraries as more scholarly and more research-oriented, a liberal arts focal facility as well as a social place. Look at a community library on any evening; it is filled with students who are reading, using computers, working on projects, exploring the collection, and chatting with friends. Library design and school design mix and blend. Sharp demarcation of areas and functions is gone.

We now see a library that looks much like a school, and we see a school that looks like a library. In this vision of the future, the entire school becomes the library, the instructional resource center (IRC), the learning resource center (LRC), the media center, or whatever term evolves to best describe the library. Some people still prefer the word *library* to describe the principal place where print and electronic media are prepared, ordered, stored, and used.

Regardless of what it is called, a new kind of facility is emerging. It is not bounded by the traditional walls that separate it from the rest of the school; in fact, the entire school is the library. The instructional materials are distributed throughout the school; science books, periodicals, tapes, films, records, and compact disks are closely associated with science laboratories, classrooms, science reading and research

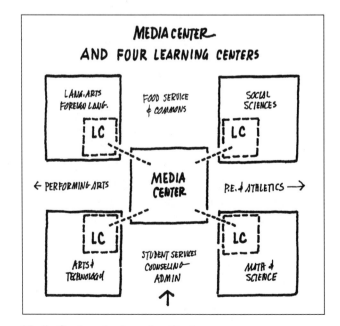

**Media Center plus Learning Centers.**

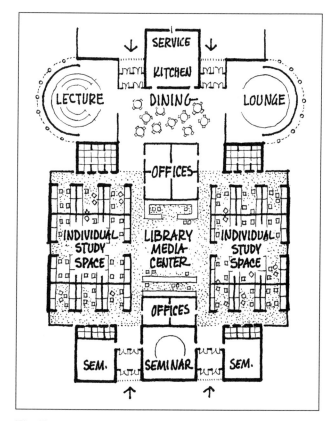

**The library and individual study space.**

spaces, and offices. The print and electronic resources for the arts are stored and used in the arts areas.

In the recent past and today, the library has been thought of as a receptacle and an information center that contains all the books and other media collected by the school. In the future, the entire school will be the library. The field of library science has changed dramatically, but it is still dedicated to finding, organizing, evaluating, and processing information. However, it now requires a greater use of electronic data and computer networks. Library school graduates have new names: data base manager and webrarian. No matter how you look at it, tomorrow's library will have a new look. It will be less rigid and less institutional, more open and more flexible; it will be linked to various schools in the region, the state, the country, and the world.

## Windows to the World

Sooner or later in the design process the many questions concerning windows will emerge as a topic for intense discussion. Not everyone will agree with the final decisions; even people with broad experience in design and construction have prejudices that are sometimes based on facts but sometimes are not based on anything factual at all.

Some of the questions about windows (and our basic answers) are as follows:

1. *What are windows for?* Windows admit light, sunshine, and fresh air; they provide views into and out of spaces while restricting the transmission of cold or hot air and odors and noises. They give people a sense of orientation and visual contact with changing weather and with the other parts of the school, the neighborhood, and the world.

2. *What factors influence school design?* Classrooms and other spaces range from windowless, to moderate use of glass, to large walls of glass. West-facing glass walls can be a mistake. In Florida, when schools were being air-conditioned, the state legislature passed a law saying that classrooms should be windowless to save energy. The rooms were unpopular with teachers, parents, and students, and so the state legislature passed a new law making windows mandatory. The windows must be operable. On pleasant days the classrooms are naturally ventilated; HVAC fans are necessary only on hot or cold days.

3. *How do windows affect energy conservation?* Windows must be oriented properly. South-facing windows in the northern hemisphere can easily be protected from south sun through the use of "eyebrows" above windows. In the summer, windows are shaded; in the winter, when the sun is low, sunlight can enter the school, gaining the advantages of solar design. Proper orientation also means avoiding west-facing windows. Trees on the north side of a school can protect it from north winds; trees on the west side can protect it from west sun. These are lessons our ancestors learned when they planned and built their farmhouses.

4. *Can interior window walls be useful?* In public spaces and in corridors and on stairs, interior windows can be incorporated into the design to put some of the most interesting activities, equipment, and spaces on display, especially the library, computer centers, art studios, shops and labs, the gym

and pool, the dining room, and the administration and reception area. Glass block, being partially translucent, allows light but not views to be transmitted. Skylights can provide great relief for interior spaces. Glass above corridor lockers frequently is used to "borrow" light for interior spaces, just as corridors borrow daylight from adjacent classrooms. In some states firefighters won't allow borrowed light in corridors, but how better to detect smoke? Electricity will be relatively more expensive, and so designing for the utilization of natural light will be more important.

In the twenty-first century, exterior walls of glass and metal (or stone, brick, or composite materials) will be called upon to work harder then they did in the twentieth century. The translucence and emissivity of windows will change during the day to adjust to the changing temperatures. The glass will be controlled electronically to serve as a solar energy collector and to become a shading device at noon, keeping the windows semidark while collecting solar energy. East-facing windows will admit early morning sun, and west-facing windows will shut their blinds to minimize heat input.

Glass walls, both interior and exterior, may take on the new job of converting old twentieth-century "movable metal-frame flexible office walls" from their passive nature to become dynamic new computer-related teaching and learning walls that incorporate the electronic thin panel technology which enthusiasts promise for "tomorrow." The thin panels can be any size, such as 8 feet high and 25 feet long (useful when the science team needs a really big table of elements or when a geography group wants a big map of Los Angeles), or can rapidly change to accommodate 25 rectangular pictures of Korean ceramics or 200 smaller pictures. Letter-size and wallet-size images will rely on paper-thin panels. The computers exist; what we need to do now is replace the bulky and heavy tubes with thin, economical, and lightweight panels.

## Restoration of Existing Schools

It is stimulating and intriguing to plan new schools for the twenty-first century, but one should remember that in the year 2020 we will still be using most of the schools that exist today, just as we continue to use twenty-year-old school buildings constructed in the late 1970s. The task of bringing school facilities up to higher standards, including more flexibility for future change, cannot be solved by new construction alone. We also must improve existing buildings by restoring and improving existing space, removing poor-quality space, and adding (where sites allow) additional space in an imaginative and economical way.

There is no need to apologize for this procedure, because incremental improvements can be deemed proper, encouraging continuous and ongoing restoration and improvement. A region can benefit by having both old and new schools and by having schools with both old sections and new sections and both restored and unrestored areas (i.e., spaces that provide opportunities for new programs that require new interior spaces).

This is what many of our older schools lack: continuing improvement and responsiveness to changing needs.

In the section "Accounting for Costs" below, we note that the structure and exterior shell of a building can last for centuries but that mechanical and electrical systems wear out or become obsolete in a matter of decades. This sometimes creates an unexpected problem. A renovation program may be aimed at high-priority mechanical-electrical improvements which are mostly out of sight, while overall improvement of the learning environment is not planned, and so the improvements are not seen by the users. Successful restoration is a multidisciplinary task; not only should the engineering systems be updated, the whole quality of the spaces should be thoughtfully designed, recognizing and restoring the older elements and adding new space where appropriate.

Colleges and universities—and school districts—have learned that the restoration of old buildings can be more expensive than new construction because restoration is a very labor-intensive operation. Nevertheless, some old structures are key parts of a community's environment, history, and culture. There may be valid reasons for repairing and reusing an older school even though the cost of doing so may not justify preservation.

If a school has landmark status, it is especially subject to broad community interest and support. Colleges and universities have recognized the "old grads'" interest in saving and continuing to use "Old Main." Since the alumni contribute dollars for historic presentation, the rules have changed; what was once thought to be impractical sometimes becomes quite practical.

## Obsolete Buildings and Inadequate Sites

Not all existing school buildings are worthy of restoration; some should be demolished.

Each case must be evaluated individually to determine whether a school should be torn down and the land should be sold. The reasons for demolition vary but can include safety (earthquakes, storms, structural problems) air quality, illegal fire exits, accessibility, changed demographics (especially when the students have moved away), the high cost of maintenance and operations, land-use conflicts (such as plans for a new expressway), and aesthetics. A beautiful building will tend to be loved and cared for, while an ugly building will be allowed to disintegrate. The beautiful building in the long run is the practical and economical design.

A school system is frequently faced with the decision about which existing buildings or parts of buildings should continue to be used and which buildings or parts of a complex should be demolished. Age alone does not answer this question.

Some turn-of-the-century buildings and some schools from the 1920s are more promising for renewal and continued use than are some of the "cheap" facilities of the 1950s, which are poorly insulated and have roof problems and obsolete mechanical and electrical systems.

In some instances the decision to replace an old building with a new one is determined by site conditions. If school sites are too small to satisfy new program needs (for buildings, parking, landscaping, and playing fields), a new location should be considered. Even space-saving ideas such as high-rise design, mixed-use occupancy, structured parking, and tennis courts above parking sometimes do not adequately solve the site-size problem.

## Accounting for Costs

There is remarkable inconsistency in how areas and volumes are measured and how they relate to con-struction costs per square foot or cubic foot. Most commonly, areas should be measured from the outside surface of outside walls, with sheltered but unenclosed walks counted as half their areas. The inevitable transition to metric measurements complicates the issue. Meanwhile, cubic feet and metric volumes are less important than they were in the past.

The program ("the ed specs") lists space requirements in net usable areas, such as classrooms of 750 square feet each or a cafeteria–multipurpose room of 7,500 square feet, including the kitchen and serving areas.

When all the space requirements are added up, we have the total net usable area for the school. To this net usable area must be added corridors, lobbies, stairs, mechanical and electrical equipment rooms, toilets, lounges, central storage, maintenance space, grounds, equipment storage, and walls—all the additional parts of a workable building that are not specifically identified in a typical program. An allowance of an additional 40 or 50 percent of the net area in the northeastern quadrant of the United States gives us the total gross area. In the south, a lower percentage is required.

The gross area is most often multiplied by dollars per square foot to calculate the construction cost, such as $100 per square foot. To this line item must be added site acquisition fees, landscaping and site development costs, equipment costs, a contingency fee, administration costs, and other fees, depending on which state standards and local customs are followed.

Comparing costs is dangerous and misleading if inconsistent facts are used. The costs of educational facilities are influenced by many factors, for instance, climate. A high school in California has an area of 90 square feet per student if the school is financed by the state. In the northeastern quadrant of the United States a high school could have a gross square footage of 180 square feet per student, twice the area provided by the California school. Why? California's benign climate means that "campus plan" school design is welcomed; classrooms open directly outdoors or onto sheltered walks. There are few or no corridors; lunch, physical education, and many recreational activities are conducted outdoors. Meanwhile, a northeastern school needs corridors and indoor assembly spaces, which boost the gross area.

In the future we will probably account for costs in a more comprehensive and sophisticated life-cycle manner, recognizing differences in the useful life expectancy of different school building components. For example, the structural frame of steel and/or concrete will last for 200 or 300 years with few major additional costs over the years. Some of Chicago's most famous and flexible office buildings are 100 years old; exterior walls have been restored, and interior walls and spaces have been remodeled to satisfy new tenants. The mechanical and electrical systems became obsolete decades ago, and the new systems can be expected to be replaced again every generation or two.

## Public-Private Partnerships and Choice

Public schools are besieged with proposals to privatize some or all of their tasks, from providing food service and bus service to turning all schools over to private companies which would provide educational services, welcome competition, and collect fees via vouchers from parents who therefore would have "choice," one of the hot concepts at the end of the twentieth century.

The concept has been widely discussed, and trial programs are in progress. Our interest is in how school design may be influenced by various forms of privatization or public-private partnerships. Will investors plan, design, build, operate, and speculate about the provision of education for students from kindergarten through the twelfth grade plus day care and adult education along with computer networks? If so, marketplace discipline will force some changes in school design. For example, a school theater with a big stage and a small house (seating) or a school auditorium with a small stage and a big house should not stand empty most hours of the day, evening, and weekend. Other fee-paying organizations will have to be found to support and justify the space. Community fitness centers probably will emerge that will link schools to adults whether they have children in school or not. Adult education with computer networks and resource centers can feature innovative public-private partnerships that give more citizens access to increased continuing education opportunities. The learning resource centers will generate new spaces linking the home, the school, and the workplace—a great design opportunity.

## Building and Site Security

The conflict is obvious, and the solution has not emerged. On the one hand, the "community school" concept, the community participation idea, and the trend toward involving more individuals in the schools (as teacher aides, visiting lecturers, private vendors, and adult students) all tend to open up the doors and welcome everyone to a learning center, cultural center, and fitness center.

On the other hand, educators and parents are more concerned about safety and security, worrying about potential trouble with "outsiders," drug dealers, computer thieves, auto thieves, vandals, graffiti sprayers, mentally deranged people, and kidnappers. These concerns tend not just to close the doors but to chain them shut. This is a sad situation, a problem to be solved.

More students in a greater age range will probably have ID cards, and the cards will be charge cards for lunch, keys to the parking lot, and keys to school doors and lockers.

Site planning will be influenced by security concerns. Structures around quadrangles, as at Oxford and Cambridge, are easier to supervise, and this makes it easier to plan walls, fences, and entrance gates. Note the plan for Warsaw High School in Chapter 3.

With increased adult education at night and more community use of cultural and fitness facilities in the evening, night lighting of entrances, walks, drives, and parking lots has become priority.

## Indoor Air Quality and Energy Conservation

Rachel Carson published her influential book *The Sea around Us* in 1950 and published *Silent Spring* in 1962. These books were indictments of a chemical war against insects, weeds, and fungi—a war against nature. Environmental awareness has been a part of our lives ever since.

The recent concerns are water quality and indoor air quality, which affects every breath we take. Americans first became aware of air pollution in industrial cities, especially Pittsburgh, and of smog problems in cities caused by automobiles. Then, rather suddenly, indoor air quality became a life-threatening problem which was evidently caused by microorganisms growing in stagnant air-conditioning ducts. In Philadelphia, Legionnaire's disease killed twenty-nine people who were attending a convention at a large old hotel.

Indoor air quality is enhanced by the introduction of sufficient fresh air into an air-conditioning system. That means that outside fresh air must be heated or cooled, using more energy and that increases the operating costs.

Good indoor air quality equals high energy use and high energy costs!

Another unsolved problem.

## Help!

How can one keep up with the maze of rules and regulations? Professional organizations and conferences help. Superintendents attend AASA meetings; business managers go to ASBO conventions; architects keep in touch (and earn continuing education credits) at AIA meetings. Board members prefer NSBA conventions. Meanwhile, the journals published by all these organizations keep one informed. *Education Week* is excellent.

If you want to learn more about architecture for education, sign up for a CEFPI conference—local, regional, or national. CEFPI, with headquarters in Scottsdale, Arizona, stands for the Council of Educational Facility Planners International. In addition to meeting school district planners, you will meet architects and educational consultants, construction managers, and building equipment suppliers.

The most effective way to learn about the state of the art in educational facilities is to visit a half dozen excellent schools. If you visit more than that, you will be tired and confused. Don't assume that excellent examples are nearby. The visiting group could include board members, administrators, teachers, planners, and architects. Everyone will benefit; it will be well worth the time and cost.

# 3

# STATE-OF-THE-ART SCHOOLS

The state of the art in school design, today and in the future, is and will be the responsibility of the design team. That includes not only the architects, planners, and engineers but also the school board, the administrators, and the faculty. When each group's interests are coordinated, innovative, superior-quality learning environments can be produced.

With financial backing from recent legislation, increases in school enrollment brought about by immigration and a growing global population, and the continual outdating of current facilities, school design once again has become a hot topic. New facilities designed today, which will serve us into the twenty-first century, will incorporate a number of new designs, new types of technology, new concepts of space, and new construction techniques.

An important thing to note is the vastly different design approach that today's school requires compared with the schools of only a few years ago. The emerging "information technologies" are affecting instruction methods and curriculum delivery systems and changing the school learning environment, giv-

ing rise to a new type of high-tech classroom. The role of the teacher has shifted from one of "delivering education" to one of "facilitating learning." "Multimedia" teaching and learning tools that require the inclusion of computers affect the size and shape of a "standard" classroom. Telecommunication and the "information superhighway" require on-line capabilities which can expand the boundaries of the classroom infinitely.

There are a number of emerging trends for the twenty-first-century school. Many of those trends, along with a variety of others, are investigated in the following descriptions of "state-of-the-art" schools. Flexibility of space allows for a variety of learning methods. Specialized school facilities will respond to specific curricula and disciplines. Community schools in which the school is a center for citizens of all ages provide a variety of social services. Outdated buildings are recycled for new educational uses.

Twenty-two state-of-the-art schools are reviewed in this chapter. Each design is unique. Every project presents an imaginative response to a different set of conditions and constraints. School types vary from elementary, middle, and high schools to schools for kindergarten through grade 12. Locations extend from the east coast to the west and to Asia. Site and climate determine the construction type. Budgets vary widely, and programs are always different. Yet in the end, each collaborative solution satisfies the wishes and needs of the expectant client through the production of innovative solutions that can be produced only by the teamwork of design and education professionals.

## SUNLAND PARK, NEW MEXICO
# A Prototype Elementary School

The concept of prototype school buildings serving as models to be imitated has been with us for hundreds of years. Large, fast-growing city school districts such as Las Vegas, Nevada, and Virginia Beach, Virginia, often repeat a school building in their own districts. Early one-room, four-room, or ten-room schoolhouses were constructed throughout North America, often copying existing prototypes. The purpose was to save money, time, and creative effort and/or to build a better school on the theory that a completed prototype school building can be studied and analyzed to learn how the next new school can be improved.

Obviously, there are both advantages and disadvantages to the prototype concept. One argument for prototypes is that design and construction costs might be lower if the owners and users would avoid changing the program and if the site conditions could be duplicated. The hope, nurtured by some school boards, is that architects' and consultants' fees might be reduced if programs and plans were reused, and that is always a possibility.

**Approach**

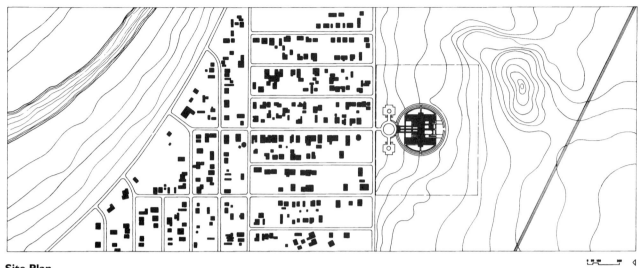

**Site Plan**

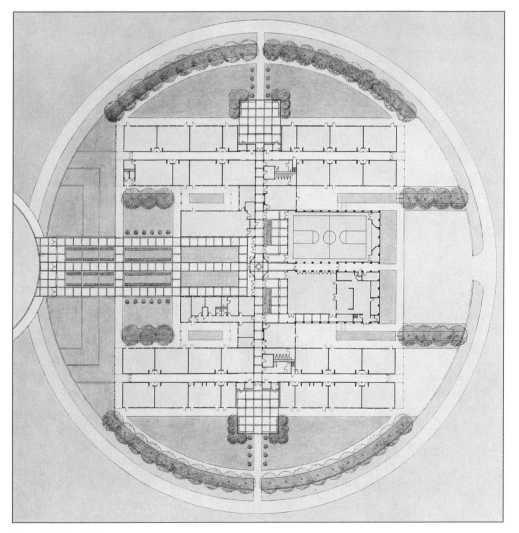

**Ground Floor Plan**

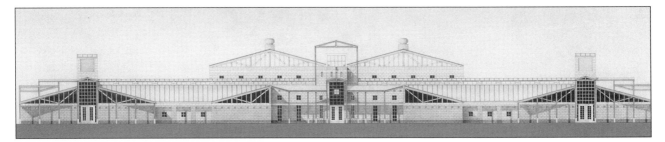

**North Elevation**

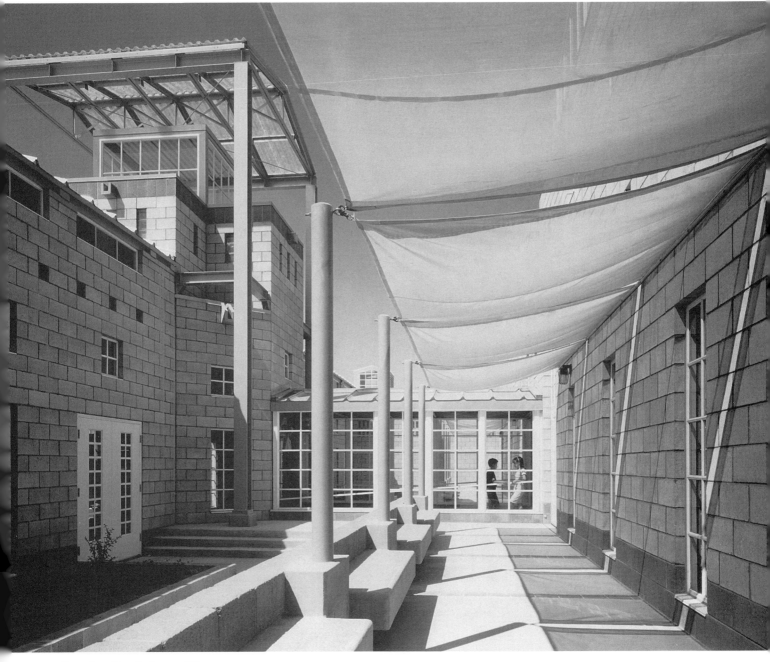

**Exterior Circulation and Tower**

**Interior Corridor**

Similar sites for a few elementary schools in New Mexico gave us an opportunity to design a prototype school for the Gadsden School District, across the Rio Grande, west of El Paso. The immediate building program was to plan, design, and construct one 600-student K–6 elementary school and then, reusing the same plans and specifications, to build two more schools. A modest budget called for modest architecture (influenced by local materials and methods of construction) and a simple, straightforward plan, H-shaped, with classrooms at the four corners and shared facilities (library, multipurpose room, dining room, and offices) at the center. This H plan, almost a house plan and easily converted to one in the twenty-first century, is then surrounded by a low circular wall of local stone, recalling the stone walls local residents enjoy. From the air, the big circle is a green oasis surrounded by the desert.

The building, which was designed in association with Mimbres, Inc., is organized into three functional subtypes: classrooms, which are repetitive units; library and administrative areas, which are shared by the whole school; and a multipurpose pavilion and cafeteria, which are shared by the school and the community. The school's architecture is a collage of sloped metal roofs, pastel-colored masonry walls, decorative wrought-iron railings, and a circular rock wall inscribing the site. Walled courtyards, canvas awnings, and deeply recessed windows create a "cooling interplay of light and shade," as *Architectural Record* observed, and offer protection from the arid desert climate. Building walls are of concrete block, and the roof structures are steel trusses.

The building reflects the regional influences of New Mexican climate and culture with "a rigorously rational design that translates the local rural environment

The secret to "reusing plans" is easy to describe: School designs can be reused if the program, floor plans, size, sites, grounds design, access, and plans and specifications are reused without making substantial changes. Only then will costs be reduced. If the prototype school design can be site-adapted to serve as a model for additional buildings, this idea can be explored, but experience reminds us that educational programs usually need special and creative attention and that sites vary in regard to size, shape, slope, and relationship to their neighbors. Sometimes, however, the sites are similar, and so the archetype idea may make sense.

**Classroom & Stone Wall**

into convincing civic architecture," said *Architecture* magazine.

The prototype was built and analyzed, and then two additional schools were erected. The second school (on a similar site) was the same size as the pro-
totype, but the third school was made larger with the addition of four more classrooms, leaving the center alone. All three schools worked well, and the inexpensive prototype building, called the Desert View School, won a national AIA Honor Award.

## NEW YORK CITY, NEW YORK

# Protoparts Schools

The New York City sites could not be more different from those in New Mexico. The urban sites are mostly in the Bronx and have helped revitalize a part of the city just north of Manhattan. What were once blocks of burned-out apartments, abandoned buildings, and vacant rubble-strewn lots now attract new investment. Young people with children in school have moved back to the Bronx, street trees are returning, and new schools are needed.

In an effort to accommodate its rapidly growing school-age population, the New York City Board of Education commissioned us to create a prototypical elementary school design which could be repeated on a variety of urban sites and could influence urban

**Proto-Part School**

school design in the twenty-first century. We approached this project by distilling the facility program into basic functional components which were then developed as smaller prototypical building blocks. These blocks can be juxtaposed in a variety of ways to respond to specific site issues. The resulting "protoparts" approach provides a kit of parts consisting of four basic modules: classrooms, administration-resource, lunchroom-auditorium, and gymnasium. The modules can be configured in a variety of ways, depending on individual site conditions and school capacity requirements.

Prototype building design is hardly a novel idea. Most American examples of such buildings, however, lack quality design. It is difficult to design one building that responds successfully to a multitude of unknown sites. Even though the inside of each repetition of the building satisfies the same functional program, the building must fit into the immediate site context and its neighborhood.

The kit of parts consists of four basic building blocks: a four-story teaching center, a four-story

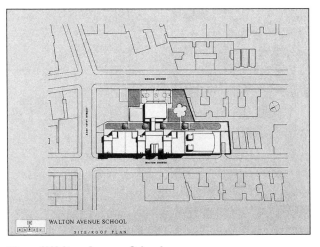

**Plan of Walton Avenue School**

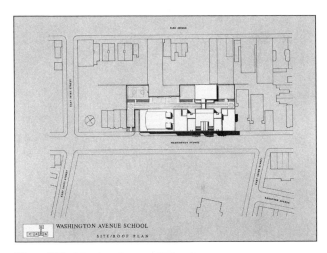

**Plan of Washington Avenue School**

**4 Story Resource Center and Entry Clock Tower**

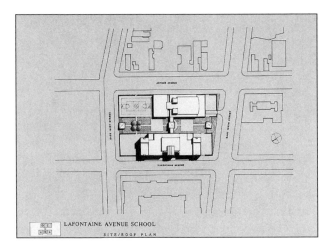

**Plan of LaFontaine Avenue School**

**Walton Avenue School Elevation**

**Washington Avenue School Elevation**

**LaFontaine Avenue School Elevation**

resource center, and two blocks that compose a community center: a two-story lunchroom-auditorium and a one-story gymnasium. The overall building program for each school was established to accommodate three variables of population density: 600 students, 900 students, and 600 students with allowance for the future addition of 300 more.

The teaching cluster is the pivotal piece of the protoparts concept. So that children don't get lost in a crowd, the block is designed for 300 students and is envisioned as a microcosm of the entire school. The teaching cluster is the only protopart that is repeated in a given building; it vertically segregates age groups, starting with preschool and kindergarten classrooms on the ground floor and rising to the upper grades on the top floor.

The resource tower—the heart of the complex— houses the building's shared academic and support infrastructure. Its central tower, crowned with a clock and traditional bells, marks the school's formal entrance at its base. Its shaft houses shared resource areas for science and arts classes as well as the most honored space: the two-story library and belfry reading room.

An urban school must play an important role in its neighborhood as a civic building. The community center protopart meets this need by providing a lunchroom for both student and community meals programs, along with an auditorium and a gymnasium. It was designed as two subcomponents that can be located together as a unit or separated, depending on the requirements of the site.

With this kit of parts, rather than a single building design, many building configurations can be achieved.

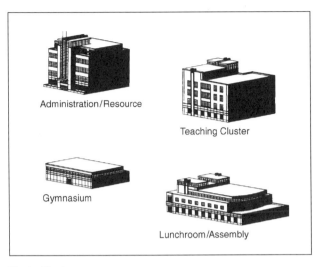

Administration/Resource

Teaching Cluster

Gymnasium

Lunchroom/Assembly

**Proto-Parts**

**Auditorium/Lunchroom Block**

The alphabet soup of possible building plans (L-shaped, U-shaped, H-shaped, etc.) contains many options. The four primary blocks form the basis of the prototype language, the vocabulary of which is expanded by the use of 180-degree rotations and left- and right-hand versions of each protopart.

As building sites are identified for potential use, the prototypes are utilized to quickly test each site's viability.

To adapt the prototype to a given context, new facades may be developed or changes in the building skin materials may be made.

The initial application of the prototype school was demonstrated on three specific sites in the Bronx and two schools in Brooklyn, for a total of five schools in the first phase. The studies, which are shown here, illustrate how the four protoparts can be interrelated and assembled to fit their unique urban sites. While this is an example of an elementary school prototype, other architects have been developing imaginative designs for middle schools and high schools. It is apparent that New York City is facing up to the huge demand for new schools and the updating of existing schools in the twenty-first century.

## SOLON, OHIO

# Shared Facilities Link the Dual Schools

The administrators, faculty, and board at Solon rallied around the idea of using space (and staff) more efficiently at the existing educational park where the high school, middle schools, elementary schools, and a kindergarten were situated. At this central location in the community, the park district also owned land for future park and recreational facilities. With the population of the district continuing to rise, a planning and design team was identified, after the successful floating of a bond, to plan and build a new elementary school and a new middle school on the existing central educational park.

The original assumption was that two separate buildings would be built. However, a new concept emerged during the process, and the new idea—a dual school—won the support of all the members of the planning and design team.

A "dual school" meant that the elementary school and the middle school would each have its own buildings and campus while certain supporting facilities, located between the two schools, would be shared. The goal was to achieve better schools at a lower cost. The superintendent of schools, Joe Regano, stated upon completion that the goal had been achieved.

**Exterior Courtyard**

The 170,000-square-foot facility, which was designed in association with Burgess & Niple, accommodates 500 students in the first through fourth grades and 750 students in the seventh and eighth grades. Each school has a separate entry and library as well as dining, art-media, and physical education facilities, while economies are provided to the district through a shared kitchen, a mechanical-central plant, and multipurpose facilities. Each school has its own gym, but the elementary school, after regular school hours, leaves its gym empty at the precise time when the middle school needs a second gym for after-school activities.

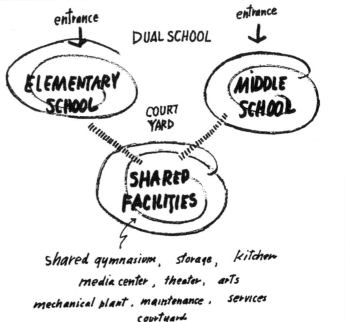

**Planning Diagram**

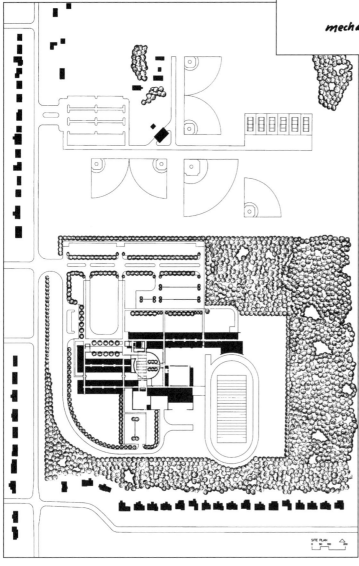

**Site Plan**

Sharing these spaces had a significant impact on the original cost of the schools, especially the HVAC capital costs, and also on the cost of fuel and electricity.

The total cost of one entire kitchen is saved, including the building space and the kitchen equipment. Also, significant savings are made every year with a smaller kitchen staff.

The elimination of one gymnasium of 5,000 square feet saves the school about $500,000.

At Solon, a community southeast of Cleveland, the centrally located nonclassroom functions are clustered around a courtyard to maximize public accessibility. This configuration allows views of the courtyard from the library, dining, and multipurpose facilities while separating academic space from the public areas. However, the elementary school students are not aware of the middle school and the middle school students are not aware of the elementary school. Public areas are accessible after school hours, while the academic wings are secured.

Each school has its own entrance, bus-loading area, and parents' area for dropping off students as well as its own principal's office near the main entrance. Each school has its own playing fields.

**Entry and Student Drop-Off**

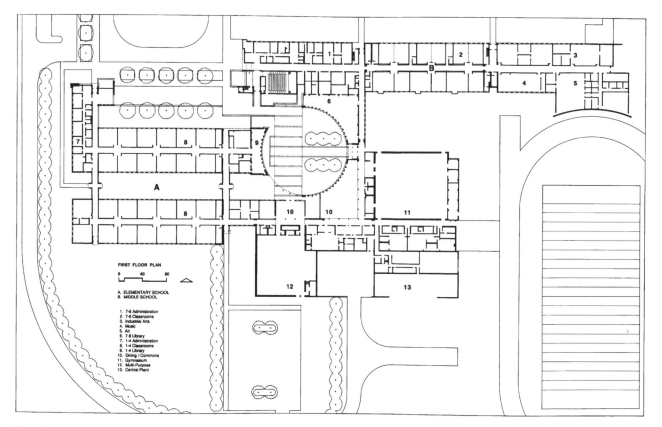

FIRST FLOOR PLAN
0    40    80

A. ELEMENTARY SCHOOL
B. MIDDLE SCHOOL

1. 7-8 Administration
2. 7-8 Classrooms
3. Industrial Arts
4. Music
5. Art
6. 7-8 Library
7. 1-4 Administration
8. 1-4 Classrooms
9. 1-4 Library
10. Dining / Commons
11. Gymnasium
12. Multi-Purpose
13. Central Plant

**First Floor Plan**

Cafeteria with View of Courtyard

Library with View of Courtyard

The elementary school is a one-floor cluster of classrooms with windows. The middle school classrooms are on two floors and are clustered as 125 student houses, or schools within a school. Each house is on one floor and consists of one classroom each for English, languages, social sciences, science, and mathematics, plus a teachers' team planning and work area.

Recognizing the fact that schools are open for community activities each evening (and recognizing the possibility of adults going there for continuing education each evening), special attention was given to the lighting of parking lots, walks, entrances, and lobbies.

The dual schools have become part of the education park in Solon. The community park system is a close neighbor, but only use and custom define the areas managed by the park district and the areas managed by the school district.

The Solon school district enjoys certain advantages from having a large central campus which contains all the community's schools. Space is more flexible and more adaptable. Adjustments in enrollment are easier to manage. The "education park" concept is alive and well in Solon.

This concept is not appropriate for every school district, but for this community in Ohio it makes sense. The unique nature of the site (a large central park) and the unique nature of the program (including a middle school with 125 student houses) drive the planning and design concepts.

# MASHPEE, MASSACHUSETTS
# Middle School and High School

A few miles after crossing the Cape Cod Canal, one comes to an area that remained undeveloped for hundreds of years because in the seventeenth century it was set aside as an Indian reservation.

Now Mashpee is experiencing development. An innovative shopping center looks more like the typical downtown of a small city, with offices above shops and a gridiron street plan with corner stores, curb parking, and service alleys.

This new 183,000-gross-square-foot school building in the town of Mashpee, Massachusetts, has been designed to be adaptable for use as a junior or senior high school. The school will accommodate a total of 1,150 students on a picturesque wooded site along the banks of the Quashnet River. Incorporating the latest educational technology, the building symbolizes the community's commitment to the future of education.

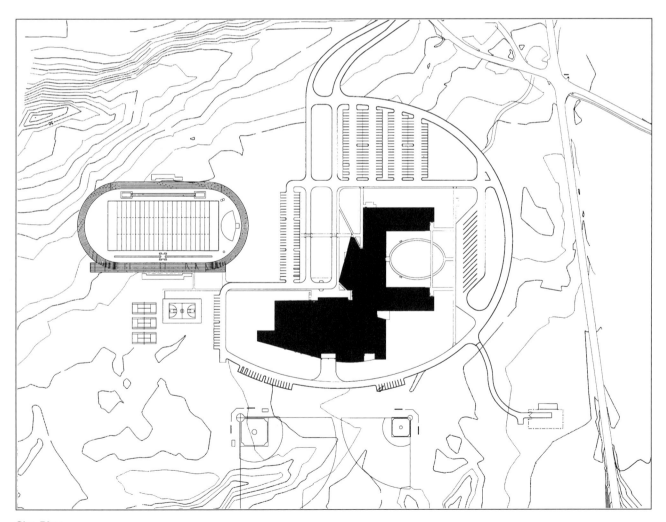

**Site Plan**

70

Conceived of as an "academic village" celebrating its constituent programmatic elements, the building has thirty-two state-of-the-art classrooms that were designed in two distinct wings, using the idea of house planning. These wings, along with the arts and athletic components of the program, serve as a pristine backdrop to the more sculptural media center–administration block and the dining areas, which serve as a visual focus for the entire complex. Incorporating native American symbolic forms from the area's indigenous Wampanoag tribe, the design creates a unique and contextually sensitive composition of building parts, contributing to the structure's organizational clarity. Keeping the

**Interior Corridor**

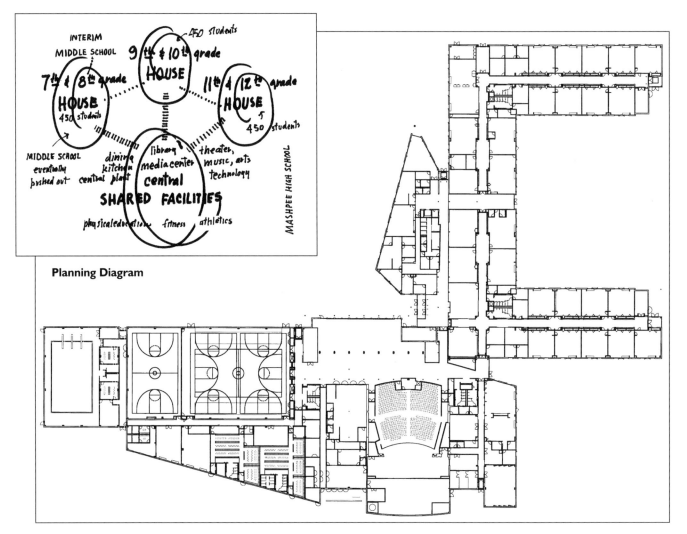

**Planning Diagram**

**Ground Floor Plan**

issues of cost and institutional mission at the forefront, Perkins & Will, in association with Symmes, Maini and McKee, made every effort to keep the building systems economical while preserving the building's formal attributes. The final design, which draws heavily on regional Cape Cod aesthetics, is bold, innovative, and deeply rooted in a rich tradition.

This design includes a full complement of sporting facilities for community use. Included are a football and track and field stadium with 1,200 seats, ten tennis courts, two baseball and two softball fields, two basketball courts, and two practice fields. The site, which was designed with academic programs and community use in mind, successfully fulfills all pedestrian, vehicular, and emergency access requirements. Also provided is a fifteen-space bus parking and dropping off area with enough parking to hold 200 faculty and staff cars and 300 student cars.

## SAUK RAPIDS, MINNESOTA
# Mississippi Heights Middle School

The Mississippi Heights Middle School is situated on a flat site in a green open space surrounded by wetlands, sports fields, and residential structures. In response to the educational concepts and the client's needs, a 950-student middle school was designed around the idea of the schoolhouse.

Interdisciplinary houses facilitate more individual instruction and reduce the scale of the teaching environment to a more manageable size. The sense of identity of each house

**Entrance**

the spaces in the building have ample amounts of natural light, good views, and an opportunity for cross-ventilation. Three basic colors are used throughout the building to emphasize the vernacular nature of the design and to delineate in a diagrammatic fashion the planning logic of the school.

**Approach**

has been extended from its internal organization to its exterior expression, and this idea became a basic language of architecture for the entire structure. All three houses are connected to support spaces and facilities which house a library and areas for music, fine arts, and physical education.

The two-story structure is organized around the courtyard, which fulfills the role of a natural light source for the surrounding spaces and a "stage" for outdoor activities. All

**Building Exterior**

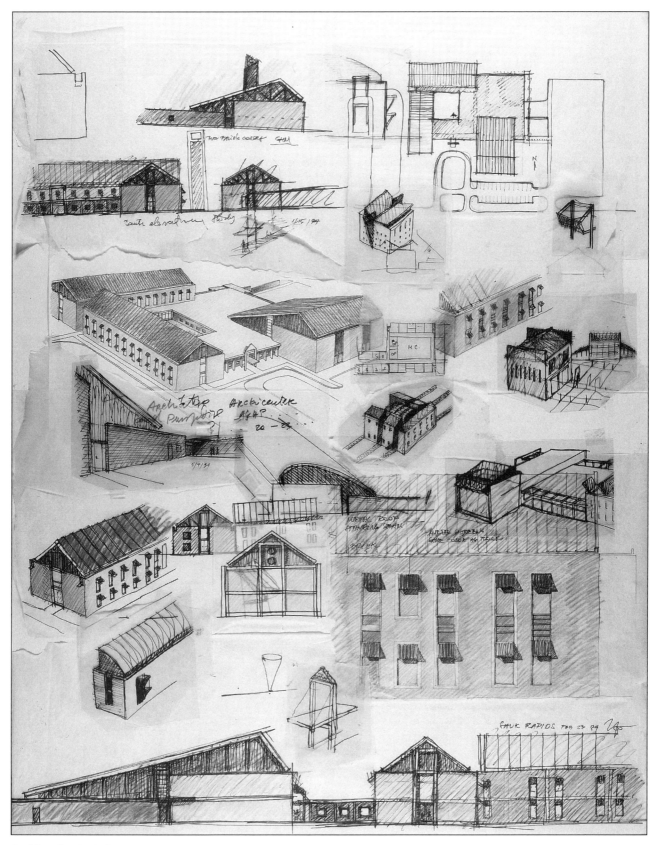

**Building Study Collage**

The structures enclosed in warm yellow brick house the core of the academic portion of the school and a double-story gymnasium. One-story administration and support spaces are built in red brick. Roof and window shades are green to suit the aesthetic program and symbolically extend the green environment that surrounds the school. The vernacular and abstracted image of a historic schoolhouse is in harmony with the surrounding residential structures and the natural environment. Programming, design, and execution of construction documents were done in association with Grooters, Leapalt, Tideman Architects.

# High Desert—A New Kind of Middle School

The middle school at High Desert is a proposed new building for the independent nonprofit school on a dramatic, sloping site at the foothills of the Sandia Mountains in Albuquerque. On 10 acres of sand and rocky desert terrain, the design of the building accentuates the natural slope of the site: a 40-foot drop in elevation.

Intended to become a model for other educational facilities, the new school has been designed to comply with Albuquerque public schools guidelines and cost models. However, its educational approach is markedly different. Without a reliance on traditional textbooks, the building itself, supported by the use of advanced instructional technology, will serve as a three-dimensional learning tool. Supporting sixth-, seventh-, and eighth-grade-level developmental objectives as well as traditional curricular subjects such as geometry, physics, history, and science, the building displays its various systems to create opportunities for interactive and cross-disciplinary learning.

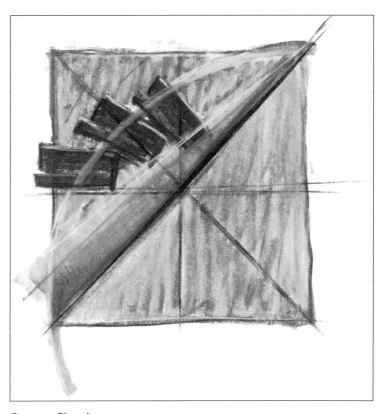

**Concept Sketch**

Program spaces such as administration, food service, music, and the performing arts, along with the gymnasium, are grouped together. Each grade is housed independently. Open public space serves as a link between the support spaces and the three houses and contains a multipurpose great hall and a stepped performance and dining area. A bilevel kiva provides insight into the cultural context of the project.

An unusual interpretation of a library takes place in this project: The entire building is designed as a media center where each student will carry a personal laptop computer with access to local, regional, and global networks. However, a traditional reading room is included to serve as a place for students to "curl up with a real book."

Divided by grade level, each "academic house" will offer a curriculum focused on the learning styles and developmental needs of its students; the sixth-grade house will reinforce themes of self-awareness and independence; the seventh-grade house, community awareness and interdependence; the eighth-grade house, global awareness and transition.

Shared facilities such as administration, the media center, dining, the gymnasium, performing arts, and public space link together the academic wings, which house up to 140 students each. Siting, massing, and building materials are influenced by the unique characteristics of the region and have strong connections to the rich cultural heritage of the Albuquerque area.

Programming efforts are done in association with Anne Taylor Associates. Architectural design services are provided in association with the Albuquerque architect Garrett Smith Ltd.

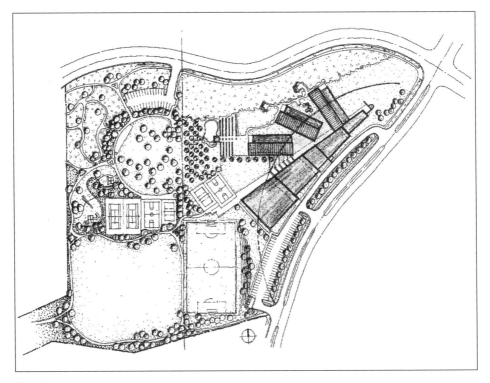

**Site Plan**

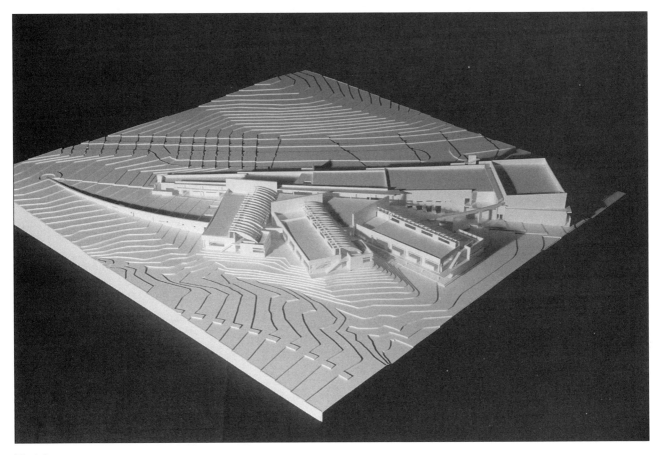

**Model**

# Silverado Middle School—A School Village

The Silverado Middle School is the second middle school constructed in the Dry Creek Joint Elementary District near Sacramento. The 18-acre site is situated in the northwest corner of the city of Roseville and has been planned in conjunction with a 10-acre city park. The Silverado Middle School is the result of a planning process that included (1) the development of comprehensive educational specifications for middle schools in the Dry Creek District based on the California Department of Education's *Caught in the Middle,* (2) a community planning forum with participation from parents, teachers, middle school students, middle school and district administrators, business leaders, park and recreation representatives, other school districts, several state agencies, the Dry Creek Board of Trustees, and the Perkins & Will design team, and (3) the review and inclusion of a comprehensive postoccupancy evaluation of a recently constructed middle school in the Dry Creek district.

The vision of the Dry Creek school district in designing and constructing a middle school is based on a curriculum for middle grade students which addresses the transition from self-contained primary classrooms to the departmentalized programs offered in comprehensive high schools and the emotional and physiological changes that occur in this age group of

**Outdoor Theater and Academic Building**

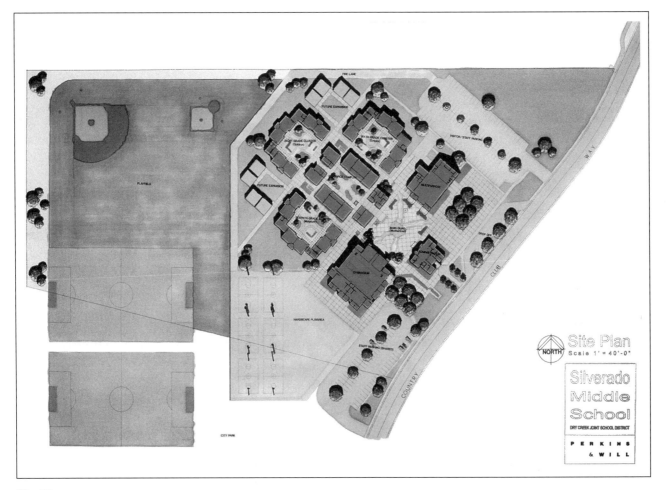

**Site Plan**

children. It is also important that the middle school be a unique facility that provides a source of identity and pride to the students and their community as an educational landmark. The vision also includes a campus that fosters educational excellence and community participation.

To achieve the goals of Dry Creek's vision, the planning process began with an early decision by the board of trustees to operate middle schools in the district that would contain grades 6, 7, and 8. The district facility master plan provided the basic requirements for land and the location of the two district middle schools. The first middle school was constructed and used as a prototype for the Silverado campus. The instructional program decisions that were used to develop the educational specifications for district middle schools were reviewed and modified slightly for the Silverado campus. The main concepts of middle

school education remained consistent, and the program offerings will be similar in the two middle schools. A postoccupancy evaluation of the initial middle school will be used to guide the design process.

The planning process included a design task force with representatives from the Dry Creek community and school district. The design task force included middle school teachers; members of the middle school student council; the parents of the children who will be attending the middle school; middle school administrators; district administrators; business representatives from local companies such as Hewlett/Packard, PASCO Scientific, Roseville Telephone, Del Webb, and Jones Intercable; members of the Roseville City Park and Recreation Department and the Placer County sheriff's department; a member of the Dry Creek Board of Trustees; and representatives from the California Division of Mines and Geology.

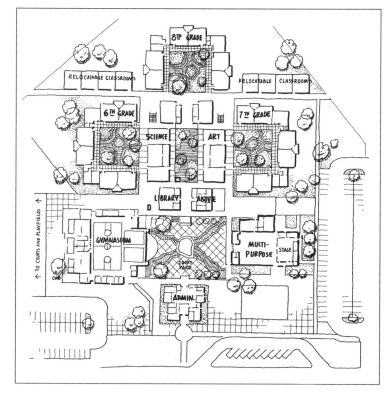

**Plan**

A thematic element was used by the district to unify the elements of the instructional program in the first middle school. Its success in providing a unique facility that was a source of pride and identification for the students and community was repeated in the Silverado Middle School. After research and discussion, the design task force selected the concept of a mining village during the gold rush era of California's history. The design task force felt that the theme and the name *Silverado* would link the events of the past, the history of the surrounding community, and the mining industry into the instructional programs of the middle

school curriculum. The design and the facility layout will emulate the mining villages of the mid-1800s, and the facility will endeavor to remind and teach the students and community about the important role mining has played in California's history and economy. Each of the main facilities will remind the students and staff of the unique architecture that was found in mother lode mining villages. The grade level quads will unify their instructional programs around an outdoor teaching theme. The main student gathering area will provide an overview of the mother lode region and identify the mines that played a role in California's history. The two-story instruction center will remind the students and community of the pioneer spirit that opened the west. Integrated in the facility will be outdoor teaching stations that may appear to be architectural or landscape enhancements. The use of sloped roofs will add to the design of the facility but also will remind the students and staff that mines were required to use and fight the effects of gravity in their operations. The flowing stream that passes through a quad or the open run of channel will be constructed to allow water flow analysis by students in physical science classes. The landscaping will portray the flora of California. These features will provide the new Silverado Middle School with an instantly identifiable heritage and serve as an instructional and community landmark.

It is believed that through the design and construction of the Silverado Middle School the Dry Creek School District will give the middle school students and staff a state-of-the-art facility that will connect the past to the future.

# PERRY, OHIO

# The Community Education Village and Fitness Center

The Perry Local School District's new Community Education Village consists of four elements: a school for kindergarten through grade 4, a middle school for grades 5 through 8, a high school for grades nine through twelve, and a physical education and community fitness center.

More than a K–12 school, 35 miles east of Cleveland and 1 mile from Lake Erie in a heavily wooded region where the most important economic activities are growing trees and generating electricity at a nuclear power plant, the Perry Community Education Village and Fitness Center is clearly the cultural, fitness, and educational center of the community. The big taxpayer is, of course, the power plant. The Perry community is fortunate to have this financial resource, which supported the design and construction of an outstanding campus.

**Athletic Complex**

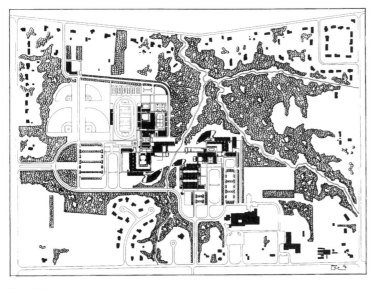

**Site Plan**

The 160-acre site is divided into two halves by a wooded ravine. The planning team, led by the superintendent of schools, Dr. E. E. Goodwin, along with the design architects, Perkins & Will and Burgess & Niple, engineers and architects, decided to locate the elementary school and middle school east of the ravine and the high school and the fitness center west of the ravine. Then the two halves were joined by an enclosed pedestrian bridge across the ravine to encourage the sharing of facilities.

Each school is designed to accommodate 1,500 students and fits into a natural clearing. The woodlands surrounding the buildings provide scenic views from most of the classrooms. Three tributaries of Red Mill Creek

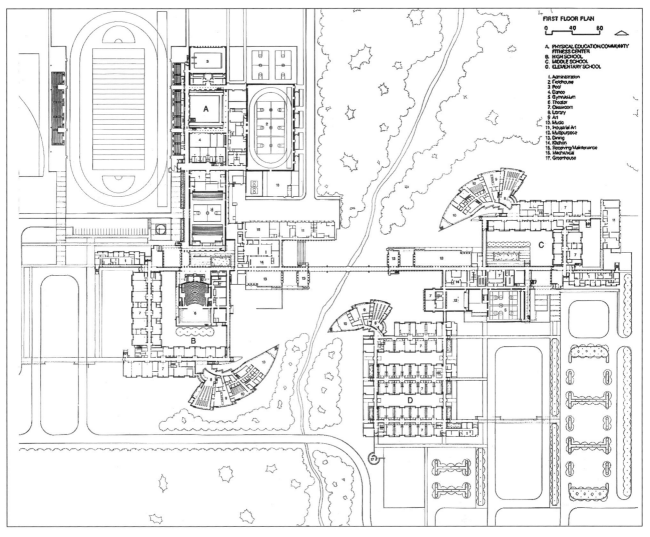

**First Floor Plan**

**Approach**

have cut natural ravines, one of which separates the lower grades from the upper grades. The facilities are organized around formal courtyards and are connected by the enclosed bridge.

The spaces shared by the three schools include a boiler plant, a chiller, a receiving and maintenance area, a kitchen (but no dining rooms), a theater, a technology system, a field house, and a swimming pool, track, and stadium. The savings in capital costs, maintenance, and operating costs are important to the owner, which wants low long-term costs.

The spaces that are not shared are the classrooms, labs, library, principal's office, dining area, teacher's parking area, and bus loading area.

One striking feature of the campus is the communications tower which marks the main entrance to the high school and community facilities; another is the use of gently curved open web steel beams. An innovative plan involves the use of "special forms" for art,

**Bell Tower**

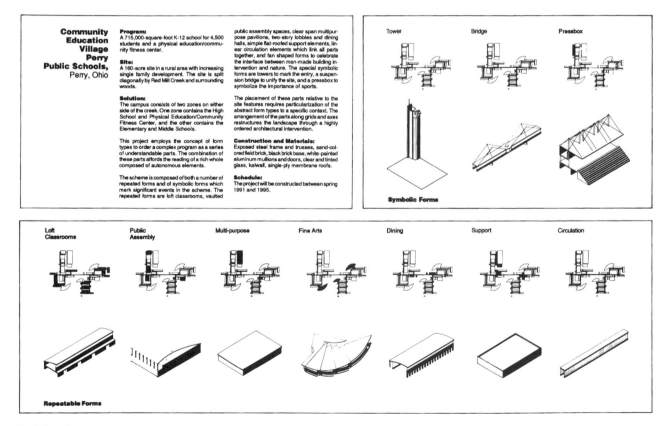

**Community Education Village Perry Public Schools,** Perry, Ohio

**Program:**
A 715,000-square-foot K-12 school for 4,500 students and a physical education/community fitness center.

**Site:**
A 160-acre site in a rural area with increasing single family development. The site is split diagonally by Red Mill Creek and surrounding woods.

**Solution:**
The campus consists of two zones on either side of the creek. One zone contains the High School and Physical Education/Community Fitness Center, and the other contains the Elementary and Middle Schools.

This project employs the concept of form types to order a complex program as a series of understandable parts. The combination of these parts affords the reading of a rich whole composed of autonomous elements.

The scheme is composed of both a number of repeated forms and of symbolic forms which mark significant events in the scheme. The repeated forms are loft classrooms, vaulted public assembly spaces, clear span multipurpose pavilions, two-story lobbies and dining halls, simple flat-roofed support elements, linear circulation elements which link all parts together, and fan shaped forms to celebrate the interface between man-made building intervention and nature. The special symbolic forms are towers to mark the entry, a suspension bridge to unify the site, and a pressbox to symbolize the importance of sports.

The placement of these parts relative to the site features requires particularization of the abstract form types to a specific context. The arrangement of the parts along grids and axes restructures the landscape through a highly ordered architectural intervention.

**Construction and Materials:**
Exposed steel frame and trusses, sand-colored field brick, black brick base, white-painted aluminum mullions and doors, clear and tinted glass, kalwall, single-ply membrane roofs.

**Schedule:**
The project will be constructed between spring 1991 and 1995.

Tower    Bridge    Pressbox

**Symbolic Forms**

Loft Classrooms    Public Assembly    Multi-purpose    Fine Arts    Dining    Support    Circulation

**Repeatable Forms**

**Building Parts**

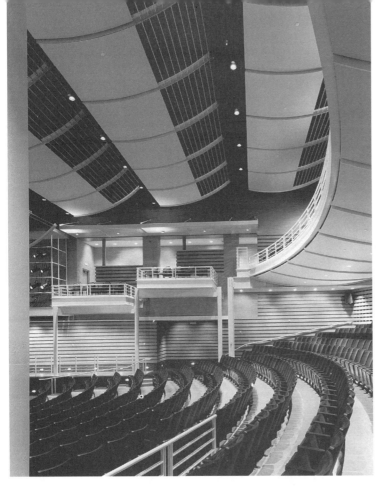

**Theater**

music, and the three libraries. All these special spaces enjoy views of the ravine.

Athletic facilities, which include a football stadium, baseball fields, and a swimming pool, serve both the schools' physical education programs and the community's recreation programs.

The fitness center is important to the community because Perry has no park district and no commercial fitness facilities. The fitness center is shared by students and adults and is integrated with the design of the track and stadium. Additional shared facilities include the high school's 850-seat theater and more than 15,000 square feet of band, choir, and orchestra facilities. The entire complex is designed to be audiovisually interactive and offers television broadcasting and receiving capabilities and communication hookups in all the classrooms.

This project was a successful collaboration between the two firms of architects and engineers.

**Corridor**

**Vestibule**

**Music Room**

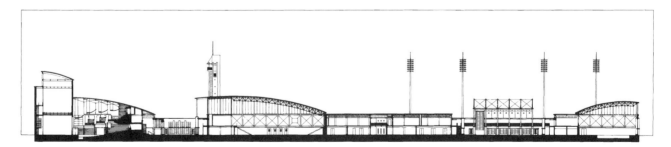

**Building Section**

# NEW ALBANY, OHIO

## School and Community Center

To comprehend this unique project, it is essential to first understand the context in which it is set. The New Albany–Plain Local Schools are located in the village of New Albany, approximately 16 miles northeast of downtown Columbus, Ohio. The school campus occupies about 70 acres on an irregularly configured parcel of land situated near the center of the village.

New Albany has seen tremendous change in the last ten years. The landscape of a typical small rural Ohio community has been gradually supplemented by new private development, and the influx of a new citizenry to the community has exerted new pressures on the existing infrastructure and community facilities.

Within the village of New Albany and Plain Township numerous entities are at work: the village and township governments, several private developers, the school district, and various other private and public organizations. To help fund public projects in the community, a tax assessment district was created by a private developer to levy taxes on new property owners within a set boundary. The taxes have been used to fund new infrastructure and roadways, public buildings, public parks and walkways, and schools.

Arising from the need to manage this growth effectively and ensure the wise use of available resources, a set of "Principles of Understanding" were drafted by Dr. Ralph Johnson, superintendent of the Plain Local School District, in 1993 and were agreed to by the various entities at work in the community. While not legally binding, this document set forth and articulated how these various organizations might interact with each other and established guidelines for the successful completion of various projects: a municipal center, a senior citizens' center, a Columbus metropolitan library branch, a community health and wellness center, a township fire department and administrative center, and a new high school–middle school.

The influx of new citizens had a great impact on the school district. As the results of enrollment projections became available, the need for additional facilities became apparent. The Plain Local School District's response to this dilemma was the creation of a revolutionary concept: the learning community campus. This concept stresses learning as a lifelong process and extols the virtues

**Reading Area and Library Stacks**

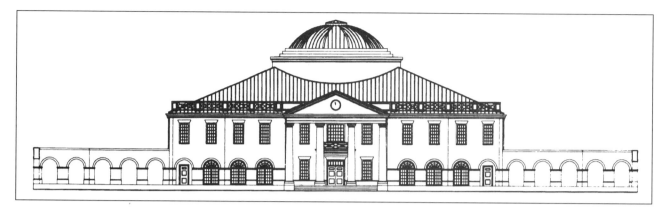

**Information Resource Center**

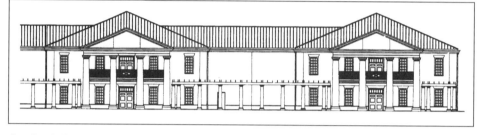

**Academic Buildings**

and necessity of advocating the education of the young and the old alike. It sees education in a community as a continuum—a lifelong process—and promotes a campus which values the education and well-being of the entire community, regardless of age.

In accordance with this concept, the campus master plan included a new high school–middle school with community recreation facilities, a wetland mitigation area which can be used as an outdoor environmental laboratory, and a reconfiguration of the elementary schools on the east side of the campus, along with a senior citizens' center, a branch library, a wellness center, and a day care facility. This master plan relied heavily on and ultimately reinforced the learning community campus concept.

The prototype for the new high school–middle school was Thomas Jefferson's University of Virginia. His notion of an "Academical Village" where students and faculty would work in close collaboration was decidedly in step with the goals and ideas of the learning community campus. Jefferson's use of Georgian architecture (this style is prevalent in the community

**Campus Quadrangle**

**Information Resource Center Rotunda**

**Athletic Buildings**

**Natatorium**

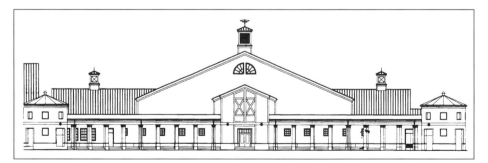

**Gymnasium**

and is strongly encouraged by the Village Architectural Review Board), with its scale, detail, and house-like quality, lent itself to his concept of this village. Jefferson wrote:

> Much observation and reflection on these institutions have long convinced me that the large and crowded buildings in which youths are pent up, are equally unfriendly to health, to study, to manners, morals and order.

This notion of smaller-scale buildings, or "houses," again paralleled the school district's curriculum objective of breaking the high school–middle school down into interdisciplinary and disciplinary clusters. It also paralleled the desire to break the mold of large, scaleless, windowless education facilities that was so prevalent at the time. Georgian architecture fit the program.

The new high school–middle school is organized around a central quadrangle or commons area, while a shaded promenade-pathway connects the school to the east campus of the learning community and the village center. Three sides of this commons are formed by traditionally detailed brick buildings which house academic classrooms, the library, arts-related functions, and administrative offices. The fourth side of the commons is formed by the physical education complex, which is a series of barnlike structures clad in vertical metal siding. These structures pay homage to the rural agricultural setting. Thus, along the primary north-south axis one finds the "whole" person symbolically represented in the form of the campus, with the mind (library) as the termination on the south and the body (physical education complex) as the termination on the north.

## FORT WORTH, TEXAS

# Trinity Valley—A Replacement School

Trinity Valley School, southwest of downtown Fort Worth, Texas, is a private school campus for students from kindergarten through upper school. The 190,000-square-foot campus, located on 75 sloping acres, will have an eventual enrollment of more than 900 students.

Designed to reflect the historical character of indigenous southwestern architecture, the school takes advantage of the moderate climate, declaring that outdoor space can become exciting teaching areas. Thick arches, deep overhangs, an exposed structure, and intimate courtyards containing native plants and wildflowers play an important role in giving the school its comfortable character. Seven different buildings, organized by a central axis and connected by covered walkways and arcades, define the campus; each building plays an important role in creating a necklace of outdoor space that steps its way down the Texas terrain. Nestled into the side of the hill, the buildings occupy the steeper slopes, allowing the playing fields and stadium to be located on the flatter areas of the site.

The campus is designed to promote a sense of community while preserving the age-centered instruction which is currently utilized in the individual schools. Each school (lower, middle, and upper) has its own courtyard, administration wing, and drop-off areas for buses, while the other facilities are shared. The middle school and upper school share science classrooms, the library and media center, and the art building. One central dining hall will be used by all the students, while courtyards and outdoor circulation will encourage visual connection and interaction. A central administration building is adjacent to each school while maintaining a "front door" presence on the site. Athletic facilities include competition baseball and softball fields, tennis courts, a football and track and field stadium, a central gymnasium, and two auxiliary gymnasiums. Other amenities include a theater and a "black box" performance space. These parameters help define the proximity among buildings and the quiet, intimate spaces between buildings.

**Courtyard**

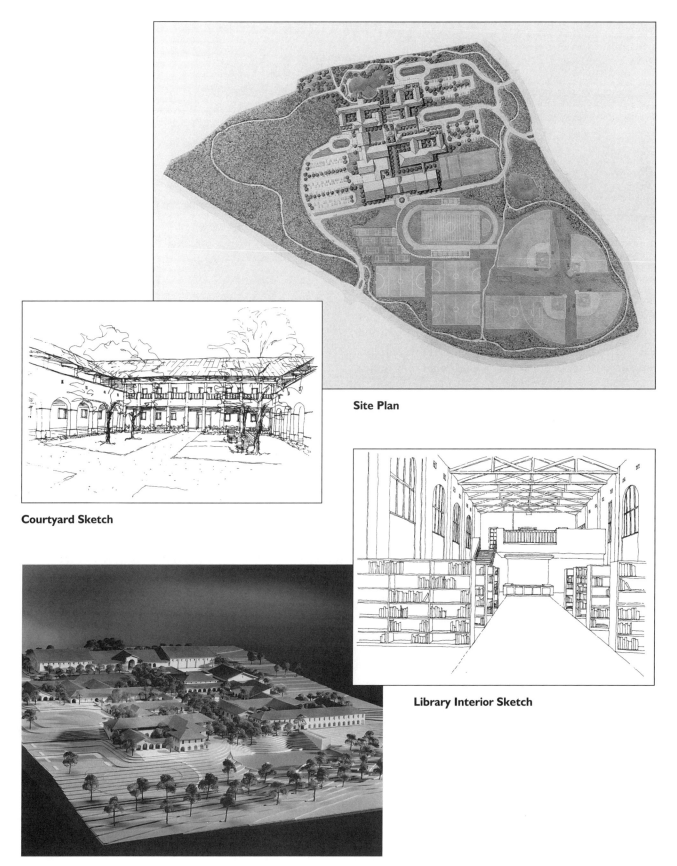

**Site Plan**

**Courtyard Sketch**

**Library Interior Sketch**

**Model**

# International School

Recently completed, this new K–12 private school serves the international community in Singapore. The 500,000-square-foot campus accommodates 3,000 students in four separate components: two elementary schools, a middle school, and a high school.

The use of shared facilities such as libraries, fine and performing arts centers, food service facilities, gymnasiums, pools, and playing fields maximizes the available resources of the school. An 800-seat auditorium for music and assembly and a theater for drama serve the entire campus. Campus facilities provide amenities to the entire Singapore American School community and serve as a social and recreational center for students, parents, and faculty members.

Forms and materials establish the design image and character of the campus and relate it to the local architecture. The demands of the tropical climate—the need for shade, ventilation, and protection from the severe rains—were the chief concerns in the functional and design solutions. The stucco and brick buildings contain single-loaded corridors of classrooms, with roof planes extending to provide shade for the exterior corridors and courtyards which serve as circulation and gathering spaces.

**Courtyard**

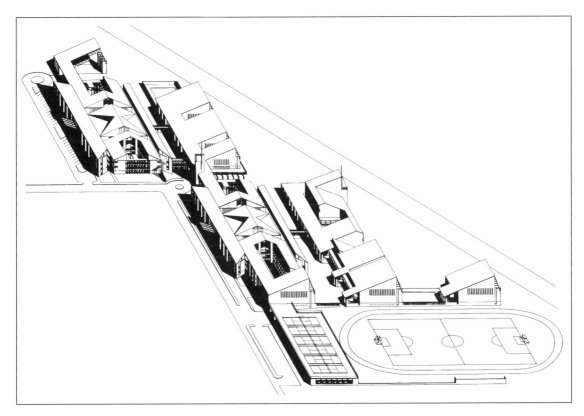

**Axonometric**

**Courtyard Concept**

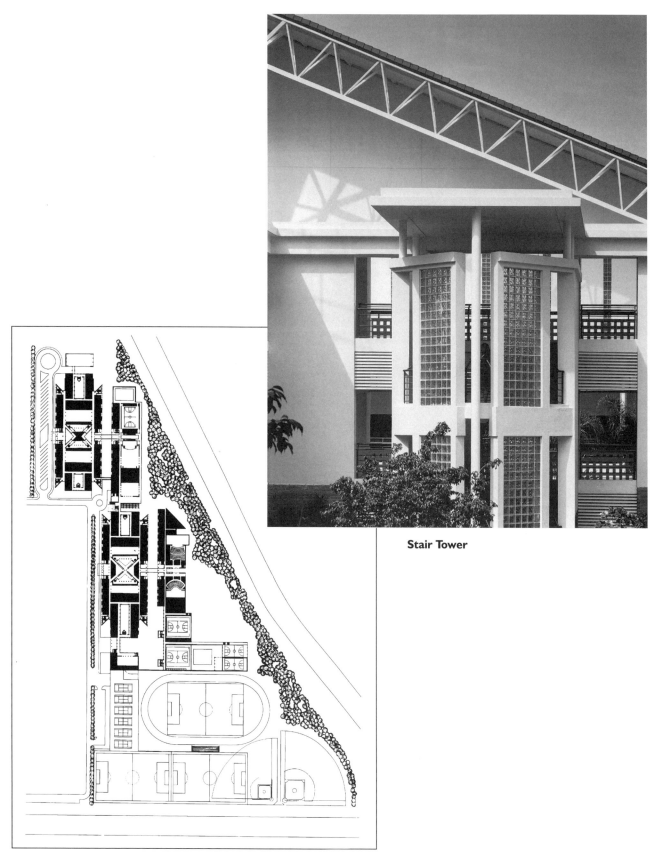

**Stair Tower**

**Plan**

**Library**

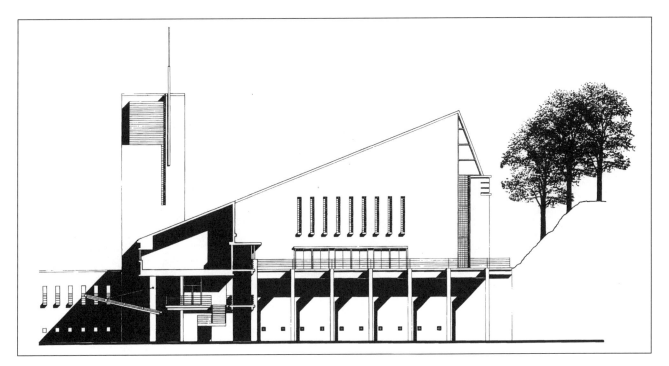

**Section**

## MANILA, PHILIPPINES

# International School

The International School Manila (ISM) is an independent, community-sponsored school for English-speaking children of all nationalities. The faculty and staff come from all over the world as well as from the Philippines. A balanced American-style curriculum, broadened to include curricula from other systems throughout the world, forms the basis for a sound liberal education.

The school stresses equally the mental, physical, and social development of the students. It strives to instill a sense of self-worth and achievement in each student and to teach respect and appreciation for other individuals and cultures. Appropriate facilities are integral to successful delivery of the educational and extracurricular programs offered at the school.

ISM is planning to construct a new replacement campus for 3,000 students on a 7.5-hectare site (18.5 acres) in the Fort Bonifacio development site of Metro-Manila. The new facility will contain an elementary school, a middle school, and a high school in approximately 39,000 net square meters (420,000 square feet) of program space.

The 1,380-student elementary school houses primary and intermediate grade levels with some shared

**Corridor**

**Courtyard**

facilities. A 690-student middle school is adjacent to a 930-student high school. Facilities for the cafeteria, media center, art, music, performing arts, practical arts, home economics, physical education, and other similar programs of the two schools are grouped to provide for sharing between the various grade levels. This planning approach is intended to achieve maximum flexibility as well as economy. The campus also includes a central administrative core and a central receiving, storage, and maintenance facility.

Other campus features include parking, a 400-meter track and two soccer fields, a multipurpose field, two swimming pools, including a 25-meter competition pool, seven rooftop tennis courts, and many outdoor covered play areas.

## DESIGN NARRATIVE

The facility design is sensitive to the individuality of each school component while establishing a unified whole. The majority of elementary, middle, and high school classrooms are organized in a continuous arc of space which gently slopes from two stories at the elementary school up to five stories at the high school. Each individual school component overlooks a courtyard which is landscaped to respond to the needs of each level of students. The classroom arc is linked across these open courtyards to the shared facilities component. A wedge of space running the length of this shared facility serves as the "Main Street" or public corridor. This space links all the components to the school's main entry, with opportunities for student work and displays at key points all along the path.

References to local culture and traditional architecture are included throughout. The portion of "Main Street" which is not enclosed is sheltered from the tropical sun by a trellis with traditional geometries. Native woods and stones are used on handrails, sunscreens, and stairways to provide color, texture, and

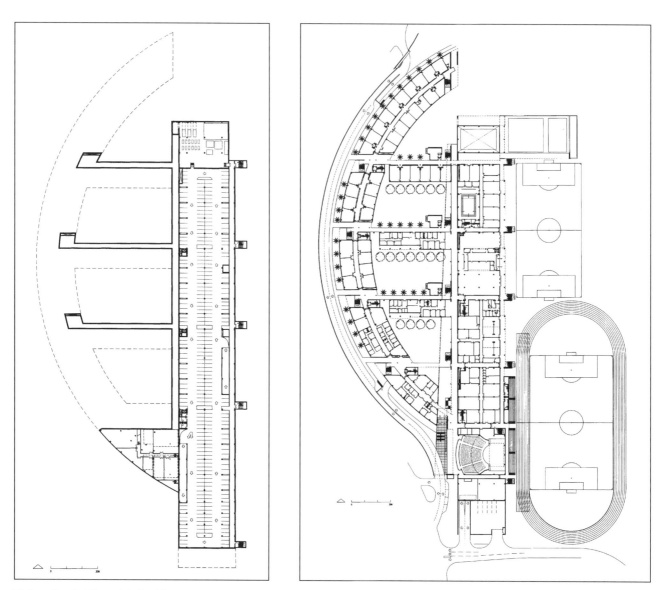

**Below Grade Plan with Parking**          **Ground Level Plan**

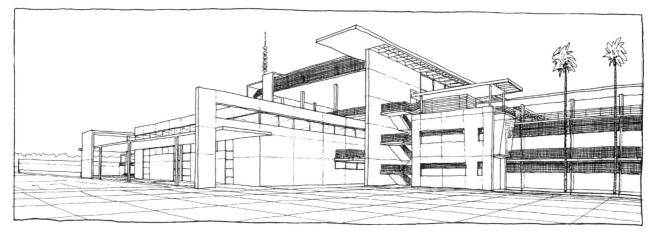

**Elementary School Courtyard**

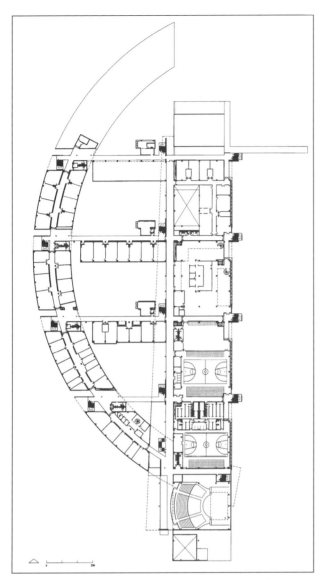

**Typical Classroom Plan**

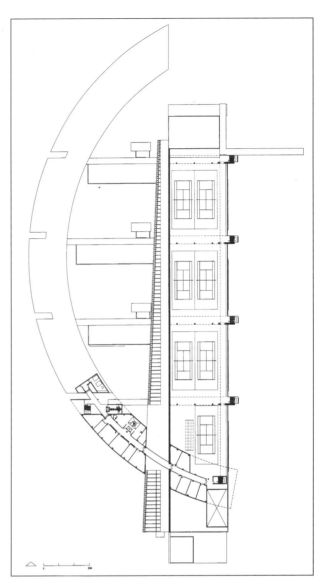

**Roof Plan with Roof Top Tennis Courts**

**Competition Pool**

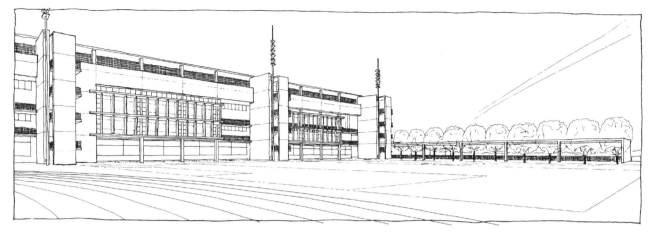

**Playfields**

durability. Three towers designed with traditional proportions and materials house teachers' work spaces while adding character and individuality to each courtyard space.

The building design resulted from sensitivity to the scale of students. From elementary school children to high school students, the vertical scale of the building increases, maximizing the area of the site to be used for educational purposes, and a sense of discovery for students, faculty members, and parents is achieved in the organization of classrooms and communal areas but also in the variety of places found in and among them. These are the spaces which support an even wider variety of activities instrumental to the development of children.

## PROJECT DESIGN CRITERIA

As was discussed throughout the programming and master plan phase, a number of key criteria for the design of the project have been recognized, including the following:

- Appropriate quality and standards for modern educational facilities
- Effective support of the educational and extracurricular programs provided by the school
- Support of the school's commitment to preparing its students and faculty to meet the challenges of a technologically changing world
- Promotion of the identity of each school component: elementary, middle, and high
- Cultural sensitivity to the Philippine context and environment
- Security and safety of students, staff members, parents, campus, buildings, and grounds
- Efficiency of site coverage to allow for open spaces and adequate exterior sporting facilities
- Constructive support of equitable opportunities for all students regardless of nationality, race, gender, or physical ability
- Support for flexible instructional techniques which respond to individual teaching and learning styles
- Recognition that the role of the school includes serving a diverse international expatriate community and must accommodate the recreational and adult education needs of parents and others within this community
- Effective balance of the project's scope, quality, and cost

# Capital High School—A School with Regional Character

Like most southwestern cities, Santa Fe is growing in spite of the efforts of some citizens to slow down the type of growth which brings with it social-cultural and environmental problems. With its continued growth, Santa Fe needed a new high school to supplement the existing secondary school.

When the project was announced, Kass Germanas, an architect with Mimbres, a Santa Fe firm, asked us if we would be interested in an association. The board of education had already selected a site, and Dr. Melendez, the assistant superintendent, was preparing the educational program.

The existing high school had a campus plan with a dozen separate buildings scattered around a hilltop. Students, teachers, and parents complained that the outdoor walks exposed them to rain, snow, cold, and wind in the winter. As architects, we liked the separate buildings, thinking the fresh air was good for the students, but the users felt strongly about wanting a "single-building campus" with indoor circulation. Another concern was the desire to maintain the scale and spirit of Sante Fe architecture and to be influenced by the small, humanistic spaces and the unique details of buildings that were of both Hispanic and

This project is for an 800-student high school for the Santa Fe Public Schools in Santa Fe, New Mexico. The site is at the southern edge of town in an unpopulated area characterized by a desert landscape crossed by a series of arroyos or drainage swales. Views of several mountain ranges surround the site, especially the Sangre de Cristo mountains to the northeast. The area surrounding the school will eventually contain single family homes as the city grows in a southerly direction. The arroyos will serve as green belts and open space for the future community.

The solution is conceived as a series of symmetrical interconnected pavilion blocks asymmetrically placed in relation

to one another as a response to site topography and vistas. These pavilions are organized along two axes, the axis of an arroyo crossing the site and the view of the Sangre de Cristo mountains to the northeast, and a north-south axis corresponding to the optimal orientation of playfields. The arroyo axis organizes the main classroom block while the north-south axis organizes the football field and other playfields.

Typological elements of the Territorial style of architecture unique to the Santa Fe region form the basis for the language of the scheme. The Territorial style has traditionally been associated with public buildings such as schools and government

buildings, and is essentially a mix between adobe and neoclassicism. The scheme employs elements of this style such as portals or long porticos, regularity of window treatment, decorative brick cornices, and window trim to reinforce and symbolically recall this local tradition for public architecture. Towers found in many public buildings in Santa Fe mark the three main entrances - the classroom block, gymnasium, and theater - and define two entry plazas. This project uses elements found in the town to create a new urban place and clearly identifiable public building which acts as a marker in the landscape around which future residential growth can occur.

**Concept Sketches**

**Gymnasium & Theater Entrance**

Indian descent. We admired the plazas and sheltered walks of old Santa Fe.

We developed a plan which the design team could rally around. The school consists of five building units, closely related and linked around five outdoor spaces and three entrances. The heart of the school is a student commons plaza that is surrounded by buildings housing classrooms, a library, offices, labs and shops, music and art studios, and an auditorium and a physical education facility. The 800-student high school can be expanded to serve up to 1,300 students.

In keeping with the region's distinctive territorial architecture, structures are relatively low with major sections connected by exterior walks and interior corridors. Entry plazas, covered walkways, and landscaped courtyards enhance the buildings, which are clad in light earth-tone stucco. Three cupolas mark the three main entrances.

**Site Plan**

# High School

**Project:**
High School
Santa Fe, New Mexico

**Program:**
This project is for an 800 student high school in Santa Fe, New Mexico. The School Board did not want a "factory like" school, but a facility which would be appropriate to the traditions and scale of the buildings of Santa Fe.

**Site:**
The site is at the southern edge of town in an unpopulated area characterized by a desert landscape environment. A major arroyo or swale crosses the northwest portion of the site an an angle. This natural feature had to be maintained. The area surrounding the school will eventually contain single family homes as the city grows in a southerly direction. The arroyos will serve as greenbelts and open space for the community. The school is to serve as a community center for this new neighborhood. Views of the Sangre de Cristo mountains dominate the view to the northeast.

**Solution:**
The school is organized along two axis. The academic axis responds to the arroyo and the mountain view. It organizes the library and classroom units. The sports axis is the ideal orientation for play fields (north-south) and also organizes the gym.

The school is conceived as a series of elements organized along the two site axis. The elements of the school are comprised of 5 form types which relate to function. These elements are loft (classrooms), portal (covered exterior movement), tower (major entry), columnar hall (dining) and specialized pavilions (gymnasium, theater). The language of the scheme is based on the territorial style which has been traditionally associated with major public buildings in Santa Fe.

The elements are arranged in such a way as to form a series of courtyards and plazas. These intimately scaled exterior spaces form outdoor classroom areas as well as major entry zones. There are three public plazas. A public entry plaza for the gymnasium and theater, a student entry plaza and a central internal plaza (a town square) off of which is located the cafeteria. This

is the heart of the school. The school in its spaces and forms is a microcosm of the town of Santa Fe.

**Construction:**
Concrete frame and masonry bearing walls with stucco. Construction completion 1988.

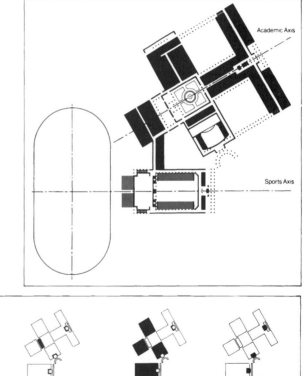

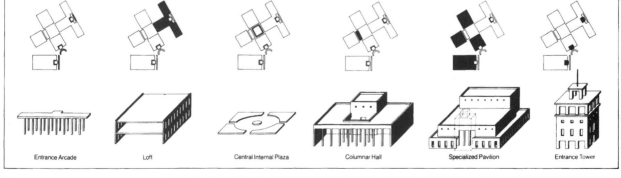

Entrance Arcade    Loft    Central Internal Plaza    Columnar Hall    Specialized Pavilion    Entrance Tower

**Diagrams**

**Main Entrance to Classrooms, Library and Administration**

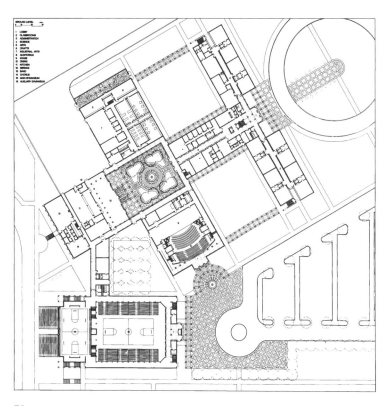

**Plan**

The plan acknowledges the special character of the site by using two planning grids. One is the original land survey gridiron, which we followed for the athletic fields, stadium, tennis courts, and indoor athletic facilities. The other grid is rotated to align with the natural drainage pattern; the site is bordered by arroyos which provide excellent drainage. Classrooms, labs, the library, and dining and arts facilities are planned to follow this second grid. The main student entrance, for bus loading, is oriented to this grid and faces a snow-capped mountain in the distance in the winter months.

Capital High School, as the new school is named, reflects the history and culture of Santa Fe with forms, materials, color, scale, and details associated with the southwest. In bestowing an American Institute of Architects National Honor Award on the school, the jury noted that "proud and dignified in stature, this school also has a rough-and-tumble quality that welcomes the students and the community to it."

**Library**

**Central Plaza**

# Planning a Community High School

A thriving northern Indiana town on U.S. 30, 130 miles east of Chicago, 40 miles west of Fort Wayne, and 40 miles southeast of South Bend, Warsaw is the county seat of Kosciusko County, serving an agricultural area that contains Tippecanoe Lake, Wawasee Lake, and Winona Lake. Warsaw also has high-tech industry, including the home base for bone fracture appliances, and a huge color press plant owned by R.R. Donnelley & Sons.

As high school enrollment increased, a decision was made to build a new freshman high school, but after a year of operation, the board of education changed its feelings about that idea and decided to build a new high school for grades 9 through 12 which would be part of an educational park on a large site and would include a middle school and an elementary school. The freshman high school was to be absorbed into the new construction.

**Courtyard**

**Exterior Wall Detail**

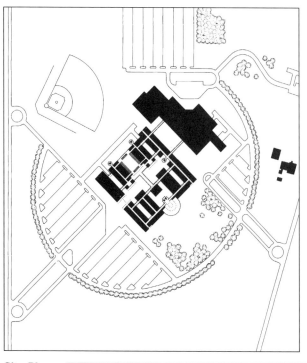

**Site Plan**

**Media Center Stair**

The board selected an association of two architects—Perkins & Will of Chicago and Odle Burke of Bloomington, Indiana—and commissioned Dr. Bill Day of Bloomington to prepare the educational specifications. Dr. Day was one of the first educators to effectively use the computer for programming. He would bring a floppy disk to each planning session with the superintendent, board of education, teachers, and architects and use it in one of the school computers, making revisions during the meetings. At the end of each meeting he would print and distribute up-to-date copies of the program.

In previous years a week would be lost as the consultant made revisions in the office and printed and mailed copies to the participants. The architects found the new technique effective in planning and designing the new school, since the team always worked from recent data that had been prepared with the participation of many individuals.

The planning team made a significant discovery early in the planning process. The existing classrooms and laboratories of the one-year-old freshman high school beautifully matched the space needs of the career education part of the program, while the gym and swimming pool were good spaces "as is." However, a large "exhibition gymnasium" also was needed.

The idea of a compact plan around a central quadrangle was developed during an early meeting, and that idea survived. Two-story academic wings relate closely to the semicircular library, which is in the front yard of the school and was the education community's focal point. The library has a high ceiling at the entrance which provides a dramatic introduction to the resource center.

The classrooms have windows. This decision involved many people and eventually won board approval, and so in addition to the main quadrangles, a few small courts give classrooms and labs a

**Model**

view, natural ventilation when appropriate, and natural light.

One of the important community high school facilities is the large new gymnasium. It seats 5,000 people for a basketball game, a reminder that high school basketball in Indiana is as important as high school football is in Texas. The gymnasium primarily serves the sports and physical education needs for secondary school programs but also serves the broader community's need for lifelong-sports and recreation with softball, baseball, and soccer fields and a swimming pool. One of the best ways to gain broad community support and use of school facilities in the future will be to include special parking spaces for senior citizens and let them use the pool a few evenings a week. The Warsaw school board provides these spaces for the entire community, but it all is charged to education.

Warsaw is on the right track. The school system gets support from the citizens. For example, when school planning was in progress, public hearings were scheduled, publicized, and held. All the testimony was favorable; no one objected. The state of Indiana approved the sale of bonds, taxes were adjusted accordingly and the architects proceeded with the design.

Planning and financing are not that easy in some states.

Warsaw's new school doesn't look like a high school, as many visitors observed. Some thought it was a corporate headquarters, office park, high-tech manufacturing facility, medical center, or new competitor for R.R. Donnelley & Sons.

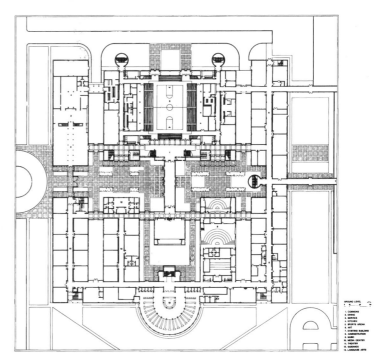

**Ground Floor Plan**

**View From South**

This should not be too surprising. The school of the future will be related more closely to other activities of the community. Learning will take place (easily scheduled, thanks to computers) at the hospital, the office building, the industrial park, and the agricultural facilities. In previous paragraphs we have emphasized the multipurpose nature of the physical education space, which serves both traditional students and adults.

The principal lesson for the future here is acknowledgment of the fact that the community high school serves both adults and teenagers. The high school will become a learning center for all ages, a fitness center for the community, and an arts center for the district.

## TROY, MICHIGAN

# A Replacement High School

Troy, Michigan, a suburb of Detroit, needed a new high school. The "old" building had grown without a plan since 1950 on a site of inadequate size, leaving only very costly ways to expand the property. Because of that limitation, the board and administration thought that the old campus was hopeless, but they commissioned P&W as architects and Barton-Malow as construction managers to explore the options and compare the costs and desirability of various schemes: (1) building a new high school on the already over-crowded site and then demolishing the old building, (2) saving and renovating the best parts of the existing school and adding new wings, (3) building a new high school on the great new 70-acre site the board had purchased years earlier and then selling the old school, which was already zoned to be commercial, so that the land was worth millions of dollars.

The architects and construction manager found that renovation of the existing school would be the most expensive option and that a new school on the

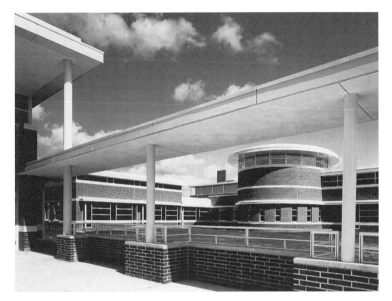

**View of Library**

new site would be the most economical solution. The voters supported that finding.

The new site was ideal. The 70 acres included 15 acres of woods and wetlands and ample space for the new building, playing fields, stadium, and parking

**View of Theater**

113

**Entry Tower**

**Interior Stair Tower**

area. A three-story design was developed, but the school appeared to be only two stories high, thanks to the rolling landscape.

Based on the philosophy that mind, body, and spirit must all be part of education, the 300,000-square-foot school is organized in three elements—academics, physical education, and art—along a circulation spine. The main entrance of the school is indicated by the location of a tower at a circular bus driveway. Classroom wings overlook the natural woods of the surrounding grounds.

Special design and curriculum features of the school include a television studio, several computer labs distributed throughout the facility, a special education unit with a self-contained classroom and four resource rooms, a 750-seat theater, and a 3,000-seat stadium. The facility also features a fully integrated voice, video, and data system with an ITV distribution center.

**Theater**

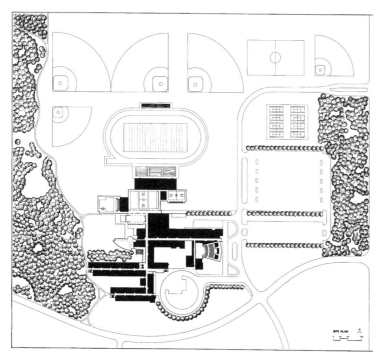

**Site Plan**

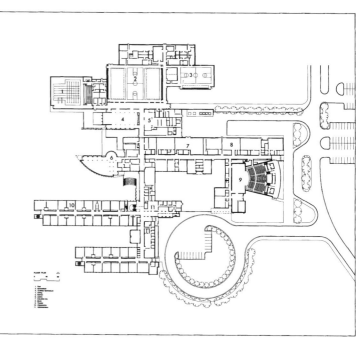

**Ground Floor Plan**

**Section**

# J. L. Stanford Middle School

The design builds on the circulation pattern of the campus in recognition of a system of movement in the school, a system of connectedness that builds the infrastructure of learning. Students have a chance to interact with one another at varying levels inside and outside the classrooms.

At the intersection of the main pedestrian axis, a long arc-shaped building begins the entrance lobby to the school, a double-height space. The structure con-

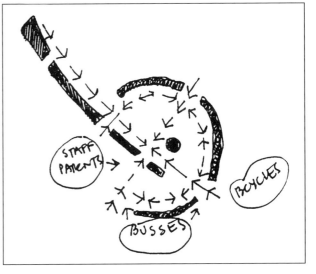

**Concept Sketch**

tinues with administrative offices and stretches through art, drama, and music classrooms, including double-height band practice and choir rooms and science tech labs on the second floor, to extend finally to a cafeteria–multipurpose room with outdoor dining under the expanded canopy at the end.

On the cross-axis, academic classrooms are arranged around a circular courtyard, indicating an expression of connectedness and togetherness. The circular arrangement of the classrooms gives each room a view of a different direction. Each classroom has a different quality of daylight and solar orientation. Between classes, the students circulate through covered walkways.

At the focus of the circular courtyard where pedestrian access routes intersect, several important elements appear: the media center, which includes a library and computer classrooms; administrative offices; the teachers' lounge; and the main entrance of the school.

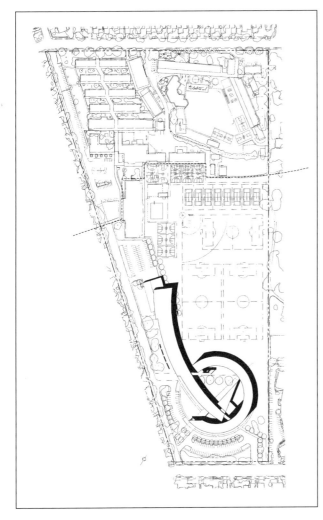

**Site Plan**

**Entry**

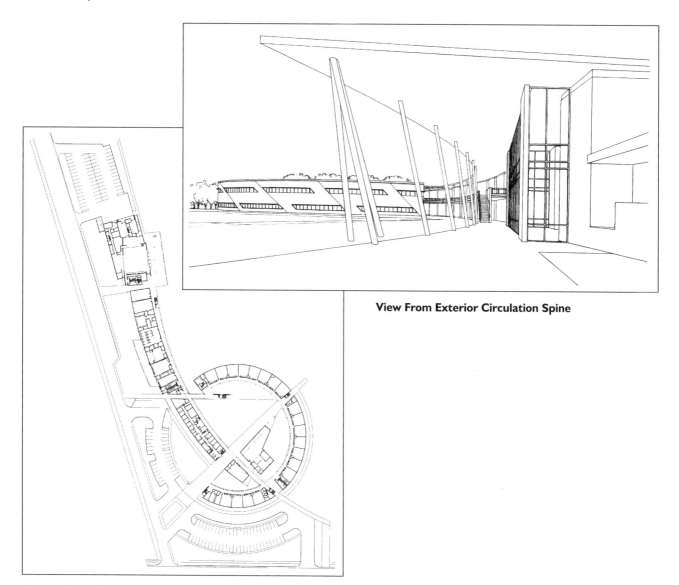

**View From Exterior Circulation Spine**

**Ground Floor Plan**

# WOODLANDS, TEXAS
## A Texas-Size Secondary School

The Conroe, Texas (north of Houston), school board began the planning process years before it hired an architect to design a new 2,000-student high school in a booming new town accurately named Woodlands by its founder, George Mitchell. Woodlands management demands a buffer of trees and other vegetation separating all buildings visually, acoustically, and functionally from the boulevards and streets. The resulting residential and business areas are popular places to live and do business. The community is already famous because in the tough financial years of the 1970s, Woodlands was the only American new town that did not go bankrupt. The community continues to thrive. A new high school was needed. Perkins & Will was selected, and work began on developing the program and analyzing the handsome wooded site. From this analysis, schematic design concepts began to emerge as ideas were passed back and forth.

Then the district's demographer provided startling new information; Woodlands was growing faster than had been predicted. The superintendent of schools and the board abruptly changed the program. We

**Bus Drop-Off Canopy**

**Model**

were to design a school for 3,000 students, not 2,000 students as originally planned. Furthermore, the "old high school" was needed for a middle school.

Alternatives to this plan were explored, but the big decision was made: Woodlands High School would be built for 3,000 students. The architectural design implications were challenging. Some of the new program requirements were obvious. The number of classrooms and laboratories had to be increased, and 1,000 more lockers were needed. The size of the faculty parking lot and the student parking lot and the

number of practice fields had to be increased. However, some spaces could be adapted from the original program, and only minor increases in square feet were needed. In fact, some labs and studios would be used more efficiently by using a specialized lab six times a day instead of four.

In the large school, equipment in the kitchen, mechanical equipment, the swimming pool, and the theater would be used more efficiently.

The toughest problem was the size of the site. The site was selected to satisfy an agreed-upon list of out-

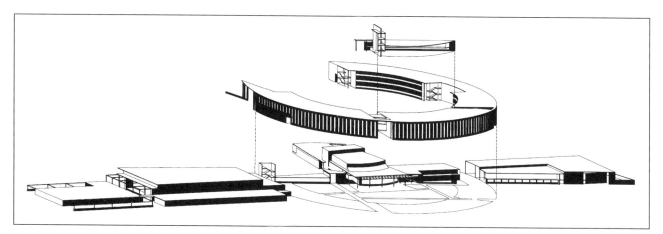

**Exploded Axonometric**

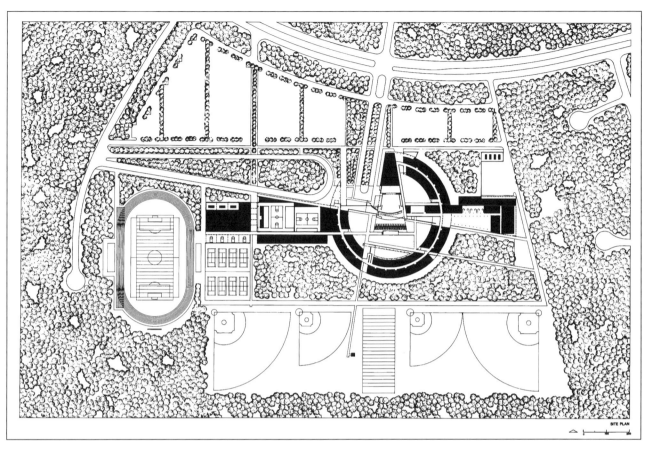

**Site Plan**

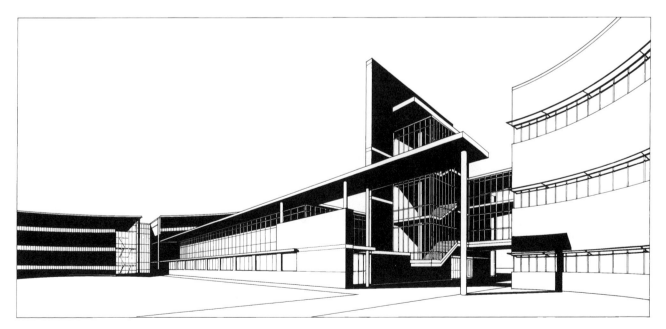

**View of Library**

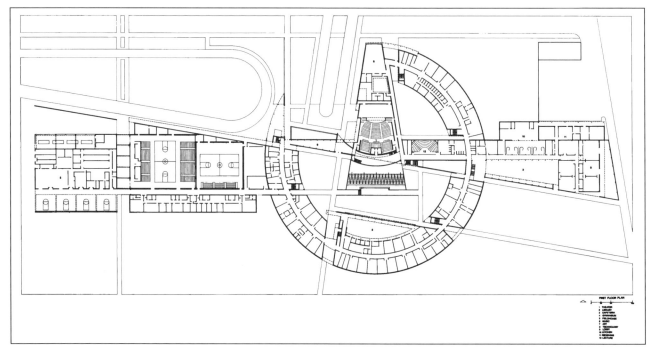

**First Floor Plan**

**Library Interior**

door spaces. The site worked well for 2,000 students, but for 3,000 students some space had to be sacrificed. What would be the first to go? Some people would say, "The green spaces, of course, the green buffer zone." Fortunately, the buffer held; most of the green spaces survived. Expansion of the parking lots and playing fields would use part of the allowances made for future additions to the school.

Note the importance of extra land for future improvement, not necessarily to make the school bigger but to make it better. Also, remember that boards change; today's board may promise to never let the school get too big, but a new board ten years later may not even know that it has a problem.

Changing the program was a difficult task at Woodlands, but we tried hard to balance conflicting demands for buildings, outdoor physical education and athletics (especially football), and the green buffer space.

The resulting Woodlands High School is a new facility which indeed accommodates 3,000 students.

The central feature of the 385,000-square-foot facility is a three-story circular classroom building housing administrative functions, classrooms, lecture halls, science laboratories, and a 16,000-square-foot technology center. This circular element forms a courtyard with space for a future amphitheater at its center. The 40,000-square-foot library and 1,000-seat performing arts center are adjacent to the courtyard.

A wing to the west of the central building houses a 2,000-seat gymnasium, a 250-seat auxiliary gym, separate locker rooms for each sport, and a football field house with training and weight rooms. Another wing to the east contains food service and dining facilities and technology labs. It is connected to the circular building by a three-story atrium.

The wooded 73-acre site includes a 1,500-seat football stadium with a press box, competition baseball and softball fields, eight tennis courts, an agricultural compound, parking for 1,000 students and staff members, and acreage set aside as a forest preserve.

# FORT COLLINS, COLORADO

## High School and Community Center

Fort Collins needed a new high school, because the old building, though much loved by the community, was overcrowded, technologically out of date, not flexible enough, and landlocked.

The old Fort Collins High School was on "Main Street," a few blocks from downtown, and was surrounded by other developments, making a substantial addition difficult, if not impossible. The high school was Collegiate Georgian in character, with a temple front featuring big white classic columns and a big white cupola as the focal point—all this arose from an undistinguished base of dark red brick relieved by white-framed windows. The community loved it. Perhaps it was the best building in town back in the 1920s, when white-columned temple fronts were popular, or perhaps it was the site that the citizens and students admired. The building was set back from Main Street, preserving a whole block of lawns and mature trees. Using that block for expansion of old Fort Collins High School was unthinkable. We architects quickly found out that it was a sacred space.

Let's back up now and discuss how we were selected to design a major high school in Fort Collins, 40 miles north of Denver. Two years earlier, the Fort Collins architect Bob Sutter had invited us to join him in seeking the commission to design a new elementary school. Fort Collins was growing as Colorado State University grew, and major corporations were discovering the advantage of this community for research and the production of electronics. The young citizens knew that this was what Boulder had been twenty or thirty years earlier. Executives, as expected, volunteered to help the board of education create an even better school system. Our team consisted of Architectural Horizons (as Bob Sutter called his small firm of architects), Perkins & Will (out-of-town experts in school design), and Colorado consultants for various engineering services, acoustics, kitchen equipment, soils, and landscaping. It was a good team, but we didn't get the elementary school job. However, we met the school board and school administrators and learned how to pronounce the name of the district.

A year later Bob Sutter called because a new middle school was needed. Again, the trip to Fort Collins was pleasant (it's a great place for skiers and others attracted by the mountains). We were interviewed by the school board but were not selected. Then, about a year later, Bob Sutter called again. The board was requesting qualifications for a team to design a new high school to replace the old downtown Fort Collins High School.

This time we felt quite confident that we would be interviewed and seriously considered for the job. We felt at ease. The interview "went well." The board hired us, and we got off to a quick start.

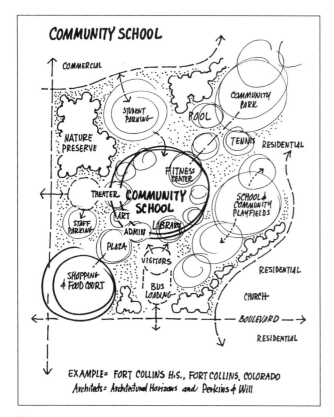

**Diagram**

**Circulation Spine**

The program was being prepared by Dr. Keith Dixon and the high school's principal, Dr. John Brzeinski, while the site was being acquired. The new 1,800-student Fort Collins High School is on a 92-acre site which includes a prime corner that is zoned to be commercial; the board and its consultants visualize a neighborhood shopping center which could include a supermarket, a drug store, a cleaners, and two or three fast-food restaurants. Such siting was purposefully chosen to foster interaction with the school. The school also asked the park board that owned some of the adjacent land to consider the development of a community school. All the parties agreed to ask the architects to explore the possibilities by preparing a master plan with the developer, who was building hundreds of houses within walking distance of the high school. Therefore, the school, the park system, and the commercial corner were assigned and built as a coordinated community center.

The park district acquired some adjacent land for a community park with the idea that the high school and park would be planned and developed concurrently to serve both the open space and the recreational needs of the high school as well as the broader needs of the community. The lot line between the school and the park was to be only a dotted line on this site plan, not a fence or a wall separating the two. When planning was in progress, the site was rural, with access from two roads on the 1-mile grid.

When the new school opened in 1995, the site had changed from rural to suburban, and developers were completing the construction and sale of new homes.

**Model**

**Circulation Intersection**

**Entry Tower**

The people who bought the houses liked the idea of living near a high school, a park, and a neighborhood shopping center.

In the past, most high schools were planned, designed, and built with little input from the faculty, students, and board of education. Instead, the "school planning experts" began with the assumption that standard classrooms would be utilized in standard configurations that were already known by all the planning participants. Before the inclusion of air-conditioning, the "standard" classroom wing plan was "the finger plan" in Florida, Texas, California, and other warm states. Classrooms were set in rows, with windows looking north and with a sheltered outdoor walkway on the south side to protect the south-facing classrooms from the midday sun. With the advent of air-conditioning, windowless classrooms were too

often incorporated "to save energy," a misleading concept because the fans have to be run forever to make the spaces habitable. A more enlightened concept is to provide most or all of the school with windows and air-conditioning and then use judgment in deciding whether to air-condition learning spaces or simply open the windows and use nature's own climate control—natural ventilation—on many days of the year.

The Fort Collins faculty, board, administration, and students recognized that the standard classroom plan used most often nationwide is the double-loaded corridor with classrooms, labs, and other spaces, plus lockers on both sides of a 10-foot- to 12-foot-wide corridor. It's hard to beat that plan for efficiency. The only more efficient scheme is the campus plan, where outdoor circulation is utilized and corridors are eliminated; this plan is great for benign climates.

However, the Fort Collins people emphasized some other considerations. They assumed that some standard classrooms would continue to be used when the new school opened, but many of those spaces would change during the following decades, and so a high level of flexibility had to be achieved in the design. Some faculty teams thought that double-loaded corridors were still the most functional, while other teams wanted open space with no permanent partitions or

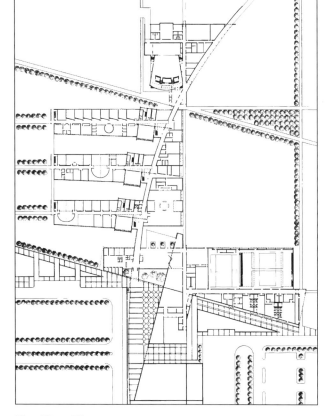

**First Floor Plan**

idea) in all disciplines, each team should decide which subdivision of spaces best satisfied its own space needs. That decision did not have to be made until late in the construction process; instead, each team was thought of as a tenant in a flexible office building. Each tenant (or "department," house, or cluster) examined its own space and equipment needs separately. The building management (the school administration) then instructed the architects and the construction manager to finish each of the six academic wings to satisfy six different learning situations.

Illustrations of options were prepared to help everyone visualize some of the space possibilities. Some of these sketches are reproduced here in the belief that others can benefit from this tailoring of space as opposed to making standard decisions at central administration and asking every faculty team to adopt the same list of spaces.

Three school components—academic, performing arts and music, and physical education—plus the commercial center and the park are organized along a central spine, creating a campuslike atmosphere. The curved "Main Street" corridor (with no lockers obstructing it) is a popular space for socializing.

The school has a number of special features, including classrooms and laboratories equipped to accommodate present and future computer applications, a television studio, a biosphere, advanced computer technical centers, a 750-seat auditorium, and sports fields for baseball, softball, soccer, tennis, football, and track. A tower marks the main entrance and will be the electronic communications tower in the future.

wanted to push the corridor over to one side to make the clustering of spaces better.

The architects listened to convincing arguments for three or four different plan configurations for a typical (base building) 70 feet wide and 125 to 175 feet long. The planning teams reached an interesting conclusion: Instead of imposing one plan (one concept, one

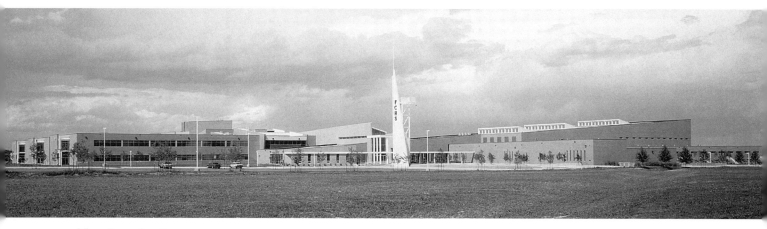

**View From South**

## CHELSEA, MASSACHUSETTS

# A High School Reuniting the Liberal Arts and Career Education

Chelsea, Massachusetts, is part of the Boston Harbor region. This small city of 25,000 people is surrounded by waterways, railroads, highways, elevated expressways, Logan Airport, and old and new industries. Near downtown Boston, the old residential neighborhoods of Chelsea are areas where low housing costs attract new immigrants. Many of the young people are highly motivated, want good jobs, and recognize the importance of education, especially career education.

Like all urban communities, Chelsea has had problems. The city went bankrupt. A receiver was appointed to run Chelsea, and Boston University was given the job of running the school system. Talented and energetic administrators were appointed. Among many other decisions, a review of Chelsea High School, the middle schools, and the elementary schools led the managers to the conclusion that the city needed an entirely new set of school buildings. For the new Chelsea High School they selected SMMA (Symmes, Maini and McKee), in association with Perkins & Will.

With the planning team in place, the team members began the process of preparing the program (the educational specifications) and concurrently analyzing the site.

The form of the new school was strongly influenced by this process. The program included a fresh look at vocational-technical education and its relationship to liberal arts education. The two have grown apart. The program for Chelsea High School was intended to reestablish a close relationship between these two realms. The bottom line was a simple and straightforward concept: The new school was to be subdivided into four houses, and each house would be both a liberal arts school and a career education

school. The ninth-grade house, however, is a transitional school between the middle school and the high school. The tenth-, eleventh-, and twelfth-graders are in three houses. Each of three houses has a different career program. The three initial offerings (subject to change each term) are

1. Telecommunications and technology

2. Health and human services

3. Transportation and commerce

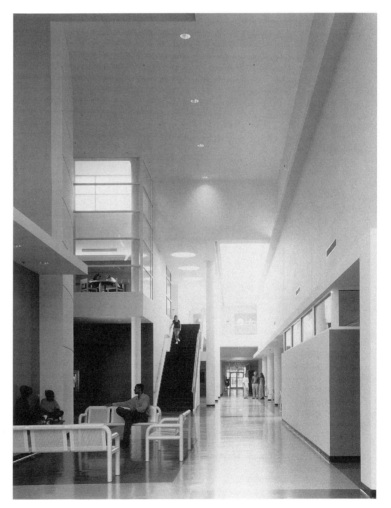

**Interior Corridor**

129

**Classroom "Houses"**

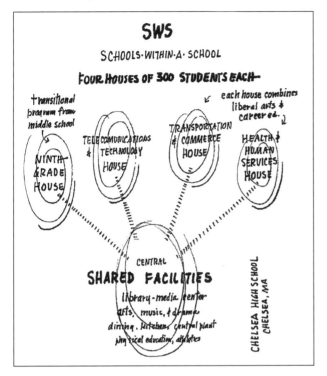

**Building Concept**

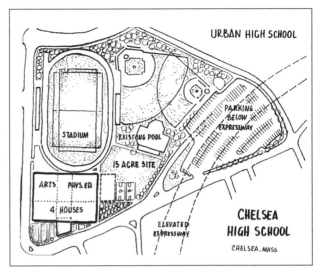

**Site Plan**

Each cluster of careers includes some of the jobs that are prominent in the economy of the Boston region. For example, MIT and the Route 128 ring expressway around the Boston suburbs are famous for the development of electronic technology. Visible from Chelsea is Logan Airport, which offers a great array of jobs. As in most cities, health care firms and social service agencies are big employers. Part of the strategy is to give students knowledge of and exposure to different kinds of jobs.

Having considered the importance of the program in design, we now consider the importance of the site.

The site for Chelsea High School is small. For a 1,600-student high school in a northeastern city suburb, a site of 40 acres was considered adequate a few decades ago; now a site of 60 acres can be justified. What changed? A lot. We passed a law saying that women's physical education is as important as men's physical education. This increased the number of playing fields. More citizens now expect to find tennis courts at schools. Also, whether we like it or not, more students drive to high school.

The site for Chelsea High School is only 15 acres, and a good part of that is consumed by an existing stadium and track, a facility that is important to the

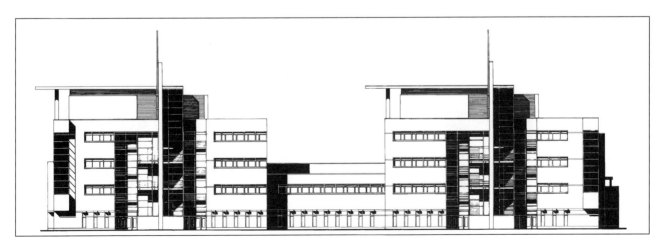

**Elevation**

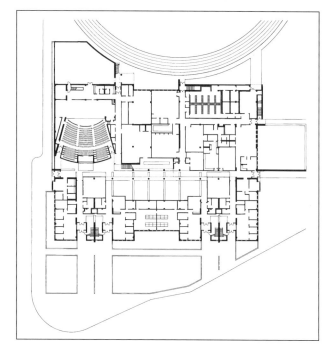

**First Floor Plan**

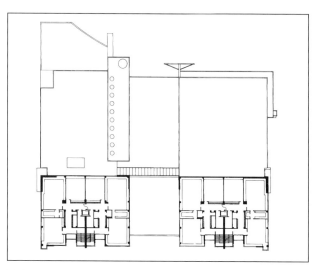

**Third Floor Plan**

community as a landmark. An already existing swimming pool is on the site.

The school building, playing fields, and parking consume the site. An elevated expressway soars over the eastern part; this was the logical place for parking. Early in the planning nearly everyone agreed that a four-story building would be appropriate and that it should be quite compact. A plan began to emerge: The school within a school concept has driven the planning and design of this new urban high school. The school is divided into four interdisciplinary houses

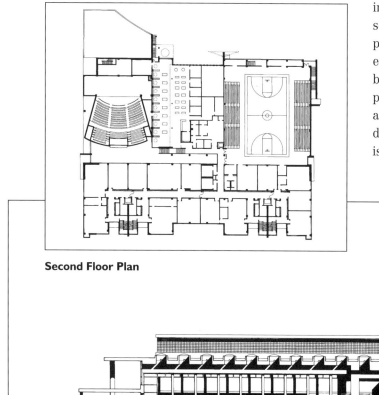

**Second Floor Plan**

**Section Through Library**

**Playfields**

which enjoy the front yard position on the site, like four row houses, and provide the students with a home within the large school environment. Immediately behind them are the shared facilities for the four schools. All the students share a library and media center, computer labs, performing arts spaces, a kitchen, a pool, playing fields, recreational areas, and day care facilities. The tight urban site is adjacent to a city park and shares programs and facilities with the community at large. This factor, as well as evening courses for working students, makes security a special consideration in the design of the two- and three-story structure. A police liaison office is located within the building to facilitate community outreach programs and handle security and safety issues. The resulting form for the building is a compact rectangular plan with an interesting composition of the houses that recalls the forms of early modernism.

## SAINT PAUL, MINNESOTA

# Arlington High School—The House Plan

Interdisciplinary curricula and a commitment to life-long learning are concepts that have been embraced by Saint Paul public schools. These ideas shaped the planning of a new urban high school for 2,000 students designed by Perkins & Will in association with Winsor/Faricy Architects. The school is situated on a 29-acre urban site and serves a diverse constituency of both college-bound and vocationally oriented students.

The program for the school divides the facility into four zones, each of which has a specific functional use. Zone 1 is composed of five ninth- and tenth-grade "houses." Each house serves 200 students with classrooms, laboratories, study space, central gathering space, and faculty office and prep areas. Zone 2 serves eleventh- and twelfth-grade students with a liberal arts house, health science house, government and public policy house, and communications and technology house.

A community core of shared facilities makes up the third zone. All grade levels take advantage of business, fine arts, physical education, and technology education spaces. This zone also contains food services, administration, guidance, health services, and a child care center. Zone 4, the information commons, consists of the media center, the study center, and a multicultural resource center.

Instead of six periods of fifty-five minutes each, the school day is divided into four periods of eighty-four minutes each to encourage and facilitate innovation, team teaching, small groups of students sharing work on projects, and independent study. For example, a study of France could include the French language along with French history, geography, government, culture, cuisine, and art. To accommodate such ambitious and ever-changing educational programs, the school building spaces should be diverse, readily changeable, and easily adjustable to different needs, and ongoing projects should be encouraged by the provision of work and storage space.

Vocational-technical study doesn't describe the Arlington High School program in Saint Paul. An integration of career experiences with the liberal arts and all the other courses one associates with traditional high school programs comes closer to the spirit of the school. The study of the evolution of a new product (or a new idea) could include history, geography, sociology, science and mathematics, design and engineering, production, promotion, sales, law and finance, team teaching, and team learning, along with individual learning.

The school has a state-of-art library and resource center and a districtwide multicultural resource center. Three hundred fifty computers are distributed throughout the school (not just in computer labs), 170 television sets are equipped to play laser disks and videocassettes, and the telephone has been rediscovered—teachers have voice mail numbers so that they can more easily communicate with administrators and parents.

Arlington High School has an unconventional auditorium. A study of ordinary auditoriums in existing schools showed that they were seldom used. As a result of planning

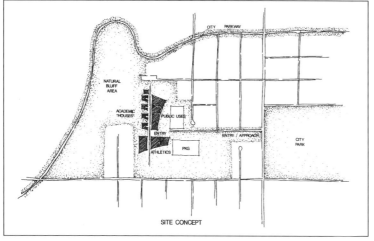

**Site Plan**

134

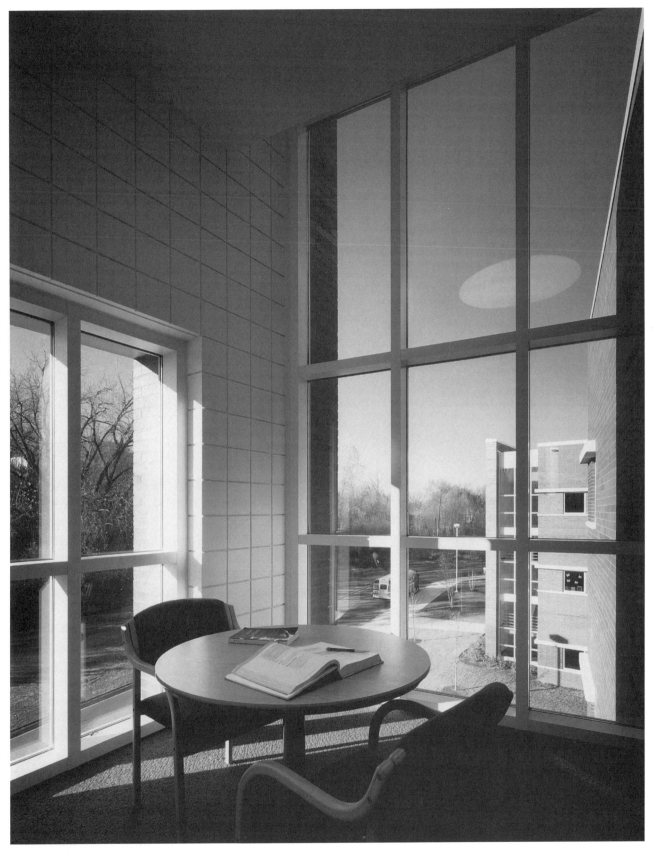

**Study Space**

**Classroom Bars**

meetings with the faculty and administration, the architects developed a "Great Room" to serve as an appealing assembly space (with windows), flexible theater space, and dining space. It is an attractive, well-lit, multilevel event space which is in high demand for various meetings and activities, day and night, for both the school and the community.

Community input was a very important part of the planning process. When the architects were selected, the school system was already incorporating the community into the planning process. The people in the immediate neighborhoods took an active interest in where and how the proposed new high school would be developed. At one of the early meetings with the neighbors, the architects arrived with a large map of the neighborhood, which was rolled out on the floor. Everyone was invited to take off his or her shoes and crawl over the neighborhood map, jotting down ideas, problem areas, opportunities, and needs. It proved to be a good icebreaker and provided some useful ideas and information.

The site might be considered too small, but this is an urban, not a suburban, site. The size, however, did suggest that a compact plan be developed and that a three- or four-story building would be appropriate. The site plan shows how the site accommodated the building comfortably along with adequate parking, a special bus-loading drive, playing fields, and adequate open space.

Part of the site problem was solved by the fact that the park district owns a large park adjacent to the new high school so that many softball and baseball diamonds are available during school hours. The concept of sharing such facilities makes good sense everywhere. Meanwhile, indoor spaces for physical education and athletics and for community fitness activities include a large gymnasium, an auxiliary gymnasium, and a six-lane swimming pool.

Individual houses are expressed as separate wings of the building, connected by a spine which links them to one another and to the support spaces, shared facilities, gymnasium, and the "Great Room."

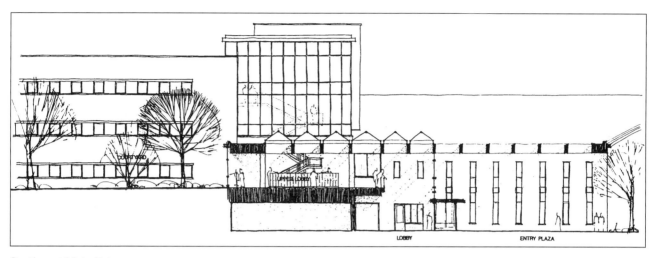

**Section at Main Entry**

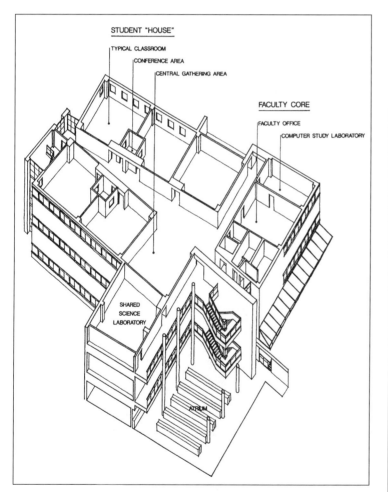

**Typical House Axonometric**

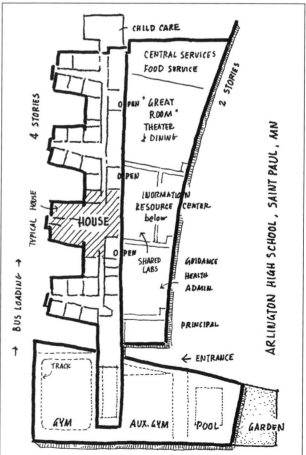

**Planning Sketch**

**Lobby**

## CRYSTAL LAKE, ILLINOIS

# Prairie Ridge High School—
# Program and Site Generate the Form

Prairie Ridge High School is in Crystal Lake, Illinois, northwest of Chicago. Crystal Lake is primarily a residential community that has experienced steady and continued growth in its district enrollment. Consequently, the district made plans for this new 1,800-student facility, envisioning a school that would serve the needs of its students and community.

The school is located on a 140-acre L-shaped site that gently rolls to its southern boundary of protected wetlands and prairie. Formerly used for farming, the site is bounded by lines of trees and hedges along its eastern and western edges. The site is within the context of residential development to the north, east, and west. It is the combination of these distinct site features and the district's vision of a multiuse facility that shaped the planning of the school.

The building is placed near the high point of the site. This placement was selected to take advantage of the shape of the land. The primary form of the building—the arc-shaped classroom bar—is derived from the line of a ridge that occurs naturally along this part of the site. The three-story building visually relates to the site and offers panoramic views to the south of the wetlands and prairie. The upper levels of the curved bar house the general classrooms and science laboratories. The lower level of the curved bar contains the school's learning resources center. The concept of the center is based on the school's educational philosophy, which mandates that its resources, including the staff, should be easily available to the students. The plan of the building responds by providing access to the library and media center, study hall, computer labs, and teachers' offices from a centralized area. These areas, which may be closed off from the remainder of the school, also provide space for community educational programs and activities after normal school hours.

The performing arts, music, and athletic facilities are situated north of the classroom bar in a rectangular wing. This wing, which includes a 500-seat theater, two gymnasiums and their supporting locker rooms, art studios, and band and choral music rooms, is cradled by the shape of the classroom bar. The main entrance to the school is defined by the intersection of sloped roofs that form the administration and dining facilities as well. The varied roof forms of the northern wing respond to the functional requirements of the spaces that wing contains. Because these uses are

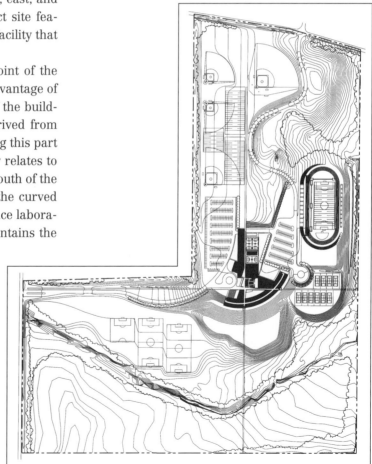

**Site Plan**

**139**

placed in a separate wing, access through the main lobby to the competition gymnasium and theater may be provided after hours without operating the entire facility.

The remainder of the site development includes a track and football stadium; tennis courts; practice fields for soccer, football, baseball, and softball; and separate vehicular access to faculty and student parking.

The design of Prairie Ridge High School is based foremost on functional relationships that give form to the architecture. While this design approach is not uncommon, the manner by which the building's functions and the site's distinct physical attributes are made inseparable defines the school's unique architectural character. The importance of designing the school as an integral part of the landscape was motivated by the desire to preserve the site's wetlands and prairie, which once defined the midwest and in particular this region of Illinois.

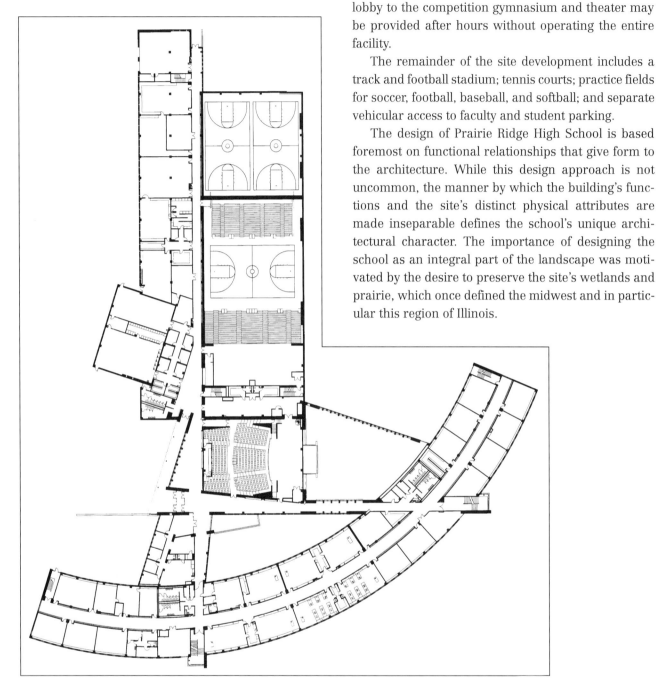

**Ground Floor Plan**

## NORTH FORT MYERS, FLORIDA
# Combining Old and New Buildings

The need in North Fort Myers was to save, improve, and reuse the best parts of an existing one-story high school while demolishing the unsuitable parts and building new two-story parts. All this building activity would proceed in two phases while all 1,800 high school students continued to receive their education on the campus.

New buildings will continue to receive attention from both educators and architects, but the renewal of older existing buildings also needs attention. Often the old and new components occur on the same site, giving the school continuity and a sense of history and local culture. The existing buildings may be 20 years old or 100 years old or more and only a few of our schools will be designated as architectural landmarks, but the need to renovate and improve the quality and comfort of 20- to 100-year-old buildings is a nationwide priority.

**Library From Courtyard**

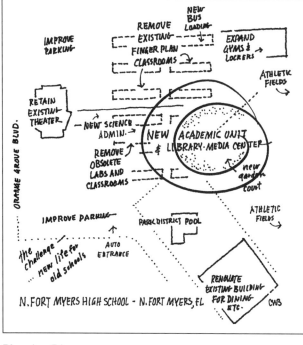

**Planning Diagram**

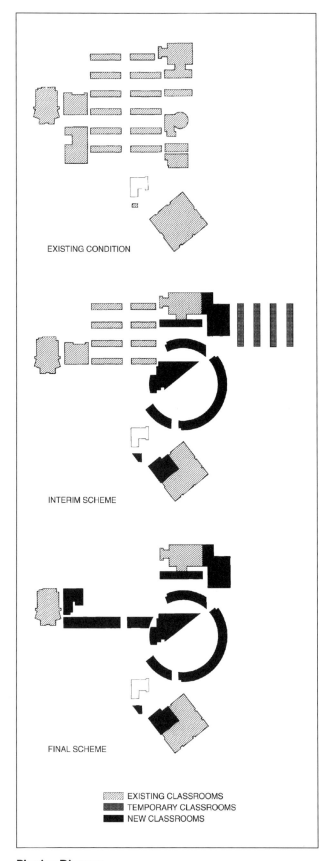

EXISTING CONDITION

INTERIM SCHEME

FINAL SCHEME

▨ EXISTING CLASSROOMS
■ TEMPORARY CLASSROOMS
■ NEW CLASSROOMS

**Phasing Diagram**

If the existing buildings on the campus are landmarks and are listed on local or national historic registers, improvements on the campus are of a different nature. The exterior of a building of historic importance probably will be restored to its original appearance by removing inconsistent doors, windows, roofs, and the almost inevitable small additions that have been "tacked on over the years."

A landmark building may have a completely new interior designed to satisfy new needs, while the exterior respects the context of the campus and the community.

The important idea is the possibility of a "rich mix" of old and new building units. Such a school grows (or contracts) and changes over the years.

The board of education of the North Fort Myers High School in Lee County, Florida, had already decided that some existing high school structures on the old one-story finger-plan campus were no longer suitable; therefore, the classrooms, labs, library, and food service facility needed to be replaced by new units, while other parts needed renewal. A fine auditorium, only a few years old, had to be a part of the new campus, and a park district swimming pool was to be retained.

The school was designated a "STEM" school, a local term that means that the school has enhanced programs in science, technology, environment, and mathematics.

The size of the school site was not up to usual standards, and so a compact plan with two-story buildings seemed appropriate. The educators and architects, including Parker Mudgett Smith of Fort Myers, met many times with the faculty and administration to

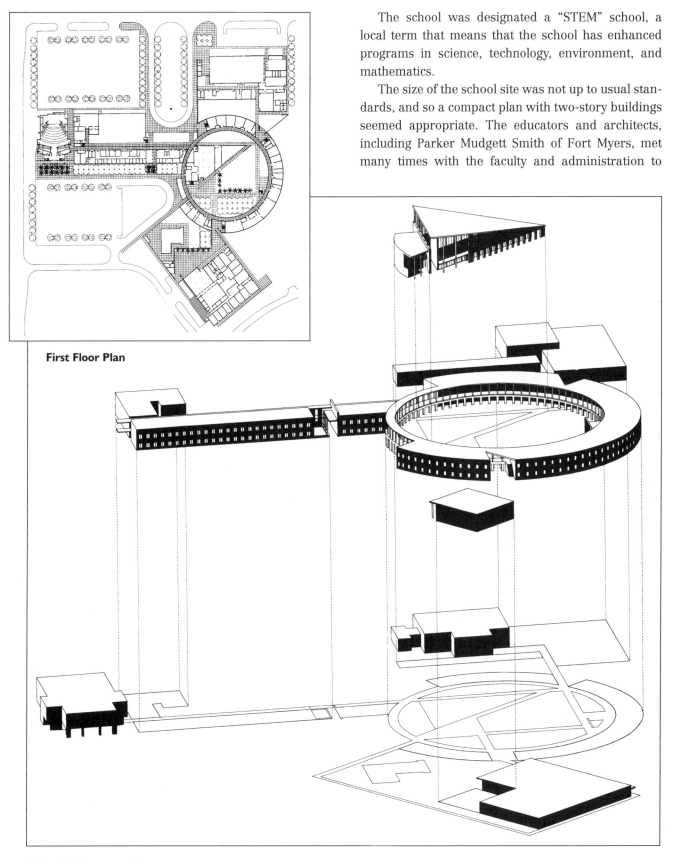

**First Floor Plan**

**Exploded Axonometric**

**Library Interior**

clearly establish the space requirement for a high school serving 1,800 students. Concurrently, a master plan for the campus was developed to guide future expansion or improvement of the campus in the year 2010. The planners, involving the administration, teachers, students, community representatives, and the board of education, all agreed that the school needed a new look in addition to being redesigned to function more effectively.

Working around the old classrooms, which were being phased out, and some temporary portable classrooms, the architects designed a two-story circular academic unit around a circular garden, with a ground floor "stoa" (a Greek sheltered promenade) providing access to classroom entrances. At the sec-

ond floor the open balcony also provides outdoor circulation to the classrooms.

The geometry of the new classroom buildings—a bar and a circle—connects the existing elements in a straightforward manner and establishes a series of intimate exterior rooms. A new media center is housed in a triangular building within the circular courtyard which forms the heart of the campus.

The supervision of the central garden courtyard is superb, since from any spot on the sheltered walk at the first or second floor a person can view the complete circulation system. Only the library protrudes into this tropical garden. Therefore, everyone has equal visual access to the library, which is the most prominent building on the campus, and the garden constitutes the prime open space for the campus. The second open space consists of the vehicular entrances and parking near the offices, and the third open space is the science department's outdoor work space and botanical garden. The fourth space is around the outdoor swimming pool, which is run by the park district, and the adjacent playing fields provide the largest open space, which, as with other facilities, is shared by all the people in the community. An addition to the existing gymnasium allows an expanded physical education program. An existing classroom building has been renovated to accommodate a new cafeteria, art rooms, business studies areas, and other classrooms.

The ground floor stoa and the second floor balcony, connected by stairs and an elevator (mandatory, of course), form a wonderful circulation system that gives the campus a new image and an efficient fresh air corridor. The open corridor along the classrooms responds to the climate of southwestern Florida, as do the covered walkways, terraces, and canopied entryways. Landscaping represents different Florida environments in support of the environmental magnet program. The goal of mixing old and new building components to achieve a rich mix of spaces that continues to evolve over the years has been met.

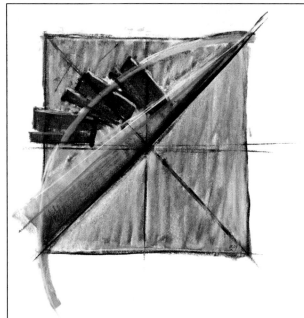

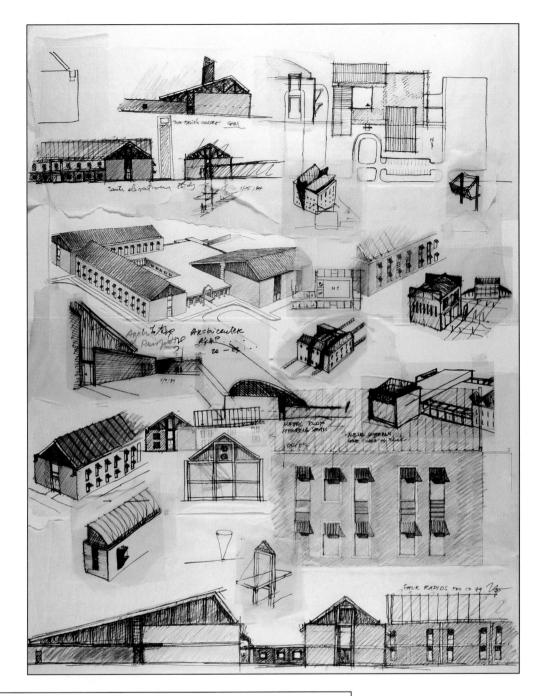

**Library Exterior**

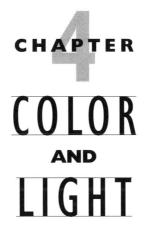

CHAPTER

# COLOR
## AND
# LIGHT

**Raymond Bordwell**

This chapter examines the influence of color and light in an increasingly sophisticated learning environment.

Information technologies are changing instructional methodologies and greatly influencing the design of contemporary school buildings. Color can affect the usability of educational spaces. Reducing eyestrain in a technology-intensive setting is now a priority. From an aesthetic viewpoint, we must recognize that we are opening our schools to a wider variety of users through expanded community participation and year-round use.

Consider also that not all schools of the future will be new buildings. Land cost and availability, community sentiment, and construction cost will dictate the reuse of many existing facilities. Renovated buildings will account for most of the educational facilities used at the end of this century. When renovation of these buildings includes a new coat of paint, consider how important the color of that paint can be.

Color and light are inseparable, and discussing them individually is difficult. However, in this chapter lighting will be addressed first.

## Light in the Learning Environment

Poor lighting can affect students' performance. Consider the word *pupil*. It can have two meanings: the round aperture in the iris of the eye and a student in school or in the charge of a tutor or instructor.

How are these meanings similar? Both deal with learning. Ensuring the health of the first can help the second. Assuming that the learning experience can be improved through uniform illumination, an indirect or diffused light source is recommended. A spectrum of reflectivity that begins with a darker floor and progresses to a highly reflective ceiling creates an environment in which school tasks can be performed comfortably.

## Lighting Effects

Eyestrain can be a major distraction for both students and teachers. The causes of eyestrain are well known: glare, adjustment to conflicting levels of brightness, prolonged near tasks such as using a computer, and poor visibility are just a few examples. If any or all

**Daylight at Chelsea High School, Chelsea, MA. Ceiling LRV (light reflectance value) near 100%. (Color Photo)**

these conditions exist, the effect can be increased blinking, muscular tension, and dilation of the pupil. All have a negative influence on a student's ability to concentrate.

Overcompensation can cause too much brightness and impede vision by creating glare, constricting the pupillary opening, and interjecting a disturbing pull away from books and tasks.

There is general agreement among the experts that school environments should have an average light reflectance value of 50 to 60 percent and that brightness ratios in the field of view should be uniform.

Interior planning should include careful consideration of a material's light reflectance value (LRV). In simple terms, LRV is the measurement of a material's ability to reflect light. All materials reflect and absorb

light, and recommended LRVs should fall into different ranges for different areas.

Floors should have a range of 20 to 30 percent (the actual range of unstained wood). The floor forms a visual base in the learning environment and should not reflect high amounts of light. Depending on the material selected, this also represents an opportunity to improve some rooms' acoustics (ceramic tiles versus carpeting, for example.) The material for a carpet, which typically has a low LRV, absorbs sound and is easy to maintain.

For furniture, equipment, doors, and door frames the LRV should be between 40 and 50 percent. It should provide contrast to the ceiling and/or light in the room. The maximum brightness difference would therefore be 2.5 to 1 (40 percent for furniture and 100 percent for the ceiling and lighting). It should never surpass 3 to 1.

Walls typically should have a range of 50 to 55 percent. Colors and materials in this range help reduce glare.

Accent walls and teaching walls should range between 45 and 50 percent. In the classroom, when students are oriented toward the teacher, this wall is sometimes called the primary teaching wall. This provides an excellent opportunity to introduce an accent color. When a student looks up from a task such as writing or using a computer, the color of this wall can do four things: relieve eye fatigue, focus attention on the teacher, reduce the overall glare emanating from the white or gray boards that are used, and provide stimulation through its reflective difference from the basic room background. An accent wall can eliminate color monotony and help reduce glare from natural light sources such as windows, an open door to the hallway, and skylights.

For ceilings an LRV of 90 to 100 percent is appropriate. It could be considered a good standard practice to use white for all ceilings. This provides a consistent appearance and an abundance of uniform, shadow-free illumination.

Depending on the ratio of floors to walls, the average range for the room as a whole should fall between 40 and 60 percent. An approach for applying color that satisfies the above criteria is illustrated here. In the example shown, cool colors have been selected as background, a practice which is especially beneficial for the secondary grades. Cool colors encourage concentration by lowering heart and respiration rates. In the development of this type of scheme, consideration of an individual's age is important, since the effect of color on the human body changes as one ages.

When the brightness ratio is 5 to 1, students' vision is smooth and unencumbered and average school tasks can be performed comfortably.

## Color in the Learning Environment

Why do we pick the colors we pick? How do we arrive at a color scheme? These are provocative question for many people. Often it is a matter of personal preference: "I like that color." At other times the rationale for repainting with the same color might sound like this: "That color matches the carpet," "We already had the paint," or "That's the color we always painted it." Each of these statements has been heard many times.

Personal preference can lead to the wrong color choice. It is very tempting to use the latest trendy color to update a school. However, this should be resisted in favor of a more scientific approach, as personal opinion or whims can complicate the choice of a color. An overemphasis on beauty and fashion may detract from the true purpose of color and from the functional dignity that should prevail in the school field. Color also should enhance the architecture of space, not detract from it. Color *for the sake of color* can be overused. Contemporary facilities with a strong geometry as part of the architecture combined with a wide pallette of colors can create visual noise. Often the best approach may be to use a uniform, neutral color to allow the architecture to create the interest.

## Color Selection

Color selection for today's schools is complicated by the wide range of users. From young children who have come for day care to senior citizens who are there for community activities, today's schools are truly multiuse facilities. A more technical approach to making color decisions can produce space that positively affects the users in a variety of ways. Color choices should be made with a clear understanding of the use of the space. Functional color that it is purposeful, as opposed to fashionable color, provides an overwhelming advantage for all the users of a facility. Functional color is concerned with measurable things and can provide identity, directional assistance, and visual interest.

The first issue for discussion should be whether to use warm or cool colors. This may seem insignificant, but there are some basic guidelines.

Warm colors have a diverting effect. Bright warm color schemes work well for elementary school students. The effect of a warm color is to draw visual and emotional interest outward.

Cool colors have the opposite effect. Softness and coolness of color and the passive effect of the surroundings permit better concentration. Cool colors are appropriate for the secondary grades in libraries, study spaces, and areas where individual tasks are the focus.

Functional color for high schools should be cool and soft. Softness and coolness of color promote a passive effect of the surroundings and thus permit better concentration. Cool colors promote a student's need to turn his or her attention inward rather than outward.

Conversely, functional colors in elementary schools should be warm, bright colors that invite an outward release of feelings and emotion. Visual and emotional interest are directed outward. Very young students do not have the ability to discern subtle changes in color, and a more sophisticated color scheme may not be effective or appreciated for these pupils. Early childhood students tend to be more introverted than are older students, and warm colors can help promote interaction.

In these classroom examples, students' concentration will be improved when the background recedes in neutral color with uniform brightness ratios for the floor, furniture, and equipment. The primary teaching wall becomes the focal point by being highlighted in medium colors of gold, green, blue, or terra-cotta. In general, school environments should use naturally finished materials or be painted in colors that have light reflectance values between 50 and 60 percent.

# CHAPTER 5

# HOW
## TO
# PREVENT
# OBSOLETE
# SCHOOLS

## Raymond Bordwell

Discussions between architects and school administrators about facility design usually include ideas about the design of "schools for the twenty-first century." How will our schools in the first half of the twenty-first century adapt to changes we cannot foresee? Consider the one-room schoolhouse. As late as 1913 almost half of all students in American public school systems attended a one-room schoolhouse. The idea of a one-room schoolhouse seems antiquated now, but how can we avoid similar obsolescence of today's schools in in the year 2020? Will it be any less startling to consider using a building constructed using many of the same guidelines that were employed in 1960 (which many schools are still following) for education in the year 2020 or 2050? How can we avoid building schools that will become the one-room schoolhouses of the next century?

Part of the answer lies in examining how we have planned and constructed schools in this century, identifying what has made them obsolete or what will cause them to need replacing. The central question is what planning or construction methods were employed in the 1950s through the 1980s that today are

contributing to our schools becoming outdated? This chapter will examine ten issues involving the American schoolhouse that must be addressed.

Often there is a difference between the stated planning objectives and what is actually constructed. If we make a priority of these design, construction, and operational issues, great improvements will be made in preparing schools for the twenty-first century. This will require us to rethink our perceptions of the schoolhouse. This involves using the knowledge from past successes and mistakes in planning educational facilities. We have seen many of the possible changes, but we have not seen all the changes. Forecasting change is the easy part. Determining what those changes will be is not as easy.

## The Issues

The list presented here contains issues that must be addressed. They have been limiting factors on the design, construction, and operation of schools in this century. They can be divided into two major areas: the use of building materials and systems that will deliver long life and flexibility with reduced maintenance and the design of flexible learning and teaching spaces.

Many of the issues are not new, but many are difficult. Some have been overlooked, underestimated, or simply not given the attention they deserve. There are many more issues, and these ten are only a starting point for designing schools for the twenty-first century. Presented below are what could be called the top ten list.

## 1. Beware of "Cheap" Construction

The effort to build schools quickly in the 1950s and 1960s produced boxlike minimalist structures. These facilities are characterized by concrete block walls, low ceilings, and minimal building volumes. There was a trend toward reducing the number of windows, which was envisioned as a way to conserve energy, even though in the same designs the roof insulation value was minimal and exterior weather protection was inadequate. Another feature was the presence of a "structural grid" where the floor and roof beams spans were designed to be as similar as possible; consequently, this plan often used masonry-bearing walls, further limiting future flexibility. If there is a choice between a bigger building and a high-quality building, one should always choose quality. Maintenance and operating costs stay with a building for its entire life and should not be underestimated. An experienced architect can help provide the necessary space to meet the objectives of programs in the most efficient way and reduce the overall size of the building.

The decision to replace an existing school can be a difficult one. Careful evaluation is necessary before a decision to add to, renovate, or otherwise spend money on a building that, economics and funding issues aside, should be replaced. If the serviceable life of a building cannot be extended past twenty-five years, serious consideration must be given to replacing that building.

## 2. No More Building "Boxes"

Interior masonry-bearing walls present a limiting factor to renovations that enlarge, reconfigure, or add space. Within the structural grid the square classroom box became the standard measure for all the spaces within a school. Few special-use areas were included in these designs in an effort to reduce construction costs. If a school plan included a library (and some

didn't), it often was allocated a single classroom block or a combination of two classroom modules. This also was true of instructional spaces intended for art and music classes. Administrative areas were typically undersized and lacked expandable space for programs such as health and guidance services. The nature of new educational programs, accommodated by tutorial and small group instructional space, require less space than does a standard classroom.

In planning new facilities, the evaluation of building structural systems must be carefully examined. This is especially important in areas where change is most likely to occur. Any space used for nontraditional instruction may fall into this category.

The use of movable walls at specific locations is an excellent way to provide flexible space. The key word here is *specific*. These wall systems are expensive and typically do not have the sound isolation and durability of permanently constructed walls, and so they are seldom used.

## 3. Planning for Technology

The technology revolution in education is well under way but at the same time is just beginning. For a clear perspective on how far we have come in fifty years, in 1946 the first UNIVAC computer completely filled a 9-foot by 12-foot room. Today technology has advanced so far that almost everyone owns a small handheld calculator that's faster, more flexible, and more available at a fraction of the price of a good slide rule (remember the slide rule?). During the 1980s, the personal computer revolutionized research and problem solving, and technology continues to advance at a staggering rate, introducing new notebook and palmtop computer systems with interactive video capabilities almost weekly.

Herein lies the problem: Despite these revolutionary changes in technology, conventional design of school buildings and instructional space in many cases has remained virtually unchanged since the 1950s. Classrooms with one electrical outlet are still common; harsh, single-level direct lighting is the rule, and insufficient mechanical ventilation is the norm. This lack of flexibility, coupled with inaccessible masonry walls, makes the integration of new instructional and administrative technology difficult and in some cases prohibitively expensive. However, computers are no longer simply tools in the experimental phase, utilized by a small percentage of interested staff members with the knowledge to understand them. They are an integral part of instruction, research, administrative tasks, and building system control. Our dependence on computer systems will continue to increase, as will the need for power and information access. Nearly every aspect of most students' lives will require the use of computer technology in some shape or form. The computer labs designed for the International School project in Manila provide a good example of a computer lab planned for use by students and teachers, with the possibility of changing the use of the space in the future. All the furniture in this room that supports technology use will be movable.

## 4. Social Changes

Societal changes continue to be a driving force in new program requirements. Implementation of state-mandated programs requires flexible spaces that can be used for small group instruction, counseling, and career guidance. These programs reflect the needs of a modern school-age population. Efforts to use public educational facilities to address important social issues related to single-parent families, drug and alcohol abuse, and crime require us to make adjustments in our planning strategies to take these issues into account.

Movement from an industrial society to one based on service, research, and technology over the last thirty years has contributed to making buildings obsolete. An educational emphasis on lifelong learning will train and retrain individuals to keep pace with a rapidly developing technological society.

School-age populations are more sophisticated than ever before. They not only know the difference between a good building and a bad one, they also care! We need to change our perceptions of our clients. If we thought of the students themselves as the buyers—with education as the product and schools as the package—we would rethink our strategy for selling education. Students are exposed to a wide range of music videos, video games, and television commercials that flash images at half-second intervals. What do our schools have to offer that can compete with the speed of the things that affect students' lives?

For inspiration we might look toward the marketing of shopping malls. Older malls have been remodeled with food courts, appealing colors, high ceilings,

new lighting, and many other features. Now think about our "buyers" going to school.

## 5. Building and Use Changes

A great deal is heard about master planning these days, and rightly so. In the past, many facilities were constructed without proper site evaluation and planning. Facilities were designed without a plan for the possibility of physical expansion, sharply restricting program expansion. Schools were built to meet current needs with little or no thought for the future. In larger districts with multiple school sites this planning must address the issue of equity. The development of an equity statement for facilities should be part of every master plan. A good example is the Building for Excellence Program master plan for the Palo Alto Unified School District in California. This program involved over 300 community residents, faculty members, and students in planning a road map for the future of their facilities.

## 6. Including the Community

Today community support and community involvement in public education are considered critical. But thirty years ago, in our effort to build low-cost functional facilities, we overlooked ways to integrate community members into school facilities. These facilities are difficult to use for community functions because access for the elderly and the physically challenged is limited or nonexistent. New federal and state legislation requiring buildings to be accessible to the physically challenged will eventually remove these barriers but will require expensive and difficult renovations. Other facilities that could be used by the public and could offer expanded opportunities for instruction, such as swimming pools and auditoriums, often were eliminated to reduce the initial building costs. Today this kind of community planning is necessary to develop public support and increase the utilization of a facility.

## 7. Maintenance

Our educational infrastructure is decaying and threatening students' ability to compete in the global marketplace. The deteriorated condition of this country's school facilities has been well documented. Administrators are faced with more old school buildings, which require additional maintenance; they also have smaller maintenance budgets to provide critical up-keep.

In most cases, school maintenance staffs have done an excellent job of maintaining facilities with the resources available to them. The problem of reduced maintenance budgets is compounded by the construction of schools with inferior materials and systems, which require a high degree of attention.

The easiest way to maintain a building on limited resources is to use materials and systems that require little attention in the construction of the facility. This returns us to issue number two and the ideal of building high-quality buildings.

### 8. The End Users

School buildings today are being used by a wide variety of users, from young children to the elderly, seven days a week and virtually year-round. In planning contemporary facilities, issues of circulation, access to different areas of the building, security, and night lighting are important ingredients. The Perry Community Education Village in Ohio is an excellent example of this type of cooperation. The involvement of students, teachers, and community members is the key to identifying needs and the potential for sharing facilities.

### 9. Adequate Storage and Support Space

A common complaint about schools built in the last thirty years is their lack of storage space. Providing adequate storage will maximize the intended and future use of buildings' programmed spaces. Classrooms, offices, athletic facilities, libraries, and art facilities will all benefit from the presence of adequate storage. To maximize the use of storage space, one should consider flexible and movable storage furniture and shelving. Systems that allow changes in the materials that are stored will support changes in the use of the adjacent educational spaces.

### 10. Flexible Furniture and Equipment

Furnishings in the technology age play a more important role than they have at any other time in the history of school facilities. One of the fastest ways to limit flexibility in learning environments is to select built-in counters, shelves, and storage units and overuse furniture and movable equipment. Using proper furnishing to support the equipment and goals of each space allows for a variety of settings and ease of future adaptability. The science labs at Fort Collins High School illustrate the use of flexible furnishings in an environment typically characterized by heavy built-in counters.

Furnishing and equipping buildings in the age of technology constitute a challenge which should be addressed early in the planning process. Planning for school furniture should begin with the development of *space standards*. This is the road map to selection and should account for the variety of learning spaces, the equipment to be used (especially computers) and the future flexibility and use of the facility.

## Summary

The schools being designed and constructed now will serve the twenty-first century. How well they do that will be a result of many factors, many of which are described in this chapter. One thing remains very clear: We can no longer look at solutions that do not provide innovative facilities for the future.

# TRANSFORMING
## THE
# LEARNING
# ENVIRONMENT

## Gaylaird Christopher

How can the environment support educational restructuring?

This question becomes much more important in a student-centered, experiential, hands-on program. Facilities not only need to support education, they must become an integral part of the experiential program.

While many states and communities have embarked on educational reform, California has developed a clear strategy for all grade levels. Through the publication of four booklets, California's state department of education has offered restructuring guidelines for individual school districts and has provided the groundwork for national educational reforms.* These documents, along with information from restructuring efforts around the country, have formed the basis for changes in the educational environment. An understanding of educational principles and philosophy will allow designers to create the appropriate environments to support the needs of students. In some in-

stances that environment will foster educational change and improvement.

A few pioneering districts are combining restructuring precepts and developing a unified framework that addresses the educational needs of all people from birth through adulthood. Notably absent in the unified approach are the real or imaginary boundaries between different grade levels.

## Points of Agreement

As educators focus on preparing students for real-world experiences, differences from one grade level to the next become much less significant. Consequently, similarities between school levels will become stronger. Here are a few of the most significant factors we see affecting the design of educational environments.

## Work Space for Students

Educators know that a handful of profound learning experiences requiring analysis and synthesis are

---

* Series of guidebooks from the Department of Education, State of California: *Here They Come: Ready or Not* (1988), *It's Elementary* (1992), *Caught in the Middle!* (1987), and *Second to None* (1992).

vastly more lasting and meaningful than weeks spent skimming reams of superficial facts for memorization and recall. The transformation of the learning environment will set aside the traditional desk or armchair student station in favor of a usable dedicated work space for every student. In these areas, students will work individually on long-term projects and also in collaborative, cooperative work teams. Bill Brubaker and Stanton Leggett in their 32-page sketchbook article published in *Nation's Schools* in March 1968 called these spaces "turf." Learning environments will be flexible, allowing for a multitude of teaching and learning strategies. Some schools may choose to provide these work areas in large open spaces, equipped with oversized tables, that are similar to the modular workstations in an open office, while others will select movable student workstations that can be wheeled to specialized work centers to be close to the equipment needed for students to work on projects. Students will spend much more time working in collaborative groups. This will allow them to learn from each other and offer them multiple opportunities to assume leadership roles within groups. Small group spaces will be provided by the subdivision of larger spaces or by the provision of dedicated areas which will be used for various activities, such as practice rooms for the performing arts. In the future these areas will be used for meetings and special instruction as well as for long-distance learning in which students are with instructors and resources thousands of miles away.

As it becomes more the rule than the exception, team teaching will allow teachers to focus on subjects or topics about which they are passionate. Learning centers will be designed to support shared teaching and easy movement from one learning environment to another and even for the grouping of environments.

## Assessments

Performance-based assessments will require an environment in which students can demonstrate their skills and knowledge. Not only will space be available to create and develop projects, students will require assembly areas in which they can share and celebrate their accomplishments and achievements with a play, musical composition, video, or speech as the vehicle. One of the most critical elements that will be provided in the future is storage space for projects in progress

and for portfolios which document students' past experiences and completed projects. Unlike today, when single-focus student projects often are geared for completion within fifty to sixty minutes, student projects in the future will incorporate cross-curricular planning and concentrated effort over a much longer time frame. Work areas and storage space will be designed to allow long-term projects to be stored or left in place until they are completed. Portfolios may be housed in built-in lockers or at home but more likely will be cataloged on an electronic medium. Students may carry a CD-ROM that records and stores their entire educational history with examples of their work, all neatly filed and easily retrievable for review. Space for the display of both two- and three-dimensional artwork will validate the relevance and richness of student expression as a part of day-to-day educational activities.

Accessibility to performing arts space for all students will be essential to give students opportunities to perform for a small group or practice in a small meeting area without interrupting others and to assemble the majority of the campus for a large group special performance. Performances as a means of student assessment will benefit students as they share knowledge and take pride in their accomplishments.

## The Teacher as Professional

With increased accountability and responsibility, teachers will be perceived in a more professional light. A teacher will be provided with professional work space with an area in which to keep personal belongings and conduct private meetings with parents and/or students. Futurists also emphasize the need to plan for an enriched, efficient environment which will be more supportive of teachers as professionals. With this in mind, preparation for teaching and planning with colleagues will be supported by well-equipped spaces for working and conferencing. Resource rooms with staff libraries and computer equipment to access educational databases and student records will be commonplace. Cross-curricular integration will mandate that teacher preparation and hands-on working sessions be accommodated through the provision of adequate white boards, flip charts, televisions, VCRs, and cable capability. A primary purpose of site administration and district administration will be to assure that appropriate resources are available for the instructional team and that students are able to dream their dreams and reach their highest goals.

## Media Center

As students assume more responsibility for personal learning through involvement in individualized study, the media center will become a supportive asset. Students will soon become researchers, following their interests and improving their research abilities. The media center will be tied into district, community, national, and global educational networks, allowing students to satisfy their inquisitiveness. A professional librarian will be available to assist and guide students through their research efforts. Once a quiet study hall, the media center will emerge as a busy, exciting hub of active investigation; it will be slightly smaller, with more and more media being stored electronically. While the media center will become a research facility for independent and group investigation, an informal area will be maintained for socialization with friends while students are studying and working together. As technology becomes more accessible, these resources will be available electronically to each building and to the entire school organization.

## Physical Fitness

Health and physical education will no longer focus only on game skills, competitive sports, and testing for minimum physical standards. Health education will be integrated with the sciences, helping students understand the effects of their physical and social actions on their bodies and lives. Physical fitness and social maturity will be the goals, with mini-fitness centers being provided in place of competitive sports facilities. Sports and sport facilities will continue to have a place but will not be the focus of instructional methodology. Learning environments will be constructed from environmentally sensitive materials, and consideration of indoor air quality will be paramount.

## Extended Operation

The addition of new opportunities for student choices, program enrichment, and specialized daily instruction will be accompanied by an extended week and year.

Schools may operate from 6 A.M. to 10 P.M. to give students access to resources and specialized instruction outside normal school hours so that they can maintain consistent progress toward the achievement of their educational goals. Extended hours will require districts to rethink security and maintenance issues, allowing accessibility after hours to buildings without piercing the veil of overall campus security. Additional wear and tear with minimal opportunities for repair and rehabilitation will prescribe the utilization of time-tested reliable building materials. Energy management and life-cycle costing are also issues with expanded building use.

## Vision

The development and articulation of a clear vision or mission are critical to the success of any organization. This is especially true within an architectural environment, where the vision is expressed through strong goals and objectives which respond to the true purpose of the project. The goals are to be achieved through the successful combination of form and function. As in the vision statement, those involved in planning must also know and support the project's purpose. The true power comes when the design concept is married both visually and functionally to the educational vision. Only then is there an opportunity to reach our highest architectural potential and develop an environment that is completely supportive of students' educational needs.

## Community Involvement

As more people participate in supporting a school's purpose, students will become part of a caring education community. The teacher serves as caregiver and mentor. Parents and members of the community join together as partners in the educational process, and students demonstrate true commitment by getting involved in both the school and the community. Expanded involvement requires additional staff and space. The skills of a congenial coordinator of community resources will pay great dividends by unfolding new and varied learning opportunities for students. An inviting welcome and control center will ensure that parents and members of the community are greeted and directed to the proper destination without wasting time or resources. Technology will play a key role in documenting the resources and making them available to individuals through the use of computer networks and cable television. Expanded community involvement also will prescribe that the appearance of existing and future schools be inviting and comfortable and that buildings and grounds be safe, clean, well maintained, and attractive.

In the future, duplication of public facilities no longer will be possible, as resources and space will continue to be limited. Media centers will double as public libraries, school cafeterias and meeting rooms as community centers, gymnasiums as community recreation facilities, and performing arts facilities as community theaters. Joint use of facilities will be a two-way street. If community facilities are available and accessible, school districts will utilize them. Cooperative agreements and the provision of essential transportation will promote the sharing of facilities. Educational opportunities will be extended to the entire learning community. Integration of social services through the educational structure will be the hallmark of many urban and suburban schools. School districts may not offer all services on each campus, but they will become clearinghouses for social services, making sure that every student receives the basic human resources necessary to support his or her educational experience.

The precepts of total quality management prescribe that decision making occur at the most essential level. This translates to students' involvement in and responsibility for their own education and teacher empowerment and control of teaching environments. Accountability will lie with the student, who also will have the power to choose from a menu of learning opportunities, essentially allowing the marketplace to govern educational appropriateness.

## It's Elementary

How will the transformed environment be different? In the early grades, the hallmark of tomorrow's thinking-based integrated curriculum will be experiential learning. Students will learn through real experiences based on familiar activities from their day-to-day life. The learning environment of the future will respond with a large centrally organized hub with strong con-

nections to life outside the school. Mathematics will expose children to open-ended encounters requiring real-world problem solving. Storage systems will allow easy student access and require student custodianship. Students will make purchases, balance budgets, and work on three-dimensional art projects which apply geometric and mathematical principles. History and social science will be explored through literature and student projects which focus on the lives and times of our ancestors. Students may simulate the societal structure they are studying in order to experience a particular society firsthand.

How can the curriculum influence school buildings? Coyote Canyon Elementary School in Rancho Cucamonga, California, was specifically designed to expose schoolchildren to the rich and varied history of their community. Four themed courtyards have been incorporated into the design to bring Rancho Cucamonga's early history to life. The design of each courtyard was the result of community input from parents, staff members, local historians, and architects, representing one of the four major periods in the history of the city.

Each courtyard reflects the period of the social studies unit for its adjacent grade level classes, allowing students to experience historic settings firsthand. A main hallway, the historic spine, links the school's two entry towers. The spine doubles as a community history gallery with pictures of early residents and of various buildings and sites important to the area's development. One can only speculate how environments of the future will allow students to simulate firsthand other lifestyles, past, present, or future. Many schools are now creating historical environments through the enlargement of slides to full-scale representations of times past. Construction of virtual reality rooms is achievable today to allow students to step into bygone eras. In the near future, headsets and goggles will allow each student to explore the culture of his or her choice.

## Caught in the Middle

The publication of the California State Department of Education document *Caught in the Middle!* in 1987 ushered in the modern era of systemic reform. The publication's mission, goals, and objectives, plus curriculum development for middle school education, have resulted in major changes in the way we will educate young adolescents. Research shows the incredible impact of these years on a student's future success. This is the time when students formulate a sense of academic purpose and personal commitment to future goals.

The creation of identifiable clusters of space that students can call their own is very important. Circulation on campus will be straightforward to minimize confusion but will be punctuated by exciting accents which appeal to an adolescent's sense of energetic vitality. Clustering by grade level will give students a strong sense of group identification, while grouping students and teachers together into intercurricular teams will reinforce opportunities to develop strong personal relationships.

The importance of students and teachers being able to work together to integrate curriculum ideas cannot be overemphasized. Adequate planning and conferring are essential in providing an integrated curriculum. Technology will allow teachers to present information and ideas through the use of televisions, VCRs, and CD-ROM with multimedia capability. To spark students' interest, the classroom experience will measure up to MTV by fully utilizing the creativity and theatrical skills of media-conscious teachers. Space at a middle school will be flexible, allowing students to quickly move from independent learning to cooperative learning. Smaller multiuse spaces will support small group instruction and group projects.

Middle school is a time for exploration. These students are trying to determine their interests and have an insatiable appetite for new and different experiences. The industrial technology program epitomizes the exploratory process. Students will be guided through a series of projects and problem-solving exercises that will give them opportunities to explore lasers, hydraulics, radio technology, computer-aided design and manufacturing, woodworking, computer technology, electronics, manufacturing, and a variety of other areas. The only limitations will be the available curriculum resources and one's imagination in developing new and different programs. A laboratory to accommodate industrial technology will be designed to meet the flexibility needs of the anticipated programs. The industrial technology model has great

potential for other curricular areas and even as a guideline for all middle school curricula. Learning through a series of in-depth, guided projects has been suggested to be one of the best ways to integrate the curriculum and develop a meaning-centered educational program.

One of the most important functions of middle schools is to provide a bridge from the secure self-contained elementary school classroom to the complex setting with diverse offerings of a large comprehensive high school. Obviously, with integrated curricula, team teaching, and community-based learning at all levels, this dichotomy will be less apparent in the future. Middle schools will still support the transition between the directed, experiential learning opportunities available at elementary schools and the self-directed, independent studies available at high schools. The design of facilities will corroborate this function. Sixth-graders will be in a common area, organized into identifiable clusters. Each cluster will be composed of approximately 100 to 120 students and three or four staff members who will provide students with instruction in all core educational areas: English, social studies, math, and science. Exploratory electives will include industrial technology, business, science, and the performing arts.

Seventh-grade classes, located within their own cluster, will be more open to the rest of the campus through direct access to specialized classrooms with more opportunities for exploration and outside activities. Eighth-graders will be integrated within specialized facilities, as these students need maximum access to independent and individualized instruction.

Adolescence is an exciting, frightening, and enlightening time. Students begin to challenge authority, experience their own sexuality, and become passionate about the issues that concern them. Future middle school design will respond to this vitality and spark student creativity.

The designs for some schools, such as Antelope Crossing Middle School in Roseville, California's Dry Creek School District, reflect local culture and history. Antelope Crossing's design was inspired by Roseville's heritage as one of the largest railroad centers in the world. Students will be greeted by a railroad motif, including sloped roofs, brick veneer, and early nineteenth-century graphics. Classrooms will be clustered around courtyards which will house displays celebrating the principles of physics: weight, motion, and resistance. The focal point will be the administrative and media center building, which will house four full-sized boxcars in a stationlike setting.

## Second to None

While just beginning a lifetime of learning, high school students are culminating their formal K–12 public education. High school plays the important role of preparing students to think in order to gather, organize, and analyze information and apply it to problem solving. Education in the future will consist of a strong core curriculum which will integrate educational themes across many disciplines. It has been said that "learning takes place when the learner regards what one needs to know as relevant to their lives; when teachers are committed to students' success: when the environment allows for differences in learning methods and style."* The high school program will encourage students to relate to the world after graduation, whether they are to enter the workforce directly, continue their formal education, or pursue advanced study.

High schools of the future will be subdivided into academic clusters or families of approximately 200 students. Students and teachers will form interdisciplinary teams (similar to those found at a middle school), allowing students and teachers to develop personal relationships built on perceptive feedback, caring, and trust. The impersonal 2,000- to 4,000-student mega-high schools of the late twentieth century will be subdivided into workable schools within a school.

It is important for the architecture to help foster a sense of community among students and staff members. Well-equipped staff work space and meeting areas will provide areas for instructors to meet with students and parents concerning personal learning plans. Each team will determine its own schedule, which will incorporate extended blocks of time for specific projects and in-depth instruction. The fifty-

* *Effect of the Physical Environment of Schools on Students,* paper presented at the Sixty-fifth Council of Educational Facility Planners, Milwaukee, October 1988.

minute passing bell will be a thing of the past. The hum of continuous activity will replace the traditionally fragmented school day.

With members of each curricular area dispersed around the campus, a means will be needed to verify that students are achieving high standards. Centrally located meeting areas will accommodate large groups of instructors from related curricular areas. Discipline, counseling, and other special services will be provided within each cluster, including offices for counselors and a vice principal. Santiago High School in Corona Norco Unified School District in Corona, California, illustrates one district's vision of how cross-curricular clusters may be grouped into four buildings, with each cluster for 250 students located on a separate floor. Two counselors and one assistant principal are housed in each building.

In addition to clusters, campuses will provide focused academic programs which explore subjects in great detail. The core curriculum will be delivered through the metaphors and vocabulary of a specific profession. Potential academic subjects might include health care, the performing arts, business and retail sales, transportation, technology and computer science, agriculture, mechanics, humanities, law, art, and design. Some districts will develop a regimented set of academic programs which will be available at each comprehensive high school. Some will develop different magnet programs at each high school site and allow students to take elective courses at other campuses. Larger districts may develop specific magnet school programs with a single, specialized emphasis. The King/Drew Medical Magnet High School in South Central Los Angeles in the Los Angeles Unified School District is an example. This school is designed to allow students to learn all of the core curriculum through the metaphors of medicine. Students who are interested in medicine can apply to attend the Medical Magnet and spend a portion of their high school years learning by doing across the street at the Martin Luther King Medical Center. Long-term student internships also will be available at the Charles Drew Medical School, located at the medical center.

The provision of career academic programs will place unique demands on facilities. Students will be provided with some equipment in settings which will be similar to the actual workplace. The academy will give a student entry-level work skills which will lead to an apprenticeship. Business-education partnerships will be reevaluated constantly to assure that the relationship is beneficial to both parties.

## Summary

Educators will note that many of these ideas are not new; some have even been tried and abandoned by teachers. Perhaps carrying out a great idea was cumbersome because of a lack of support or because the classroom or facilities were designed for only the most traditional instructional methodologies. In the past architects often set aside creative school design solutions because it was easier and less controversial to design again exactly what they had built in the past and what many teachers asked for: "a classroom just like I have now, only with more outlets, please."

Schools are identified by society as pivotal places for effecting change. We know that the status quo is unacceptable. Today, educators, community members, students, and architects must join together to share common visions which will provide quality learning experiences for our children and young people.

## Chapter 6 Bibliography

1. The Effect of Architecture on Education. The American Institute of Architects. Committee on Architecture for Education, 1990.

2. Hawkins, Harold L. Facilities and Learning: essentials of Educational Reform. Vol. 3. No. 1. 1989–90: Journey—National Forum of Applied Educational Research Journal.

3. Effects of the Physical Environment of Schools on Students, a Paper Presented at the 65th Council of Educational Facility Planners, International Conference in Milwaukee, Wisconsin, October, 1988.

4. Series of Restructuring and Reform Guidebooks. Department of Education, State of California.
    "Here They Come: Ready or Not. 1988"
    It's Elementary! 1992
    Caught in the Middle! 1987
    Second to None. 1992

5. Components of Systemic Reform, State Superintendent of Schools. Department of Education, State of California.

6. Taylor, Anne P. And George Vlastos, School Zone: Learning Environments for Children. 1983.

# CHAPTER 7

# SITE
# PLANNING
## AND THE
# MASTER
# PLAN

Whether it is a new school, an existing school, a cluster of old and new educational facilities, or a proposed campus for the future, every site for education needs a campus master plan to serve as a guide for future development.

The master plan shows how the site and the buildings can be expanded and where future structures can be located; it also shows where future structures and paving (roads, parking, and services) should not be located by establishing, protecting, and maintaining open spaces such as woods, lawns, gardens, wetlands, and playing fields. The master plan guides future development and gives future school administrators and architects the guidelines and rationale which governed the original planning decisions.

The master plan shows the size, shape, and nature of the property; its orientation; the existing and proposed topography; the views of the site and the views from the site; the location and size of trees and other vegetation; wetlands location; drainage patterns; access roads or streets; services; utilities; walks and bicycle paths; the character of the neighboring properties; legal setback requirements; and the locations of easements.

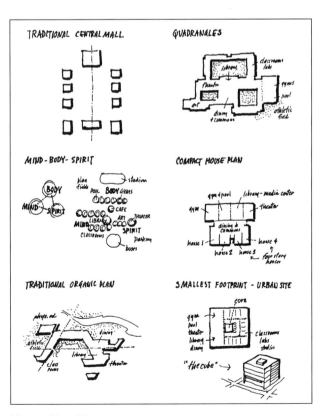

**Master Plan Diagrams**

163

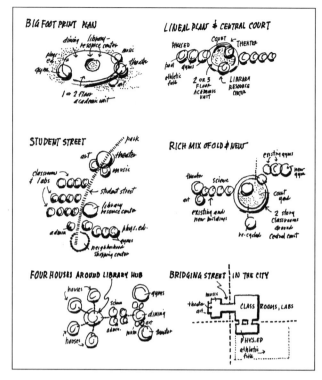

**Master Plan Diagrams**

Every school campus should have a master plan, but most existing schools do not have one that is up to date and is followed. That is surprising, because almost all colleges and universities have a plan that includes all the items listed above. Usually the plan is restudied, reevaluated, and revised every five or ten years and then adjusted to changing conditions such as increasing enrollment, changes in access, changes in the neighborhood, and changes in educational programs.

The typical college and university master plan consists of two principal documents: the master plan for future development, which is framed and hung on the wall and therefore is highly visible, and the master plan book, which summarizes the findings and proposals for future improvements. The book, filed away in the offices of members of the planning team, is not very visible and sometimes is forgotten. The master plan book is often a mine of information about the institution, including a history of the campus, all the data mentioned above, enrollment trends, college or university policies and goals, an analysis of and data on all the existing buildings, future space requirements in net usable square feet, an analysis of the space in existing buildings, and the potential for reno-

vation. The framed master plan and the book often are supplemented by a model of the future campus that shows the location and size of proposed new buildings. Obviously, the master plan is a valuable resource at colleges and universities.

Think how useful that kind of thinking could be for a high school campus or a K–12 educational park.

One of the practical reasons for a good up-to-date comprehensive plan for a public or private school is to have complete knowledge of the existing conditions, such as facts about roofs and electrical and communications systems, the quality of air from HVAC systems, the estimated cost of improvements, and energy costs. All those items help determine whether an existing school is a good candidate for renovation and reuse or whether it would be better and more economical in the long run to replace it with a new construction.

Underground utilities are shown on land surveys, on which master plans are based. That knowledge is important when additions to existing buildings are planned. A sewer installed in the wrong place can represent a costly mistake when it conflicts with an addition and has to be relocated. A good master plan, at only a fraction of the cost, could have prevented the mistake.

## Elementary Schools

Usually located in residential areas, small elementary schools make it possible for many young children to walk to school. In new towns that often means walking to school on paths and through parks dedicated to pedestrians and bicycles with only a few, if any, crossings of streets. In older communities, from small towns to big cities, students walk on sidewalks. Therefore, new towns and old communities are quite different in terms of their impact on school planning. A good idea which is applicable to both settings is to locate schools adjacent to parks, with cooperation between the school district and the park district to encourage the sharing of facilities. For example, at Irvine in Orange County, California, elementary schools are on relatively small sites, but a neighborhood park is always adjacent. The local swimming pool and game courts are on parkland but are equally accessible to the school. If the community perceives the school as a community center, the neighborhood will benefit from the presence of its own community school.

The elementary school site needs thoughtful planning of services to accommodate delivery trucks. Planners must check with the local fire department to be certain that fire trucks can be accommodated. Finally, automobile drives and parking lots should be planned with convenience, appearance, and safety in mind. Teachers' parking should be separate from visitors' parking, which should be near the main entrance. Curb space is needed where parents can safely drop off children near their classrooms. If the school includes day care, remember that parents park and take their children into the school. One doesn't drop off a 2- or 3-year-old at the curb.

These may seem like obvious items of advice, but they are meant to remind school planners that certain relationships should prevail and that these relationships are important considerations when the "preschematic concepts" are being evaluated. Bubble diagrams on a pad of paper or a chalkboard may help the planning and design team develop logical relationships which have a strong influence on school design. Such functional space relationships make more sense as generators of form than do architectural fashions or trends.

## Middle Schools

Junior high schools, as they were formerly called, or middle schools are usually situated in residential areas, though not always; like elementary schools, they can benefit from being adjacent to parkland. Community planners should be involved in the planning process.

Since these schools are larger and are spaced farther apart in the community, fewer students walk or ride a bicycle to school, though many do. School sites are larger because not only are middle schools larger, but physical education and athletics require outdoor activities which need playing fields for softball, football, soccer, and tennis. An interesting alternative to locating elementary and middle schools on separate sites is the idea of a "dual school," as was planned and built in Solon, Ohio (see Chapter 3). An elementary school and a middle school are joined by certain shared facilities, including one boiler room, one kitchen, and other facilities that make both the construction and the operation of the dual schools economical. Each of the two schools has its own identity,

library and dining room, main entrance, and principal's office. For purposes of economy, educational spaces weren't trimmed; instead, the service spaces were reduced.

Site planning requires reevaluation, but if one uses bubble diagrams, alternatives can be developed and evaluated.

## Secondary Schools

High school sites are getting larger in areas where abundant land is available. A century ago secondary school sites were measured in acres and were often a city block or two in size. In the 1920s an adequate site might be 20 acres. After World War II, a 40-acre site would satisfy the land needs of most high schools, and in 1970, 50 acres was a good size in the suburbs and in rural areas. Now we see 60-acre and even 80-acre sites. Note that some of this land may be owned and managed by an adjacent park district.

Why have high school sites grown so large?

Well, the "public" demands more space. An obvious factor is the fact that (whether we approve or not) more students drive cars to school. That means more land given over to driveways and parking lots (and the trees in the parking lots, as required in some states). Also, more teachers drive to school, usually one person per car. Since the community school is an expanding idea, more citizens visit the school both during the day and in the evening, and so more parking spaces are required. School buses used to park at main street curbs, but now more people want to provide buses with their own dedicated loading facilities.

Local citizens want more tennis courts at the high school and more playing fields for other sports and for fitness programs. In addition, remember that we passed new laws a few years ago that mandate equal physical education facilities for women. That law doubled the number of soccer fields. Finally, our constituents ask school planners to be more environmentally responsible. Twenty or thirty years ago it would not have been unusual for a site to be cleared of all vegetation and bulldozed level, except for the wetlands, which were obliterated, but those days are gone forever. Now the trees are saved if at all possible, and the wetlands are preserved or restored. The school and the community share the benefits of such actions. However, the forest preserve takes 10 acres and the wetlands take 15 acres, and so the high school site is a 70-acre property, but only 45 acres are "developable" and 25 acres are preserved for the community.

We have been describing a large high school site located where large sites are available. Obviously, a 70-acre site is not available in many parts of cities or built-up suburbs. City high schools cannot meet suburban "standards", which in most states are not mandated. Ingenious solutions develop. Compact multi-level buildings (as Chelsea high school in Massachusetts) are logical. High Rise schools exist in New York City, and in Chicago, where Clemente High School, 8 stories high, is served by the skip-stop escalators. In the Boston area, at Charleston High School, HMFH designed a pedestrian bridge which links two blocks over a busy street, and in Chicago, Whitney Young Magnet High School bridges Jackson Boulevard. In the built-up city of Santa Ana, CA, architect Ralph Allen put the automobile parking on the roof of the Century High School. A school in New Orleans is on stilts over a playground, a good solution in a wet and hot climate where shade and shelter are appreciated. Jones Commercial High School in downtown

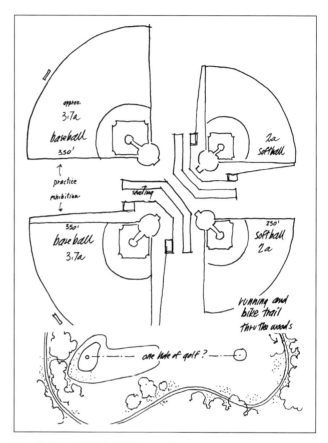

**Baseball and Softball Diamonds**

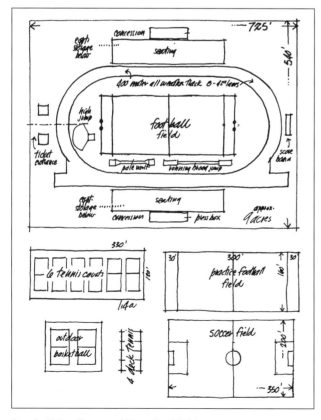

**Football Stadium and Practice Fields**

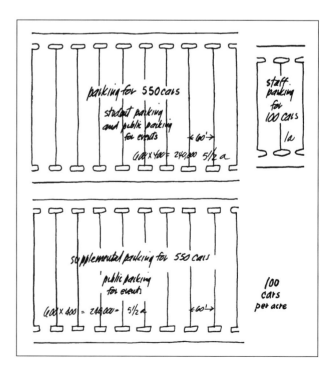

**Parking Lots**

Chicago has less than a city block for its site, so a 6 story central core office-building-like tower (expandable to 16 stories) houses all classrooms and labs, while the gym and auditorium are in low-rise units. We see a good deal of innovation in the city, where conventional sites are simply not possible.

While preparing the program or the educational specifications for the school building, the planning team should concurrently prepare the program for the outdoor spaces—the playfields, parking needs, etc. At this stage of planning a landscape architect probably joins the team to advise on the size, shape and orientation of playfields, the possibilities for landscape concepts, identification of appropriate plants, and parking lot configurations. In some cases, another consultant—a traffic planner—may be required to relate the school's traffic patterns to the traffic systems of the surrounding areas, with both convenience and safety in mind.

The program for outdoor spaces would identify every outdoor space, with numbers and sizes specified. This should reduce the possibilities for misunderstandings about how many parking spaces, what size stadium, the number of tennis courts, etc.

Outdoor space requirements might include:

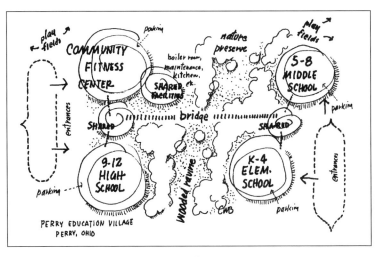

**Perry Education Village and Fitness Center**

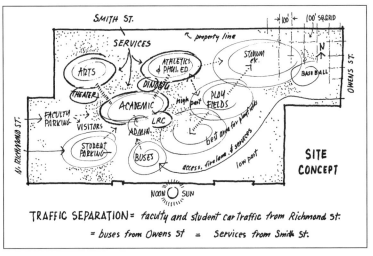

**Traffic and Site Analysis**

the building footprint (along with an assumption of the number of floors)

the main entrance area, including landscaped areas

visitor parking, drop off curbs, and sheltered waiting area

secondary entrance areas

loading curbs for school buses

service and receiving areas, loading docks, dumpsters

air conditioning chillers, electrical transformers

entrance driveways, fire lanes, service drives

student parking, community parking, faculty and staff parking

baseball and softball fields, exhibition diamonds

football and soccer fields, exhibition and practice

tennis courts, basketball courts, handball courts

stadium, track, seating, concessions, restrooms

wetlands and woodlands preservation, nature study areas

storm water retention, lake and/or ponds

amphitheater

At this stage, with the educational program in progress or completed, and with the program of outdoor space requirements completed, the planning team can more effectively analyze the site and begin sketching indoor and outdoor space relationships which logically lead to alternative concepts for the master plan. Bubble diagrams may be helpful in developing ideas.

# 8

## THE
## PLANNING
## AND
## BUILDING
## PROCESS

### Deciding to Build a New School or Renovate an Existing School

When the demographic pressure is on—when the schools in a community are overcrowded and the enrollment projections call for steadily increasing numbers of students—it's time to study the demographic changes and determine where and how changes in the capacity of various schools are needed, whether some structures should be removed, and how and when new schools should be built.

A districtwide inventory of existing facilities should be made. Good planning requires an accurate analysis of the existing schools, including their size, location, condition, and suitability. The size of each site is important in determining whether the expansion of schools is practical. Are new sites available? What are the financial facts for the district? What are the goals of the community? Good schools, of course, attract high-quality development and families that want high-quality schools and are willing to pay the taxes.

The decision to build a new school or renovate and expand an existing school influences the physical plan of the community and the educational plan for the schools. For example, what happens when an old high school is converted to a middle school and the grade organization of the district changes from K–4, 5–7, 8–12, to K–4, 5–8, 9–12? If this educational change is suggested by the desire for more efficient use of existing buildings, is it also the best organization of grades for both the middle school and the high school? It's time to assemble a planning and design team.

The board and the administration may wish to create a number of committees to focus on different topics, such as the program committee (to work with the educational consultant), the technology committee, the site committee, the architect selection committee, and the finance committee.

### Selecting Members of the Planning and Design Team

The interest in and experience with school facilities of school administrators vary, and the same is true for board members, teachers, architects, consultants, builders, and community representatives. Therefore, the selection of the planning and design team is an important early task in considering a building program.

The Board of education may want to form a building committee. Sometimes the president of the board may be on that committee, but the president may be too busy with other tasks or may be more interested in other committees (curriculum, finance). The chair of the board's building committee often is the key individual in the planning and design process.

Some school superintendents are interested in the building program. Others depend on an assistant superintendent for business or an assistant superintendent for curriculum development, and sometimes a new position is created at the administrative level to manage the planning process, with a title such as "director of facilities planning and management."

The board and the administration may then agree that it is time to contract for the professional services of architects and consultants. This is a critical task. The selection of the wrong architect and the wrong consultant can diminish the chances of creating a significant new school which is both beautiful and functional.

Hire an architect whose completed work you like. Visit prospective architects' schools, especially if they are of a type that your community needs, such as an urban high school or a suburban middle school. Check references and make phone calls to the superintendent of schools or to the persons (the principals) responsible for operating the schools. A good architect with a good track record who has been the recipient of awards may be satisfactory for the design of your new elementary school, but high schools are more complex and can benefit from input from other consultants. More important, the local architect must be interested in both education and school architecture to design a good school.

Sometimes you may find that no local architectural firm is large enough or experienced enough in school planning and design, and in that case the board and administration should look in the metropolitan area, in the state, or nationwide for a firm of architects with broad experience in designing educational facilities. This is not unusual for a new high school, because secondary schools are complex planning projects that involve the specialized talents that are necessary to design multistory schools with elevators and escala-

tors, science laboratories, large-scale food service, a theater, music and arts facilities, libraries, swimming pools, and other facilities.

To take advantage of that kind of design expertise, a large project needs the comprehensive services of a medium-size to large firm of architects, a firm that is committed to school design and has up-to-date experience in and professional enthusiasm for architecture for education. If that size and experience are not available in an existing firm of architects (either with or without engineering consultants and educational consultants), another kind of team makes good sense:

1. Form an association composed of a local firm and a "national firm" and add other local or national consultants as needed.

2. Agree on who will do what and make it part of the contract.

3. Proceed with the planning process with the custom-made team tailored to the special needs of the project. If more than one new building or more than one renovation project is contemplated, each project can be assigned to the team as its services are needed.

## Developing the Educational Specifications: The Program

It is highly desirable to assign the responsibility for preparing the program to one individual: an educator who knows the goals and values of the community, the rules and regulations of the state and city, and what is happening in education nationwide. That individual can be related to other members of the planning and design team in a number of different ways:

1. He or she can be an administrator, such as the assistant superintendent for curriculum development, working with and reporting to the board of education.

2. In a small district the superintendent of schools can serve as the head of the program committee.

3. In a large district the building program may be too large for an administrator to manage, and so a full-time educational assistant may be appointed to work with and for the superintendent of schools or to serve as the assistant superintendent. This assis-

tant superintendent, along with one or more assistants, office space, and other expenses, can easily add a few hundred thousand dollars of administrative expenses and salaries to the school district's budget.

4. An "outside" (outside the district organization chart) educator can take over the task of preparing the educational specifications. This outsider may be a private consultant hired by the administration or may be provided by the architect as one of the architectural firm's consultants. Note that many architectural firms identify themselves as "architects-engineers-planners." "Planners" may work on educational curriculum planning, facilities planning, or community and/or city planning. There is a possibility for misunderstanding here, and so tasks and responsibilities should be spelled out in detail. Some architects have "on their staff" an educational consultant who is often a retired superintendent of schools. For a large high school, a private consultant will probably save the district a substantial amount, and for a small elementary school, the savings will be apparent because of the broad experience of a private program planner.

5. The program process sometimes uses the services of one or more individuals at a college of education in a local (or national) university.

6. A new school can use the specifications of another, completed school by "borrowing" fragments of programs from one or more schools and then attempting to modify them before assembling the components.

The reuse of educational specifications rarely produces an exceptionally good building, but of course there are exceptions, most recently seen at "prototype" schools. Two examples are included in this book: the Gadsden elementary schools in New Mexico and New York City prototype schools, where large components have been designed to fit together in various ways to site-adapt the standardized "protoparts" to create unique schools with recognizable components.

For its interesting, challenging, and successful prototype school program, New York City chose a small number of architects. One of the goals was to reduce the time and expense of planning and building schools in that city. Experience showed that about ten years could elapse between starting a project, buying a site, preparing a program, and arranging financing to the completion and occupancy of the building.

The program did indeed improve the timeliness and cost of delivery. New York City hopes to use the experience gained in planning, designing, and building these schools to influence and improve school design throughout the city.

The program (the educational specifications) should include a summary of recent demographic trends, the philosophy and goals of the school, the curriculum, the desired relationships between the components of the program, the organization of the administrative spaces, a detailed summary of all the required spaces and their sizes, a description of how each space works, and a list of the equipment required.

## Selecting the Site and Preparing a Master Plan

We noted earlier that the two major "form generators" are the site and the program. Since both components are unique to each school, it is apparent that the design for a good school must be heavily influenced by the site (its size, shape, orientation, access, views, neighbors, geology, and drainage) and by the program. The educational specifications should be prepared and the site should be selected with these interrelationships in mind. For example, the program for a small or middle-size school might call for a one-story design with the components loosely organized and with courtyards and open space. If the facts of the site (its small size) make a one-story building impossible, the program and the site need immediate attention by the planning team. A master plan is needed to coordinate the various and sometimes conflicting uses of the land (the school site) and the needs of the program. If the limited size of the site suggests a four-story building but the local community plan and building code limit buildings to two stories, one of three actions must be chosen:

1. Increase the size of the site.

2. Change the community plan and building code.

3. Change the program to a smaller number of students.

A master plan is always important for a college or university campus to guide future development. K–12 schools also can benefit from the adoption of a physical facilities master plan, which shows where buildings are to be built on the site, along with open areas, parking, and playing fields, and graphically shows proposed future development possibilities and limitations. Every school needs a master plan. Sometimes a board of education and/or a superintendent will proclaim that "this school will never be allowed to expand; it is our policy to build the school as a finished project; when and if future growth calls for more school space, we will plan another new school." "Never" is a long time: Things will change, and boards will change. A future board will have the power to "change the master plan." Therefore, all the interested parties should consider how the new school can change and grow in the future.

The master plan also brings more members of the planning and design team together in response to the need for problem solving. At this level of development the active team members include the board, the superintendent, the assistant superintendent for curriculum, the educational consultant, and the architect and engineering consultants.

## Exploring Options: Preschematic Design

This is a good time to explore alternative master plans for a new school or additions and renovation at an existing school.

It is important to involve many different groups, including community representatives and city planners, transportation planners, the educational consultant, and the architect. In planning Arlington High School in Saint Paul, Minnesota, with our associate architect in Saint Paul, Winsor Faricy, we used an effective technique to involve all the interested citizens in the city, especially those who live near the school. We prepared a large map of the community (about 25 feet by 30 feet, the size of a classroom), which we unrolled on the floor of a larger meeting room. Then we invited the citizens to take off their shoes, walk on the new paper map, and write comments on it.

This was a great icebreaker. After an hour or two the map was covered by citizens' comments on problems and opportunities, such as where good views

should be unobstructed, traffic ideas, playing field locations, and access for cars, trucks, buses, and pedestrians. We learned a lot, and they learned a lot. Good ideas were recorded; bad ones were too, but not everyone agreed on the definition of good and bad. The architects returned a few days later with notes that summarized the lively planning session with the community. After a few more weeks of planning, appraisal, refinement, and consideration of many alternative schemes, two or three schemes looked most promising. Each concept had the following characteristics:

1. Compactness in response to the fact that city schools often need to develop smaller sites

2. Three- or four-story academic units

3. Schools within a school, subdividing the larger student high school into four houses, with those houses expressed as four units in the overall design of the school

In some states, California in particular, site size is determined by the rules and regulations of the state department of education. Along with money from Sacramento comes mandated advice on the number of acres for a school site and the square footage allotment for each type of space in the school, including the size of each classroom, the number of classrooms, and even the number of toilet fixtures.

Of special interest to school architects in California is the requirement that each school have a certain percentage of its classrooms in relocatable units. Finally, California has a unique assistance program for school districts that are so urbanized and built up that no sites can be found that satisfy the state's site size requirements. This is the "space saver" program, which allows school districts with site problems to consider innovative ideas, such as placing parking and tennis courts on roofs, as demonstrated by the architect Ralph Allen's Century High School in Santa Anna.

## Establishing the Concept: Schematic Design

Having identified and studied the site and having prepared the program, the team moves on from alternative design concepts to agreement on one scheme—the "schematic design"—which shows the basic idea for the school: the plan of the proposed building as developed by the architect, following the space requirements set forth in the educational specification. The schematic design also includes the first sketches of the character of the school and often some simplified models of the concept to convey the big idea to the board, administrator, teachers, students, consultants, and community.

This is an exciting and challenging phase in which all team members rally around a concept which expresses the philosophy of the school. Is the school compact, multifloored, classical, or mechanistic, or is it irregular, informal, rambling, or "humanistic"? Is it elegant and highly finished, or is it purposely unfinished and given a special character as students move into it?

Different individuals representing different interests and viewpoints advocate what they deem proper. Controversy is necessary here and is welcomed. Classroom size and class size depend on the future ability of the community to finance and support the prepared programs. Decisions made for the specific new school affect the existing schools, and the new school is influenced by all the older schools in the district. For example, if an existing three-year middle school is to be replaced by a new four-year middle school, the elementary schools will change from K–5 to K–4 and decrease in size. Or one new middle school designed specifically to be a middle school for that age group may replace two old middle schools which were built to be elementary schools. The new facilities will be larger or smaller and will be better learning environments. The schematic design includes a schematic cost estimate. A 1,500-student high school for a northeastern state may have 180 square feet per student, or 270,000 square feet in gross area. (Gross area includes not only the net usable area called for by the educational program but also the not yet programmed walls, corridors, stairs, mechanical and electrical spaces, and other services.)

If the new construction cost for 270,000 square feet is budgeted to be $100 per square foot, the construction cost will be $27 million for the work to be done by the contractors. To this "construction cost" must be added a planning contingency, site purchase and site development costs, equipment and furniture costs, and fees. The "total project cost" may therefore be $35 million.

One should not be misled by wild claims that some buildings cost much less but also should note that construction costs vary widely in different parts of the country. For instance, we have been discussing a building in a northeastern city. Note the difference if the area per student decreases to only 90 square feet in California, as dictated by state policy.

In California, a 1,500-student high school is only 135,000 square feet in gross area, or only half as large as the northeast example described above. The gross area is dramatically different in California because the benign climate encourages use of the campus plan concept with no interior corridors. Classrooms are in buildings with few or no corridors, and circulation occurs outdoors. Thus the California high school for 1,500 students (at only 90 square feet per student) is only 135,000 square feet. If the budget for construction is $100 per square foot, the construction cost is $13.5 million. In making such regional comparisons, one must remember that construction costs per square foot also vary widely.

This dramatic example is meant to demonstrate that local conditions determine costs and that one must take great care in making cost comparisons.

## Design Development: Filling in Thousands of Details

Design development means exactly that—the development of a design incorporating thousands of details which eventually are drawn on plans and written in the building construction specifications.

At this stage, the architects need many planning meetings with the owners and users of the school to determine which ideas are appropriate for the school and which are not. Remember that one can't always have it both ways. If one group wants a circular space and another group wants a square space, a decision must be made. One group will be disappointed about this detail, but it is necessary to decide such matters during this phase, not when construction working drawings are being produced. Teaching and learning technology are important considerations during design development.

Design development is the time when all spaces are studied, discussed, and reviewed, showing all building forms, complete floor plans, inside and outside wall elevations, and details.

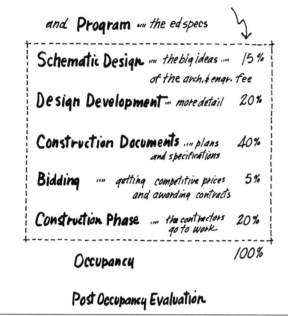

**Where Architectural and Engineering Fees are Expended**

At the conclusion of this phase, all drawings should be examined by the owners' representatives, the construction manager (if there is one at this time), and teachers and department heads to assist in making final design decisions on room layouts, storage, and working walls (in contrast to passive walls, which don't do much except block the passage of sounds and views). At the end of this phase the board should take action to approve the design plans and authorize the preparation of the plans and specifications.

## Producing the Contract Documents with Lots of Help from the Computer

Design changes are no longer welcome at this stage.

The "big idea" for the school slowly evolved during the preparation of education specifications and the master plan for the site and during the schematic design and design development. Now it is time for the engineers and architects to develop in great detail the architectural and engineering plans and specifications for the school.

The computer is an even more valuable tool at this point. It is used to keep track of thousands of details

and coordinate the architectural design with structural engineering, mechanical and electrical engineering, civil engineering, site and landscaping work, and furnishings and equipment. Computer-assisted design and drafting (CADD) has become an everyday tool in most architects' offices. Students graduating from colleges of architecture know how to use the computer effectively.

We might note that as computer use increased rapidly during the last two decades of the twentieth century, sketching concurrently declined in some architectural schools. That was unfortunate, because sketching is a very useful skill for architects who use sketch techniques as a means for developing ideas, transmitting those ideas to others in graphic form (on paper or on the computer screen), and convincing others that their ideas have merit.

Contract documents include both accurate, finished drawings and instructions and requirements in words bound into the specification book.

The "plans and specs" tell the builders exactly what is to be constructed. Whether developed in the architects' and engineers' offices using manual drafting or CADD, the drawings (plans, elevations, details) are printed on paper for use at the construction site. However, instructions and plans may more often be sent electronically via paper-thin screens in the future.

If everyone has done his or her job well, the bid opening should not come as a shock. A well-run project has cost estimates made at three or four stages: during preschematic design, design development, and the production of construction documents.

Cost estimates can be made by the architects-engineers, the construction managers, the program manager, the general contractor, or cost consultants hired by the owner or the architects-engineers.

## Advertising for Bids, Receiving Bids, and Awarding Contracts

Public schools must, of course, solicit bids from a wide range of general contractors, construction managers, and/or program managers. The invitation to submit bids for a project usually is published in local newspapers, and announcements of new projects often are sent to contractors who are known to be good builders.

We have often wondered why the plans and specifications aren't supplemented by renderings, model photos, and explanatory sketches prepared by the architect and presented to the broad planning team during the earlier phases of planning. They would help all the contractors and subcontractors better understand the nature of the building and the relationships between its parts.

Advertising for bids usually includes a period for contractors' questions. Those questions should be sent to the school district or to the architect. The prospective bidders therefore receive the same supplemental answers to questions. The owner's representative will be responsible for getting the answers back to the contractors in a timely manner.

A construction manager, or program manager, will organize the bidding differently, identifying the work to be done by the construction management firm and the work to be done by the contractors and subcontractors.

## Bid-Opening Day

A specific time and location are set for the bid opening. At the specific time, the bidding is closed; that means that no late bids are received, even if they are only seconds late.

Now the construction costs are known, not as estimates but as actual bids. If the bidding market has been favorable and the bids are at or below the estimates, the process of accepting low bids and preparing construction contracts will be relatively easy. "Under-budget" bids make this phase pleasant.

However, if the bids are above the estimate, additional steps must be taken. When they are not anticipated, "over-budget" bids (1) require adjusting the scope of the work by negotiating or by accepting and rejecting various alternates, (2) using part of the contingency fund, (3) allotting additional funds to the project, or (4) rejecting the bids and, after modifying the plans and specifications, rebidding the work a few months later.

A frequent action that solves bidding problems is to bid a number of additive or deductive alternatives, for example, adding kitchen equipment that is not in the base bid or replacing a copper roof with a less expensive metal roof. (This is a reasonable adjustment,

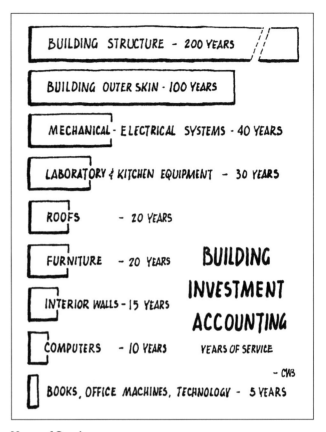

**Years of Service**

because copper is a commodity which goes up and down in cost according to the market.)

When there are a reasonable (manageable) number of alternatives to work with, the bids usually can be adjusted to satisfy the owners and users. A reduction of 5 or 10 percent of the total bid often will solve the problem and keep the project on schedule.

## The Construction Phase

Some of the work will be done on the site, out in the weather, including excavation, earth moving, underground utilities, concrete foundation work, masonry, roofing, and landscaping. Other parts of the construction work will be done in more or less enclosed or sheltered areas of the building. Still other parts will be done off site in factories all over the country, with the products shipped to the site and assembled in the building during construction. All these activities must be managed and coordinated so that the thousands of parts work together to create a unified building. To achieve this, the contractors, architects, and engineers will work together. The contractors will have questions, and the architects and engineers will have or develop answers.

One of the ways in which the needed coordination is accomplished is through the use of "shop drawings," which are the special job drawings made by each subcontractor to plan and produce his or her own work. These drawings (seldom seen by the owners-users) are checked by the contractor and the architects and engineers for accuracy and are approved if they are satisfactory.

It is desirable to keep change orders to a minimum to control extra costs during the construction phase. The best way to accomplish that is by having good-quality, accurate, and well-coordinated construction plans and specifications. Obviously, a "good architect" produces good documents which keep change orders low to control the costs.

The construction site, whether for renovating a fine old building or for building a new school, is a wonderful, interesting place to visit. However, here we have the problem of security and safety. A construction site can be a dangerous phase. Contractors' insurance companies insist that visitors wear hard hats, but other precautions are difficult to enforce.

If you want to create a convenient and safe "construction viewing place," that idea should be discussed with the builder and the architect before the job starts.

## Moving In: Occupancy of the New or Renovated Facilities

Along with people moving in, furniture, fixtures, and equipment (FF&E) move in, ideally during the summer before fall occupancy or at least the month before occupancy and the arrival of the students. However, that occupancy date is preceded by a year or two of planning FF&E. Too often the process of selecting or designing, bidding, purchasing, and delivering loose furniture and equipment is started too late for comfort and accuracy. An early question to be resolved is, Who will be responsible? Candidates for the acquisition of FF&E include the assistant superintendent for business, a person assigned full time to the task, "outside consultants" (dealers), and the architect, especially for fixtures and furniture that need materials and color

coordination with the built-in fixture furnished by the contractor. Part of the decision depends on whether the architect has a good interior design group as part of his or her team.

Another task that often is delayed is the establishment of a rational room numbering and naming system and the necessary graphics and signage systems to satisfy not only students, faculty members, and visitors but also the learning technology, fire alarm, and key systems.

Open house should be a joyous occasion, complete with introductions, music, dedication ceremony and speeches reminding the citizens, staff members, and students what the mission statement of the school system is and how the design of the new facility advances those goals.

If the community has indeed designed and built an innovative school and/or renovated an old building which citizens love, you can expect to see many visitors who, like the planning team three years earlier, want to see and experience the most significant schools planned in response to the best education programs—the state of the art.

## Evaluating a New School or Renovated Building

When the building is completed and occupied, excitement is generated by the new programs and the new spaces and equipment. Then some teachers find that something isn't quite what was expected; perhaps it's a missing storage cabinet or an incorrectly placed door.

What can one do to correct such disappointments? First, recognize the fact that you can't please everyone every time; "Space 202" probably can't be both square and round, but have you considered octagonal? Second, a "finished" school should never be 100 percent finished. Instead, as needs change (including the need for a storage cabinet), continuing improvements should be made. Third, a systematic "postoccupancy evaluation" should be made by the faculty and administration with the help of the educational consultant and the architect. Ask the following questions:

- Did we achieve our overall goals in this new facility?

- How does the school function?

- Does it have a good relationship with its neighborhood?

- What is especially successful?

- What doesn't work as well as expected?

- How do costs compare to those in other schools?

- Is it adaptable and flexible?

- Is it beautiful?

- Is it innovative? If so, what kind of publicity would be appropriate?

Such an evaluation can be useful a month after the initial occupancy, a year later, or even five years later.

# CHAPTER 9

# DESIGNING SCHOOLS WITH CHARACTER

The campuses of American elementary and secondary schools, both old and new, are often works of art, providing effective environments for learning while enhancing their communities with open spaces, green space, and interesting architecture. Some people would feel deprived if they had to live in a town or city that did not have attractive schools to complement the residential buildings. A good neighborhood means to many people an attractive place to go to school. An education park means busier, larger, more complex institutions with one or more elementary schools and a secondary school situated on a single unified site. In the 362 years since our first college was founded (Harvard, in 1636), Americans have designed and built thousands of campuses for both colleges and schools which sometimes are similar to the Harvard campus with its yards, trees, traffic-free pedestrian zones, and varied architectures but sometimes are more reminiscent of Thomas Jefferson's University of Virginia (a more formal, axial, balanced plan). Sometimes our campuses are distinctively different, if not completely unique.

We are so surrounded by the bare-bones modern architecture of many public schools that we forget part of our rich heritage of traditional brick and stone buildings constructed by colleges and universities. One should remember that many of our higher education campuses have in some ways been influenced by Oxford and Cambridge. We can call some of our older colleges and schools "Collegiate Georgian," usually with dark red-brown brick and white trim; "Collegiate Gothic," usually with gray stone and gray trim; or "Collegiate Roman," with mandatory classic stone columns creating a "temple front."

What can we learn from our higher education campuses? Harvard's older buildings tend to be Georgian, but the university has always followed a policy of erecting contemporary buildings, and so the campus is a mixture of styles, materials, colors, and details, with the yards (defined open spaces and landscaping) providing continuity.

The University of Chicago, of course, is Collegiate Gothic, as are Yale and Princeton. MIT is Collegiate Roman and adds the concept of the continuous or linked building complex, which has become more popular in hot or cold climates. On the West Coast, which enjoys a benign climate, outdoor circulation is both pleasant and economical. Stanford, UCLA, the University of California at Berkeley, and hundreds of other campuses have outdoor walks. We could call their style of architecture "Collegiate Mediterranean." The lesson is clear: High-quality architecture is worth the expense of doing it right.

In contrast, unfortunately, many public and private school campuses do not have distinctive architecture and memorable spaces. A low point occurred in the 1950s, when some institutions were built quickly and cheaply. Those buildings are now being renovated or demolished at age forty or fifty. It is much more satisfying to renovate older buildings which are gems and have become important landmarks.

In restoring the best old buildings, architects have developed a new appreciation for those existing structures which have provided a context for new buildings. We are more respectful of the work of earlier generations. It is no longer necessary to design boxy and minimalist modern schools.

Some of the new campus architecture may be identified as postmodern, which suggests that all modern design is ignored in favor of the forms of the premodern era. More promising is the concept of designing a new, respectful, and appropriate building which comfortably relates to both older buildings and modern buildings on a particular campus. Continuity may be achieved through the use of common brick, stone, or concrete; proper scale; and the joint creation of useful outdoor spaces.

Then there is the special design attitude of Frank Gehry and his followers. They like to announce that an existing campus does not have a strong context and so they will not try to be influenced by it; instead, they try to "create a new context," a new campus environment. Usually that is not likely to happen because a 100-year-old campus on 100 acres is not going to be transformed by the addition of one new building. A more comprehensive program and master plan for the entire campus and its environs are needed to guide new construction; the renovation of existing buildings; and the management, improvement, and protection of open space, traffic, and parking.

Many well-established public and private school buildings are over 100 years old. Each building must

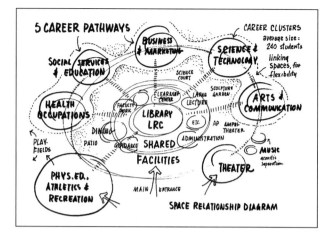

**Liberal Arts and Career Education Reunited; 5 Career Pathways**

be evaluated individually to determine whether it is worthy of renovation or whether demolition and reconstruction (at the old site or a new site) would be most effective. In the year 2020 Americans will be still using most of the existing buildings that are in use today. We hope to have the wisdom to decide which school buildings will survive and which will make way for new architecture.

## Each School Will Be Unique

To ask the question "What will the school of tomorrow be?" is to begin with the false and misleading assumption that our efforts should be and can be directed toward developing a single solution for education and therefore a single solution for school architecture. Searching for a single answer is both undesirable and unlikely to produce a solution, even though society often seeks simple and universal answers and establishes uniform standards. For school design in the future (the next generation) we should not impose standards and encourage homogeneity but instead seek diversity. We should recognize the value of creating multiple criteria for success in learning and of developing school facilities that are appropriate to each particular educational program and each school site.

Just as every person is unique, every school is unique. This is true for our existing inventory of school buildings and for tomorrow's schools. If two or more facilities appear to be identical, which is practically impossible given the fact that the people and neigh-

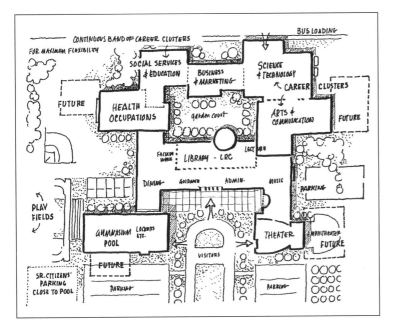

**Building Concept**

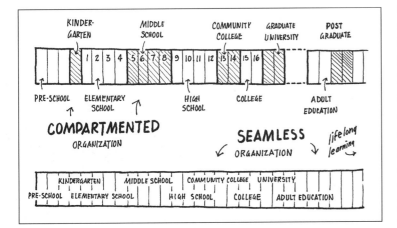

**Compartmented or Seamless**

thoughts on how schools should be designed to achieve the maximum effectiveness of education for all students. It is important to monitor the quality of education in various kinds of facilities to determine what works and what doesn't.

The school of the future will be tailored to the needs of its constituents, which include traditional students of similar age and development, nontraditional students, parents, teachers, and all the people in the neighborhood served by the school. Again, each school program and each school building will reflect the unique needs of these individuals, and each school will be influenced by the special nature of its site and community.

It is sometimes erroneously assumed that schools are identical when they are located in large subdivisions with street patterns that are endlessly repeated and with nearly identical homes. Look more carefully and you will find that the houses (and schools) are not identical. Well-known examples include the Levittowns built in the 1950s, with miles of curving streets. Each house looked about the same in the 1950s, but families grew and added bedrooms, family rooms, and landscaping. Now, with mature trees and individually changed houses, the place has character; the schools have changed too, and each one has a special character. The lesson here is that each school is unique and that uniqueness comes from responses to the changing needs of the program and the site. This is a good lesson to remember in planning a new educational facility.

borhoods they serve are distinctive, further and closer examination will reveal the inevitable differences. One-of-a-kind people and places do not create identical buildings for education.

New ideas for education and new curriculum concepts will continue to evolve and compete for favor, and school design will respond to those changing ideas. In earlier chapters we discussed the importance of innovation. Some innovative ideas will survive and influence school design throughout the country and the world. Others (a greater number) will not survive unchanged but can be deemed successful since they have brought new ideas to the planning table. This is a dynamic process in which experience leads to new

## Program-Driven Change

Why is it desirable for school buildings, sites, and equipment to have the ability to change? Why are some existing school facilities resistant to change? Whether handsome or unattractive, some buildings are difficult to adapt to changing educational programs.

Chapter 2 discussed the need for flexibility, noting that the contemporary office building is a model for flexible and adaptable space. An office building, whether a three-story structure or a forty-story tower, is designed to accommodate a broad range of possible tenants, from small dental offices with many walls and lots of plumbing to insurance company offices with few walls but with underfloor raceways for power and computers. The developer does not know who the tenants (i.e., the programs) will be, and so flexible space is created. It can be changed as the needs of the tenants change.

In the nineteenth century and the first half of the twentieth century the demand for easily altered space was not intensive in architecture for education. Then the changing curricula of some schools began to generate more of a demand for walls that could be moved easily. Before 1950 teaching and learning occurred in standard classrooms, but some teachers began asking for walls that could be slid out of the way, folded, or relocated to create a larger space for larger-group instruction or for many clusters of small groups. These teachers also wanted equipment that was movable.

Program-driven change will continue to affect school design in the twenty-first century, and we can expect to see such changes occurring more rapidly. The computer will help make tomorrow's classrooms adjustable to weekly, daily, and hourly changes in the organization and use of space. Large and small flat electronic screens will give classrooms a new dynamic quality as individuals, small groups, and large groups rapidly alter their learning environments, calling on the resource centers for data and graphics, instantly projecting everything from art and literature to science and mathematics and applied technology.

## Organization for Education

Opinions will continue to differ on how age and ability groups should be clustered.

The common K–12 system puts four grades in each of three school levels, plus a kindergarten added to the elementary, or lower, school, while the middle school is for grades 5 through 8 and the high school, or upper school, is for grades 9 through 12. A districtwide system might look like this:

Eight small lower schools with 300 students each = 2,400 students

Four middle schools with 600 students each = 2,400 students

Two upper schools with 1200 students each = 2,400 students

(plus kindergartens in the lower schools)

The planning implications of this type of grouping are seen in the community and school system master plan for the village of Woodbridge, a component of the city of Irvine in Orange County, California. The limits of the village of Woodbridge are set by the 1-mile-high traffic routes. An activity corridor where two high schools are located and two lakes divide the village

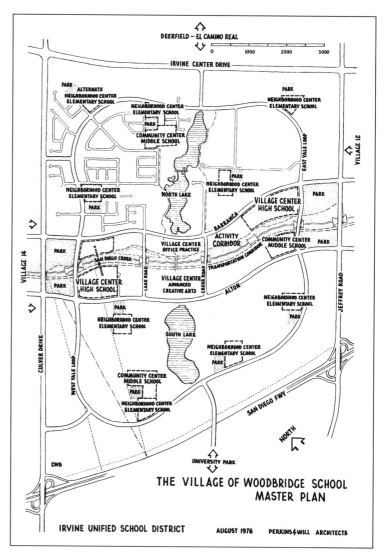

**Woodbridge, Irvine, CA**

into four quadrants, and a boulevard, Yale Loop, links the four quadrants, with each quadrant having a middle school and a park as its community center. Then each elementary school and adjacent park becomes the neighborhood center, with a park and bicycle path linking homes to the neighborhood center.

Other organizations are seen in other places, and there is little evidence that one system is superior to others. In fact, decisions on grade and ability groupings are strongly influenced by the size and location of existing schools and by how much unutilized space is available in each school. For example, if middle schools have surplus space and elementary schools are overcrowded, the logical move is to transfer one grade to the middle schools.

California has a regulation now that mandates the use of prefabricated movable classrooms for a certain number of teaching stations.

One should also consider the probability that some schools will develop entirely new organizational patterns based not on age groupings but on a more complex and more sophisticated analysis of the unique educational needs of each student. Schedules will be tailored to each individual, who will then proceed at his or her own pace.

In the 1960s, with support from foundations, some interesting and innovative ideas were developed and tried, including the concept of team teaching, the core curriculum, and house plans (schools within a school). Such ideas will be reconsidered along with new concepts in the twenty-first century.

## Specialized Space

As the birthrate rises and falls and the demographers revise their estimates on how crowded our schools will be, physical plant problems and goals will change. When enrollments rise rapidly, the emphasis in some districts may be on building as many classrooms as possible, but when enrollments decline, as they did in the 1970s, administrators look for new uses for surplus space. The emphasis may be on upgrading the specialized facilities: the science and technology labs, the library and media center, the arts facilities, and the spaces for physical education, team sports, fitness, and lifetime sports. The specialized spaces that will need attention in the twenty-first century include the following:

- Libraries and media centers will be redefined as the impact of the computer is more clearly understood.
- Science labs will partially replace more specialized and limited biology, chemistry, geology, and physics labs, and simulation and computers will be used in all labs.
- Applied technology will replace shops.
- Mathematics, business, and computers will be more closely related.
- Career education will occur in schools with liberal arts education and in community workplaces.
- The arts, including music and drama, will be closely related to the community.
- Languages will be integrated with geography, history, art, music, drama, and cooking.
- A new kind of multipurpose space will be developed, combining after-hours space and activities for students with dining, theater, and assembly areas.
- Classrooms as we know them will be supplemented and replaced by small, medium, and large learning spaces, and individual study spaces will be the home base for each student.

## Individual Learning

A new kind of education is emerging and will continue to develop in the twenty-first century: the concept of "individual learning" combined with small groups and large groups. The fundamental space will not be the classroom but a "space for individual learning" which is the office size home base for five students, in which each student has his or her own study space and project work space and storage. This is where each student starts the day at school, where coats are hung, and where small group discussions occur with other students and teachers.

In a study done almost thirty years ago, such a place was called "turf." It is for writing, reading, using computers and other media, designing and building things, and learning how to work effectively with others. According to Arthur Costa and Robert Garmston, codirectors of the Institute for Intelligent Behav-

**Turf: Space for Individual Learning**

ior in Berkeley, California, and Joe Saban, the super-intendent of schools in Crystal Lake, Illinois, "it is a school dedicated to developing homonomous individuals . . . simultaneously successful at independent and interdependent tasks."

Five students' turf, or space for individual learning, is visualized to be about 12 feet by 12 feet (the size of an office or a small bedroom), or about 150 square

feet, which means a net usable area of about 30 square feet per student. A gross area allowing for circulation and some support space could increase the space to forty square feet per student. Can we afford that amount of space? If you consider a typical high school with 170 square feet of gross space per student, the turf space is about one-quarter of the typical school's space per student. Each student will spend about half of the day in the turf space; the other half of the day will be spent in medium or large group space, such as the music room, media center, dining area, gym or pool, theater, and art room. Another way to visualize the program is to remember that a typical turf is used by only two or three students at any time, giving each student enough elbow room.

## Special Education

In earlier days special education students were placed in accordance with an exclusion policy. Special rooms or special schools were provided for students with difficult physical and/or mental problems. That system has changed to an inclusion policy. Special education students are and will be included in the regular learning spaces of schools: the classrooms (or their successors), labs, studies, gyms, dining rooms, and media centers.

## A Return to Small Is Beautiful

Responding to recent educational philosophies, curriculum developments, teacher union lobbying, and parent pressure, class size in the twenty-first century will be smaller, and so classrooms will be smaller and more numerous. Note that a 10 percent reduction in class size means that a school needs 10 percent more classrooms.

Such a reduction in class size, however, may not entail a reduction in room size if computers and other equipment need more space.

Another possibility is to reduce classroom size 10 percent, from 900 square feet to 810 square feet, and provide each classroom with 90 square feet of teacher's work space, office, conference room, and activity space. Or perhaps better yet, it is possible to locate two or three such small group rooms between classrooms. These amenities can be accomplished with no increase in the floor area of the school. A reduction in class size makes this feasible.

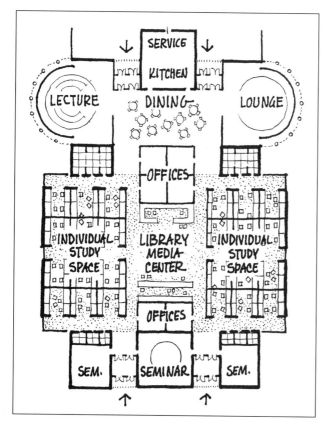

**Turf: The Library Media Center**

In addition to smaller classes, schools may be smaller and therefore school sites can be smaller. This is an important design consideration in a world that continues to become more urban.

A suburban high school with its own football stadium and other outdoor playing fields can consume a site of 40 to 70 acres. However, in the city sites of that size are rare. Smaller schools with smaller sites make good sense in an urban environment.

## The Community School Concept

It will work both ways: The community will use the school facilities for education, fitness and recreation, and culture, and students will go out into the community and use the resources of their area.

For decades the Mott Foundation has consistently promoted the idea of using the school as a community resource; getting all citizens involved and interested in continuing education at elementary, middle, and high schools; and thinking of schools as cultural and fitness centers. This is an expanding idea, and so the schools of the twenty-first century will most often be community schools.

Concurrently, the community at different levels—the city, the village, the neighborhood—can provide opportunities for hands-on learning. In Philadelphia in the late 1960s the Parkway Program used space in the neighborhood, especially businesses, art galleries, museums, other schools and institutions, and the city hall. The Parkway Program was called the first school without walls. As with individual learning, it is an idea whose time has come, in this case after thirty years of quiet experimentation and exploration.

The schools of the twenty-first century will not be walled off from community life as they sometimes were in the past. A school is a part of its community, not apart from it.

## More Regulations

We often have the feeling that school design was less complicated in the past, and indeed it was. There were fewer rules and regulations, fewer submissions, fewer approvals, fewer laws, and fewer guidelines.

Now the design of a high school requires thousands of hours of specifications, drawings, submissions, and approvals to satisfy the new rules and regulations.

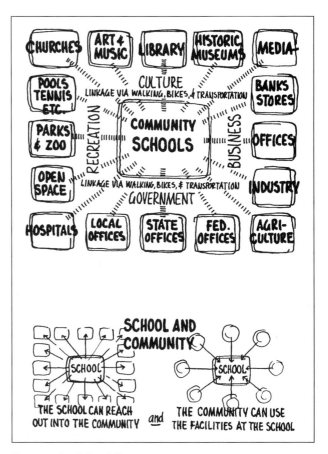

**Community School Concept**

Traditionally, the police power of government was used to protect public safety. Building codes did that, but they got to be more complex. For example, earthquake codes are very important in California and in other zones with high seismic activity. An architect is not permitted to design schools in California until he or she has passed earthquake exams and is registered in that state.

Health and building codes control plumbing and swimming pools. Electrical codes "practically design the power distribution system." Asbestos and lead paint are prohibited. Fire codes limit the use of some materials and require that yellow paint be applied to certain curbs. The handicapped must be accommodated, coastal zones acknowledged, wetlands preserved, trees protected and saved (at least in some states), energy conserved, and indoor air quality assured. The list of rules and regulations goes on and on.

Is it any wonder that tomorrow's new schools will be more expensive to build?

## Lifetime Costs and Value Engineering

These are recent buzzwords for what was earlier called *good design,* which entails building costs which give the owner long-term economy (i.e., favorable lifetime costs) and the constant search for the best possible way to design the building (i.e., value engineering).

Value (relative worth, utility, and importance) is what design is all about. Value is a matter of getting the most for one's money; that includes satisfaction, comfort, low operating costs, and beauty.

Too often in the past minimalist buildings were designed and built, with all the emphasis on the first costs and with little attention given to the long-run operating and maintenance costs.

One way to reduce costs significantly has not been widely accepted: adopting the all-year school idea. The nine-month school year means that buildings, equipment, buses, teachers, and other staff members are utilized only about 75 percent of the time.

Tomorrow's facilities will be designed to achieve a good balance between the initial building costs and the long-term operating and maintenance costs which continue forever. Forever is a long time.

## Adaptable Spaces

One of the lessons learned by school planners of this generation is the need for spaces that can easily be adapted to changing needs. With encouragement and grant dollars from foundations, especially EFL, many interesting experiments were conducted in the 1960s to find ways to change and redeploy interior space with movable walls, disposable walls, folding partitions, sliding walls, movable furniture and equipment, and mechanical and electrical systems that could be readily operated and adjusted to combine or subdivide rooms to better meet new space requirements.

As was noted in earlier chapters, the modern office building with its ongoing changes in tenancy provides an excellent demonstration of how open and flexible loft-type space can be subdivided and/or opened up.

One of the pioneering examples of the use of loft space for elementary and secondary education is Hillsdale School in the San Francisco region, designed by the architect John Lyon Reid. A large open and adaptable space was built to which users then added the walls and equipment required for current needs. The

idea implies air-conditioning and suggests that when enrollment declines, part or all of the school building can be converted easily to other uses.

Some people may object that such a loft school will not "look like a school" but will look like an office building or manufacturing plant. However, this potential problem will be alleviated when the adaptable loft space is clustered with other specialized facilities, such as a gym, a pool, and a theater, which will help create more of a traditional campus feeling.

Also, if we believe that education is a part of life, not apart from it, it is proper and even inevitable for buildings and grounds for education to be closely related in distance and character to workplaces in the community and to the neighborhood and homes of the students.

## Technology for Teaching and Learning

The implications of the computer in school design have been discussed so extensively that we need not discuss them thoroughly in this chapter, except to note the following:

- Regardless of what equipment is specified, it will be obsolete when the new school is occupied; we cannot afford that luxury forever.

- If a school is "wired" with copper or fiber optics, what happens if wireless systems are adapted?

- The school will be linked to an endless number of libraries, databases, other schools, other communities, and homes.

- Computerized programmed learning (step by step, with feedback), along with other voice-video-data systems, makes learning at home a practical alternative, and so it may change the nature of school buildings (just as working at home may change the nature of office buildings).

## New Trends in Building Systems

Structural systems (whether using steel, aluminum, reinforced concrete, masonry, wood, or new composite designs) will be "expressed" (i.e., seen, experienced, and understood), and mechanical and electrical systems also will be seen and understood, helping to give the school building a special and appropriate character. Since mechanical and electrical systems already consume one-third of the construction budget, they should have a more profound influence on design. Architectural, structural, mechanical, and electrical functions will more often be integrated to achieve efficiency and lower costs. For example, H-shaped beams and girders can provide structural support for floors, receptors for walls, conditioned air distributors, communications raceways, and lighting components.

Energy efficiency will have a high priority since a large percentage of any building's operations budget goes to the cost of energy. The energy crisis of the 1970s publicized the fact that many schools were energy hogs, consuming too much gas, oil, and/or electricity. Twenty-first-century schools will be more thoughtfully planned and oriented, better insulated, and more responsibly engineered to achieve lower operating costs and will set a good example for the community.

## Urban Schools

Urban schools are different.

The most obvious difference is the high land cost and the nonavailability of land; these factors generate very compact and very tall school buildings. A few high schools in New York City and Chicago are served by escalators, but elevators are also required to accommodate the handicapped.

City schools are influenced by neighboring properties and influence their neighbors more profoundly than do suburban and rural schools. The shortage of land and its high cost generate interest in considering the "mixed-use development" idea, in which different tenants share a common loft or tower. A few such structures exist, especially in New York City. A future mixed-use tower could have shops and restaurants on the ground floor, a parking ramp on floors 3 to 10, mechanical equipment on floor 11, a school of 200,000 square feet gross on floors 12 to 19, and offices and/or apartments on floors 20 to 36.

Urban schools can bridge city streets to gain the advantages of a traffic-free zone at the second-floor level. In Chicago, directly west of the Loop, Whitney Young Magnet High School bridges Jackson Boulevard.

An urban school may be located on smaller sites distributed throughout a multiblock area, with normal city sidewalks linking the buildings.

## Aesthetic Considerations

Chapter 1 reviewed our rich school design heritage, from early one-room schoolhouses to traditional multistory schools in towns and cities, to the gems of the early twentieth century and, after 1940, the widespread adoption of modern architecture. Fifty years later, in the 1990s, modern architecture, with its emphasis on boxy forms, flat walls, flat roofs, and total lack of ornament, was challenged by postmodern architecture (a partial return to the traditions of the richly textured forms of the past). "Contextualism" has been a driving force in school design, respecting and being influenced by "the context" of the neighborhood, city, or region. Regionalism is another form of contextualism.

High-tech design is another force that competes for our favor. High-tech architecture emphasizes sophisticated building technology, with machine-made parts bolted together like an erector set.

Modern architecture is now more closely associated with high-tech design and brings to the planning table the social goals which were developed and promoted by the modern architects of the late nineteenth century, including Louis Sullivan and Frank Lloyd Wright.

Meanwhile, most of us have a new interest in and respect for the American schools of the twentieth century. Bringing them up to date internally and restoring them externally will be important tasks in the twenty-first century.

## Additions and Renovations

In the year 2020, only twenty two years from now, most of our schools will be the ones we are using today. Even if many schools are replaced with new construction, a twenty-year building program will make a difference; however, most of our school buildings in 2020 will still be structures built in the twentieth century.

In the year 2020 we will still be using some buildings that are a hundred years old.

In the year 2020, we will still be using some buildings that are seventy years old.

In the year 2020, we will still be using some buildings that are fifty years old.

In the year 2020, we will still be using some buildings that are thirty years old.

**Whitney Young Magnet High School, Chicago**

Therefore, we must recognize the importance of getting existing buildings into good shape and keeping them that way. What does this mean? To oversimplify, it means a physical plant that is well maintained and facilities (building, equipment, and site) that satisfy the needs of the educational program (the curriculum).

The physical plant requires architectural (including roofs and walls) and engineering systems that are in good condition and that are up to date, safe and sound, waterproof, structurally sound, and well insulated. HVAC systems must work properly to assure good indoor air quality, and electrical and communications systems must be up to date.

Unfortunately, many school systems, especially in big city school districts, have let the physical plant go to pot. The cost of repairing schools in the United States and adding the needed teaching and learning technology has been well documented. It will run into billions of dollars.

Another unfortunate situation is the "crisis" nature of the maintenance problem, which usually means a concentrated crash program. It would be far better to spread out those deferred maintenance expenditures evenly over the years so that at any given time some schools are in good shape while others are in need of improvement. Thoughtful financial planning requires up-to-date real estate data.

Concurrently, the adequacy of spaces and equipment should be evaluated. Classrooms should be comfortable and large enough for ongoing projects with new teaching and learning technology. Science labs are obsolete in most schools; only a few teachers would challenge that observation. Applied technology can replace shops. Libraries and resource centers have a new look. Theater, music, and art studios in existing buildings are sometimes obsolete. Physical education, sports, fitness, and recreation need reevaluation.

Each building in each district should be evaluated and compared, using the same criteria, to give all planning participants a better idea of how each school stacks up—whether it should be saved and renovated or demolished and replaced with a new school and how much each option will cost.

Plan your evaluation survey with a simple, easy-to-read format:

- Identify physical plant problems

    Example: unit ventilators broken in science lab 204

    Example: illegal exiting from band room 403

- Identify strengths

    Example: an excellent kitchen that was remodeled in 1997

- Identify education program problems

    Example: no computers in art studio 112

- Identify education program strengths

    Example: large group lecture room 140

- Evaluate each school on a scale of 1 to 10

    Example: 8

- Estimate the cost of improvements

    Example: $4.2 million for renovation

- Consider other options

    Example: $6.6 million for a new school on the same site

## Historic Preservation

In the 1950s and 1960s many well-built and handsome old schools were demolished to make way for presumably "new and improved" schools designed in the modern idiom. Sometimes the old building was indeed ready for the wrecking ball and the new replacement school proved to be a better facility, but not always. In some cases, part or all of a well-built and good-looking heavy masonry multifloor traditional or "classical" old school was destroyed to provide a site for a new structure which was not as good as the old building.

In the twenty-first century we will experience new interest in the preservation of fine old schools. That happened on college and university campuses in the last half of the twentieth century, when "old grads" provided interest and funds for the preservation and restoration of "Old Main" buildings. Hundreds of old schools in America are worthy of restoration. That won't necessarily save money, but preservation of great old schools will make communities better places to live.

## Variety and Choice

No single solution can satisfy the wide range of school needs. Schools can and will be large or small, comprehensive or specialized, public or private, traditional or experimental, seasonal or all-year, at a single location or multilocational, with the same gridiron schedule for all students or with a custom-tailored schedule for each individual, in structures that are old or new, with flexible or rigid space, in rural, suburban, or urban locations, offering or not offering a wide spectrum of services to the community.

The end result will be a rich mix of options for education and, for each student, multiple criteria for success.

In the twenty-first century students will go to school in buildings that were constructed in the twentieth and twenty-first centuries, plus a few nineteenth-century structures. Concurrently, many important new concepts for education and facilities will evolve and be tested. Some of these new ideas will be successful and therefore will influence school design profoundly. Tomorrow's school will often be a rich mix of old and new components, while entirely new facilities will be planned and constructed. Some schools will be large, and some will be small. Each individual will have many options available.

Parents and students will have choices.

# 20/20 VISION AND CHOICE FOR THE FUTURE

S econdary schools have not changed for a hundred years or more. That was the conclusion reached by the National Association of Secondary School Principals (NASSP) in its report in 1995. Of course, some of the details of curriculum, teaching, and architecture for education have changed, but the fundamental facts of high schools remain unaltered. The high school of A.D. 1900 was based on classrooms and laboratories along with specialized facilities such as an auditorium, a library, a gymnasium, shops, a cafeteria, and a boiler room. The teachers and students of A.D. 2020 will know their way around a hundred-year-old schoolhouse, just as teachers and students in 1900 would have found the high schools of 2020 readily comprehensible. The conservative nature of education is apparent when we compare the educational programs and facilities of schools at different times. If you ask teachers and students today what changes they believe have most profoundly affected the way they teach and learn, the answer probably will involve the use of the computer, but the spaces have not changed; the sites for education continue to be laboratories, classrooms, and libraries.

However, education is changing. For example, Ameritech gave a grant to the Chicago Academy of Sciences to broadcast science projects on the Internet to classrooms and via cable to homes, giving students unprecedented access to the work of scientists. This Science Power program gives science experts a huge audience and gives students a great opportunity to participate in demonstrations and discussions.

Educators and architects continue to explore new concepts on paper, but most of their ideas don't progress beyond the publication stage. It's almost as if the policy were "Okay, we've published our ideas; now we can get back to teaching and learning the ancient and tested way."

Therein lies a great opportunity and need for the new millennium. *Millennium* is a word that can mean a period of 1,000 years or a celebration of a thousand-year-old event, but the most appealing definition is "a period of great happiness and human perfection." What better goal for the next decade, recognizing our limited ability to plan for a century or a millennium? We should not be too negative. Great goals were set for education in the nineteenth century, and some excellent school buildings were created. Some will survive as architectural landmarks in addition to being recognized as social and educational landmarks. Early in the twentieth century the architect Daniel Burnham urged us to "make no little plans." He heeded his own advice by developing a plan for Chicago that continues to influence city planners and architects today.

In 1997 President Clinton made big plans for schools. He gave top billing to his education plan with a ten-point "Call to Action for American Education" and a $10 billion increase in education spending. The federal budget for education would be $39.4 billion for fiscal year 1998. The ten-point plan included $5 billion to help communities pay for $20 billion in school construction over the next four years.

That is just a step along the way toward the renewal of our school buildings and the construction of new facilities. At a cost of $25 million for the construction of an average size secondary school, $20 billion would build only 800 high schools, or an average of 16 schools per state. We have not yet faced the tremendous costs involved in renewing our educational infrastructure.

Should our educational goals include striving to achieve a period of great happiness and human perfection? Lesser goals and aspirations will produce lesser quality in education and in architecture for education.

Excellence in school planning and design can evolve and thrive only in an environment where excellence is recognized and rewarded.

As planners and designers of architecture for education we need 20/20 vision—keenness of perception about our heritage and the needs and opportunities we will face in the near future. We must be sensitive to the issues of education and architecture, the trends of today, and ideas for tomorrow.

A single solution to school design is neither possible nor desirable. We have mentioned a number of times in this book the fact that the United States and Canada are large and diverse nations geographically, socially, and culturally. The need is for many solutions for teaching and learning, not a single solution. It is most desirable to have multiple criteria for success at all levels, including many different curricula, various kinds of learning spaces, different sizes of schools, a rich variety of learning technology, and opportunities for different sizes of learning environments from indi-vidual study at "school" (and/or in the community) to study at home.

When one considers a school system with many different sites and numerous buildings, old and new, large and small, high and low, modern and traditional, it is relatively easy to provide a great variety of spaces to accommodate different programs, giving students a broad range of choices of physical facilities as well as choices of curriculum, size, use of technology, and many other factors which give schools their own character. However, when we consider one school only, with one building, it becomes a different challenge. How do we create and maintain variety in program and variety in spaces to give students a choice of different kinds of curricula, different types of learning, and various kinds of facilities? Usually, in a single building a single style of learning dominates, but it need not be so limited. A great variety of teaching techniques can coexist under one roof.

Consider the house plan again. Three or four (or twenty) different schools can share a site and many common facilities, such as one boiler room, one kitchen, and one theater. Some older buildings are easily adapted to the small scale and charming space needs of little schools. A new, large, institutional, or "corporate-looking" building suggests tidy rows of similar spaces. Again, one learning environment need not dominate. It is better to encourage a broad variety of educational environments.

Schools, like people, should be one-of-a-kind organisms. They need space that is adaptable to changing needs. They need flexible facilities that can, at a minimal cost, be converted from classrooms to seminars, to individual study space, to study rooms for five students. Architecture for education should facilitate the evolution of future schools. The basic need is for flexibility to encourage both innovation and continuing development based on past success.

The school of the future will look more like an office and laboratory environment where small teams study, discuss, and create with the assistance of technology.

In an age when there is growing interest in creating "standards" that limit and restrict what can be done in addition to guiding and requiring certain activities and procedures, we may feel that planning and design for educational facilities can be excessively regulated, limited, and legislated. Local school districts probably are losing some of their power as state and federal agencies gain in influence and power. (Meanwhile, school districts are constantly being pressured to surrender more power to "local control."

The question in regard to this simultaneous fragmentation and consolidation is, How does it all affect the quality of education and architecture for education? Will standards limit creativity? Will they limit choice?

Choice can be effective only when there are good options to choose from.

We probably can agree that it is desirable to offer students and their parents some options, such as choosing between attending a neighborhood elementary school where most students walk to school and where the character of the school is small, local, and residential, attending a magnet school in another part of the district where a special program (such as the arts) attracts pupils to well-equipped studios and specialized faculties for music, drama, and art, and receiving a significant part of their education at home

with visits to the local school on two or three days a week.

Similar choices can be made available at the secondary level. The comprehensive high school has been the American norm for generations. However, some of the options might include the multilocation school, the school in the city, and a career education center with specialized faculty and facilities where students from other high schools visit a few half days a week while attending their regular high schools every day, as is true at Robert Morgan Vocational Technical Institute in Dade County, Florida.

The vocational-technical school south of Miami in Dade County was designed to serve thousands of secondary school students and adults. High school students have their own home-base high schools throughout the southern part of Dade County, and that is where they get most of their education, but on certain days they go to the career center on a bus, usually for a half day. On other days, another group of high

**Robert Morgan Vocational—Technical Institute, Dade Co, FL (Color Photo)**

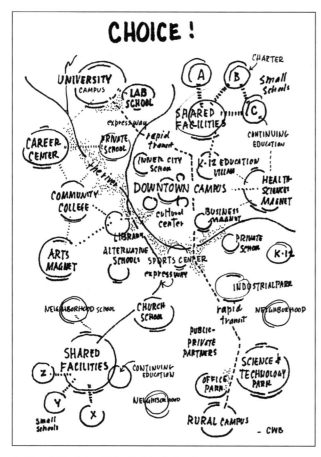

**A Great Variety of Available Schools.**

school students is at the center in the morning and a different group is there in the afternoon. Then, at 5 P.M., it becomes an adult education institute, and at 7 P.M. another group of adults arrives. It is not difficult to visualize these facilities being used intensively.

When we planned this campus, students suggested that the central mall *not* be air-conditioned; they said that natural ventilation and shade would be preferred for the social and circulation space. However, the labs, classrooms, and shops are air-conditioned.

Specialized schools can be freestanding or can share a large structure with other programs; they might include a hearing-impaired house, a school

where students teach other students with help from computers, a business school linked to a local college, or a Latin school. Choices can include religious schools, both public and private institutions, which could jointly use expensive shared facilities such as a theater and a swimming pool.

20/20 vision will give us the sharpness and the keenness of perception to create a rich mix of options for every student. A special option can be created for every individual student; it would be a custom-designed and unique program suited to a student's ability, interests, and pace. Interactions with other students, faculty members, and community residents would occur at school, downtown, at the medical center, at local factories and offices, at home, and at college and university campuses. In the past, keeping track of such individualized programs would have been difficult or impossible, but today the computer can do it for us.

Dynamic programming, active, continuous, and productive, with changing space needs generated by the unique curricula of the students, can drive the school design of tomorrow. Let us welcome the new ideas and the innovative concepts that explore possibilities for our future schools.

Dr. Joe Saban, superintendent of schools at Community High School District 155 in Crystal Lake, Illinois, has been discussing an idea for tomorrow with his consultants, Dr. Arthur Costa and Dr. Robert Garmston of the Institute for Intelligent Behavior in Berkeley, California. They visualize a high school dedicated to developing "holonomous" individuals capable of living and working successfully in a dynamic and unpredictable future. Holonomous individuals, they explain, are simultaneously successful at independent and interdependent tasks, an idea that embraces a reality that is emerging for twenty-first-century America.

Keep an eye on this kind of thinking. It may give us some very important clues to the nature of tomorrow's schools.

# CREDITS

## 1988
### Capital High School
### Santa Fe, New Mexico

CLIENT: Santa Fe Public Schools

ASSOCIATE ARCHITECT: Mimbres, Inc.

PROJECT ARCHITECTS: Kas Germanas, Sam Jamron

MANAGING PRINCIPAL: C. William Brubaker

DESIGN PRINCIPAL: Ralph E. Johnson

PROJECT MANAGER: James A. Toya

PROJECT DESIGNERS: Elizabeth Fakatselis, Mark Romack, Stuart Royalty

PHOTOGRAPHY: Gregory Murphey

## 1988
### Desert View Elementary School
### Sunland Park, New Mexico

CLIENT: Gadsden Independent School District

ASSOCIATE ARCHITECT: Mimbres, Inc.

PROJECT ARCHITECTS: Kas Germanas, Sam Jamron

DESIGN PRINCIPAL: Ralph E. Johnson

PROJECT MANAGER: James Toya

DESIGN TEAM: Elizabeth Fakatselis, Mark Romack, Jerry Johnson, Stuart Royalty, Pamela Kurz, Carolyn Smith

PHOTOGRAPHY: Robert Reck

## 1990
### Warsaw Community High School
### Warsaw, Indiana

CLIENT: Warsaw Community School District

ASSOCIATE ARCHITECT: Odle, McGuire & Shook Corporation

MANAGING PRINCIPAL: C. William Brubaker

DESIGN PRINCIPAL: Ralph E. Johnson

PROJECT MANAGER: James Toya

PROJECT DESIGNER: August Battaglia

DESIGN TEAM: George Witaszek, Stuart Royalty, Steven Ward, John Lucero

PHOTOGRAPHY: Gregory Murphey

## 1992
### Troy High School
### Troy, Michigan

CLIENT: Troy Public Schools

MANAGING PRINCIPAL: C. William Brubaker

DESIGN PRINCIPAL: Ralph E. Johnson

PROJECT MANAGER: James Toya

PROJECT DESIGNER: John Arzarian, Jr.

PROJECT TEAM: Eric Spielman, Mike Hoffman, Geoffrey Brooksher, Elizabeth Fakatselis, Susan Emmons, Robin Randall, George Witaszek

PHOTOGRAPHY: Balthazar Korab

## 1992

### Solon Middle School/Parkside Elementary School
### Solon, Ohio

CLIENT: Solon City School District

ASSOCIATE ARCHITECT: Burgess & Niple, Ltd.

PROJECT DIRECTOR: Raymond Bordwell

MANAGING PRINCIPAL: C. William Brubaker

DESIGN PRINCIPAL: Ralph E. Johnson

PROJECT PLANNER: James Woods

SENIOR DESIGNER: Ruth Gless

PROJECT TEAM: Steve Turckes, Greg Bennett

PHOTOGRAPHY: William Sheck

## 1995

### Perry Community Education Village
### Perry, Ohio

CLIENT: Perry Local School District

ASSOCIATE ARCHITECT: Burgess & Niple, Ltd.

PROJECT DIRECTOR: Raymond Bordwell

DESIGN PRINCIPAL: Ralph E. Johnson

MANAGING PRINCIPAL: C. William Brubaker

PROJECT MANAGER: James Toya

TECHNICAL COORDINATORS: James Nowak, William Schmalz

PROJECT DESIGNERS: August Battaglia, James Woods

PROJECT TEAM: Eric Spielman, Mike Palmer, Jerry Johnson, Robin Randall, Robert Ruggles, Celeste Robbins, Carlos Parilla, Greg Bennett, Randy Takahashi

PHOTOGRAPHY: Hedrich/Blessing

## 1996

### Woodlands High School
### Woodlands, Texas

CLIENT: Conroe Independent School District

ASSOCIATE ARCHITECT: PBK Architects

MANAGING PRINCIPAL: C. William Brubaker

DESIGN PRINCIPAL: Ralph E. Johnson

PROJECT MANAGER: Joseph Chronister

PROJECT DESIGNER: Jerry Johnson

PROJECT TEAM: Steve Roberts, Thomas Mozina, Phillip Kiel, Carol Siepka, Henry Lee, Susan Broadbent

MODEL PHOTOGRAPHY: Steinkamp/Ballog

BUILDING PHOTOGRAPHY: Jud Haggard

## 1996

### North Fort Myers High School
### Fort Myers, Florida

CLIENT: Lee County School Board

ASSOCIATE ARCHITECT: Parker/Mudgett/Smith Architects, Inc.

MANAGING PRINCIPAL: C. William Brubaker

DESIGN PRINCIPAL: Ralph E. Johnson

PROJECT MANAGER: James Woods

PROJECT DESIGNER: Jerry Johnson

PROJECT TEAM: Celeste Robbins, Steve Roberts, Thomas Vecchio

ILLUSTRATIONS: Brian Junge

PHOTOGRAPHY: Hedrich/Blessing

## 1996

### Chelsea High School
### Chelsea, Massachusetts

CLIENT: Chelsea School District

ASSOCIATE ARCHITECT: Symmes Manni McKee Architects

PROJECT DIRECTOR: Edward Frenette

MANAGING PRINCIPAL: C. William Brubaker

DESIGN PRINCIPAL: Ralph E. Johnson

PROJECT DIRECTOR: Ruth Gless

PROJECT ARCHITECT: Michael Poynton

PROJECT PROGRAMMER: Raymond Bordwell

PROJECT TEAM: Steve Roberts, Wendy Gill, Tom Ahleman, Elias Vavaroustsos, Brian Junge

ILLUSTRATIONS: Brian Junge

PHOTOGRAPHY: Hedrich/Blessing

## 1997

### Singapore American School
### Woodlands New Town, Singapore

CLIENT: Singapore American School

ASSOCIATE ARCHITECT: Consultants, Incorporated

MANAGING PRINCIPAL: T. C. Tham

PROJECT DIRECTOR AND SENIOR DESIGNER: August Battaglia

DESIGN PRINCIPAL: Ralph E. Johnson

PROJECT PROGRAMMER: James Woods

PROJECT TEAM: Mark Jolicoeur, Celeste Robbins, Thomas Mozina, Chris Hale, Diane Zabich, Carol Siepka, Susan Broadbent, Steve Roberts, Joe Pullara, Greg Bennett

ILLUSTRATIONS: Brian Junge

PHOTOGRAPHY: Richard Bryant

## 1996
### Fort Collins High School
### Fort Collins, Colorado

CLIENT: Poudre R.1 School District

PRIME ARCHITECT: Architectural Horizons

DESIGN PRINCIPAL: Robert Sutter

PROJECT MANAGER: Dennis Auker

TECHNICAL COORDINATOR: Richard Warvi

DESIGN TEAM: C. William Brubaker, James Woods, Ralph Johnson, James Nowak, Vojo Narancic

PHOTOGRAPHY: Torney Lieberman

### Middle School at High Desert
### Albuquerque, New Mexico

CLIENT: Middle School at High Desert

PRIME ARCHITECT: Perkins & Will

ASSOCIATE ARCHITECT: Garrett Smith Ltd.

PRINCIPAL IN CHARGE: Ray Bordwell

PROJECT DIRECTOR AND DESIGNER: Amy Yurko

PROJECT TEAM: Mike Poynton, Brian Meade

## 1996
### Mashpee High School
### Mashpee, Massachusetts

CLIENT: Town of Mashpee

PRIME ARCHITECT: Symmes, Maini & McKee

PROJECT DIRECTOR: Edward Frenette

PROJECT MANAGERS: Andrew Chartwell & Company, Robert Fournier

PROJECT ARCHITECT: Phillip Poinelli

BUILDING TECHNOLOGY SPECIALIST: Elinor Charlton

ASSOCIATE ARCHITECT: Perkins & Will

DESIGN PRINCIPAL: Ray Bordwell

PROJECT ADMINISTRATOR: Norris McLeod

PROJECT ARCHITECT: Mark Chen

DIRECTOR OF PROGRAMMING AND PLANNING: C. William Brubaker

PROJECT TEAM: Ann Marie Lewis, Chris Borchardt, Imran Ahmed, Bill Van Horn, Sung Ho Shin, Mike Poynton

## 1996
### New Albany Learning Community
### New Albany, Ohio

CLIENT: New Albany/Plain Local School District

PRIME ARCHITECT: Perkins & Will

PROGRAMMING AND PLANNING PRINCIPAL: C. William Brubaker

PROJECT DIRECTOR AND PRINCIPAL IN CHARGE: James Woods, Mike Palmer

DESIGN DIRECTOR: Ralph Johnson

SENIOR PROJECT DESIGNER AND PROJECT MANAGER: Ruth Gless

PROJECT ARCHITECT: Mike Poynton

PROJECT TEAM: Steve Turckes, Wendy Gill, Jim Nowak, Mike Fletcher, Jack Ramm, Leigh Harrison

PHOTOGRAPHY: Hedrich/Blessing

## 1995
### Sauk Rapids High School
### Sauk Rapids, Minnesota

CLIENT: Independent School District 47

PRIME ARCHITECT: Perkins & Will

PROJECT MANAGER: James Woods

PROJECT ARCHITECT: Vojo Narancic

SPECIFICATIONS: Steve Pash

ASSOCIATE ARCHITECT: Grooters Leapaldt Tideman

PRINCIPAL IN CHARGE: David Leapaldt

## 1998
### Trinity Valley School
### Fort Worth, Texas

CLIENT: Trinity Valley School

PRIME ARCHITECT: Perkins & Will

PRINCIPAL IN CHARGE: James Woods

PROJECT ARCHITECT: Mark Jolicoeur

PROJECT TEAM: Wendy Gill, Diane Zabich, Jennifer Moss

ASSOCIATE ARCHITECT: Carter & Burgess

PROJECT MANAGER: Chuck Nixon

LANDSCAPE: Brian Adams

MODEL PHOTOGRAPHY: Steinkamp/Ballog

## 1997
### Prairie Ridge High School
### Crystal Lake, Illinois

CLIENT: Community High School District 155

PROJECT DIRECTOR AND DESIGN PRINCIPAL: August Battaglia

PROJECT DESIGNER: Greg Bennett

PROGRAMMING PRINCIPALS: C. William Brubaker, Jim Woods

PROJECT ARCHITECTS: Mike Palmer, Chris Hale

PROJECT TEAM: Jeff Olson, Diane Zabich, Carol Siepka, Steve Swenson, Brian Junge, John Karabatsos, Jon Kopp, John Tingerthal, Ron Parsley, John Tsingas, Alex Ledesma, Wendy Gill, Dan Fagan

## 1997

### Arlington High School
### Saint Paul, Minnesota

CLIENT: Saint Paul Public Schools

PRIME ARCHITECT: Winsor/Faricy Architects

ASSOCIATE ARCHITECT: Perkins & Will

DESIGN PRINCIPAL: Ralph Johnson

PROJECT DIRECTOR: August Battaglia

EDUCATION PLANNERS: James Woods, C. William Brubaker

PROJECT TEAM: Tom Mozina, Chris Hale, Peggy Hoffmann, Carol Siepka, Louis Vavarosos, Mike Poynton, Jerry Johnson

PHOTOGRAPHY: George Heinrich

## 2000

### International School
### Manila, Philippines

CLIENT: International School of Manila

DESIGN PRINCIPAL: Ralph Johnson

MANAGING PRINCIPAL: Raymond Bordwell

SENIOR DESIGNER: Amy Yurko

PROJECT ARCHITECT: Mike Poynton

PROJECT TEAM: Brian Meade, Nicola Casciato, Kimberly Brown, Tim Bicknell, Scott Kuehn, Brook Potter, Joe Pullara, Peggy Hoffmann

ILLUSTRATIONS: Nicola Casciato

## 1996

### New York Prototype Schools
### New York City

CLIENT: New York City Board of Education

PLANNING PRINCIPAL: C. William Brubaker

MANAGING PRINCIPAL: James Garretson

DESIGN PRINCIPAL: Aaron Schwartz

PROJECT TEAM: Lou Bauko, Barbera D'Agostino, Ed Denny, Ed Narbutas, Roy Rogers, Deepika Ross, John Turmelle, Joanne Violanti, Ephraim Wechsler

PHOTOGRAPHY: Chuck Choi

## 1998

### Silverado Middle School
### Roseville, California

CLIENT: Dry Creek Joint School District

PRINCIPAL ARCHITECT: Gaylaird Christopher

PROJECT DIRECTOR: Godwin Osifeso

PROJECT ARCHITECT: Robert Lavey

SENIOR DESIGNER: John Dale

## Proposed

### J. L. Stanford Middle School
### Palo Alto, California

CLIENT: Palo Alto Unified School District

PRIME ARCHITECT: Perkins & Will

ASSOCIATE ARCHITECT: Anderson Brule Architects

DESIGN PRINCIPAL: Ralph Johnson

PROJECT DESIGNER: Cyngis Yetkin

PROJECT DIRECTORS: Mark Jolicoeur, Mike Palmer

PROJECT ARCHITECT: Albert Fitzpatrick

PROJECT TEAM: Steve Swenson, Alex Wray, David Poorman, Brian Junge, Greg Bennett

# INDEX

## ABOUT THE AUTHOR

C. William Brubaker is the leading designer of educational facilities in the world today. He has specialized in educational planning and design for more than 30 years. Three of his recent projects, an elementary school and two high schools, were accorded the coveted Honor Award of the American Institute of Architects. A principal of Perkins & Will in Chicago, Brubaker is a fellow of the AIA.